Slavery and the Peculiar Solution

SOUTHERN DISSENT

UNIVERSITY PRESS OF FLORIDA

Florida A&M University, Tallahassee
Florida Atlantic University, Boca Raton
Florida Gulf Coast University, Ft. Myers
Florida International University, Miami
Florida State University, Tallahassee
New College of Florida, Sarasota
University of Central Florida, Orlando
University of Florida, Gainesville
University of North Florida, Jacksonville
University of South Florida, Tampa
University of West Florida, Pensacola

SOUTHERN DISSENT

Edited by Stanley Harrold and Randall M. Miller

The Other South: Southern Dissenters in the Nineteenth Century, by Carl N. Degler, with a new preface (2000)

Crowds and Soldiers in Revolutionary North Carolina: The Culture of Violence in Riot and War, by Wayne E. Lee (2001)

"Lord, We're Just Trying to Save Your Water": Environmental Activism and Dissent in the Appalachian South, by Suzanne Marshall (2002)

The Changing South of Gene Patterson: Journalism and Civil Rights, 1960–1968, edited by Roy Peter Clark and Raymond Arsenault (2002)

Gendered Freedoms: Race, Rights, and the Politics of Household in the Delta, 1861–1875, by Nancy Bercaw (2003)

Civil War on Race Street: The Civil Rights Movement in Cambridge, Maryland, by Peter B. Levy (2003)

South of the South: Jewish Activists and the Civil Rights Movement in Miami, 1945–1960, by Raymond A. Mohl, with contributions by Matilda "Bobbi" Graff and Shirley M. Zoloth (2004)

Throwing Off the Cloak of Privilege: White Southern Female Activists in the Civil Rights Era, edited by Gail S. Murray (2004)

The Atlanta Riot: Race, Class, and Violence in a New South City, by Gregory Mixon (2004)

Slavery and the Peculiar Solution: A History of the American Colonization Society, by Eric Burin (2005, first paperback edition, 2008)

"I Tremble for My Country": Thomas Jefferson and the Virginia Gentry, by Ronald L. Hatzenbuehler (2006)

From Saint-Domingue to New Orleans: Migration and Influences, by Nathalie Dessens (2007)

Higher Education and the Civil Rights Movement: White Supremacy, Black Southerners, and College Campuses, edited by Peter Wallenstein (2007)

Burning Faith: Church Arson in the American South, by Christopher B. Strain (2008)

Slavery

and the

Peculiar Solution

A HISTORY OF THE AMERICAN COLONIZATION SOCIETY

Eric Burin

UNIVERSITY PRESS OF FLORIDA

Gainesville   Tallahassee   Tampa   Boca Raton
Pensacola   Orlando   Miami   Jacksonville   Ft. Myers   Sarasota

13   12   11   10   09   08   6   5   4   3   2   1

Library of Congress Cataloging-in-Publication Data
Burin, Eric.
Slavery and the peculiar solution : a history of the American Colonization
Society / Eric Burin.
p. cm.—(Southern dissent)
Includes bibliographical references and index.
isbn 978-0-8130-3273-3 (alk. paper)
1. American Colonization Society. 2. Slaves—Emancipation—
Southern States. 3. African Americans—Colonization—Africa, West.
4. African Americans—Colonization—Liberia. 5. Liberia—History—
To 1847. I. Title. II. Series.
e448.b955 2005
326'.0973'09034—dc22   2005042238

The University Press of Florida is the scholarly publishing agency for the State
University System of Florida, comprising Florida A&M University, Florida Atlantic
University, Florida Gulf Coast University, Florida International University, Florida
State University, New College of Florida, University of Central Florida, University of
Florida, University of North Florida, University of South Florida, and University of
West Florida.
University Press of Florida
15 Northwest 15th Street
Gainesville, FL 32611-2079
http://www.upf.com

For
Nikki

Contents

Preface for Paperback Edition   ix

Foreword   xiii

Acknowledgments   xvii

Introduction: American Colonization Society Manumissions
and Slavery   1

1. An Overview of the African Colonization Movement   6

2. ACS Manumitters: Their Ideology and Intentions   34

3. Slaves: Negotiating for Freedom   57

4. The Pennsylvania Colonization Society as a Facilitator
of Manumission   79

5. White Southerners' Responses to ACS Manumissions   100

6. ACS Manumissions and the Law   121

7. Liberia: Freedpersons' Experiences in Africa   141

Conclusion   160

Tables   169

Notes   175

Bibliography   201

Index   215

Preface for Paperback Edition

In the mid-1990s, Dr. Robert McColley, then my graduate advisor, casually remarked that the African colonization movement would become a "cottage industry" among historians. This was a bold forecast: although several good studies had recently appeared on colonization, the standard work on the subject had been written in 1961. Nevertheless, McColley's prediction proved true. In the late 1990s and early 2000s, a host of books, articles, and dissertations examined the American Colonization Society (ACS), Liberia, and related topics. Many of the new works weighed in on the perennial debate over the ACS's relationship with slavery, with some insisting that the organization advanced antislavery interests while others argued the opposite. That dispute was hardly resolved, but the outpouring of scholarship indelibly changed colonization studies, for the field of inquiry now stretched from the pre-Revolutionary period through the post-Reconstruction years, and the sites of investigation included Liberia, Louisiana, and every place in between. *Slavery and the Peculiar Solution* was a part of, and profited from, that upsurge in research. Reviewers' comments about the book, along with still newer scholarship on the ACS, suggest that colonization will remain an important if controversial topic of study.

In *Slavery and the Peculiar Solution* I examine how the colonization movement influenced slavery. Whereas previous studies tended to be narrowly focused, often investigating only one person, place, or time period, I wanted *Slavery and the Peculiar Solution* to be a more expansive work, one that assessed the ideas and actions of different peoples in America and Africa over an extended period of time. Thus, the book opens with a sweeping overview of the colonization crusade, demonstrating how this enduring campaign often subverted proslavery interests. The remaining chapters scrutinize "ACS manumissions"—that is, instances wherein slaveholders freed bondspersons on the condition that the latter move to Liberia. I analyzed the episodes from myriad perspectives, beginning with an examination of the would-be manumitters, and then discussing slaves' responses to the freedom offer, northern colonizationists' involvement in the affairs, white southerners' attitudes toward the enterprises, the legal conundrums posed by ACS liberations, and finally the freedpersons' experiences in Liberia. The infrequency of ACS manumissions, I argued, belied their significance; moreover, under certain circumstances, they undermined chattel bondage (often in ways that white colonizationists had not intended). I generally avoided using the term "antislavery," preferring instead words like "destabilized" and "undercut"—a distinction that many, but not all, reviewers noticed. The book's conclusion traces the colonization movement from the Civil War through the end of the century, when the ACS ceased sending emigrants to Liberia.

The reviews of *Slavery and the Peculiar Solution* testify to colonization's historiographic salience and contentiousness. For starters, I was surprised by what reviewers chose to showcase. I had supposed that Chapter 1, with its grand overview of the colonization movement, would be the most noteworthy portion of the book. Instead, many reviewers highlighted African Americans' impact on ACS liberations; others focused on slaveholders' manumission programs, white southerners' responses to the affairs, the legal rows that attended the episodes, and the freedpersons' fate in Liberia; still others spotlighted my ACS Database, which includes information on over 550 ACS manumitters, the 6,000 slaves they sent overseas, and the 4,000 antebellum free blacks who also moved to Liberia. The discrepancy between my expectations and the reviewers' commentary illustrates the breadth of colonization's scholarly appeal. Just as the movement meant different things to different people in the nineteenth century, so too do contemporary historians see disparate reasons for studying the ACS. What made the reviewers' diversity of opinion especially intriguing was the fact that the same items which some judged praiseworthy, others found problematic. Ultimately, the reviews of *Slavery and the Peculiar Solution* demonstrate that while scholars might dispute how colonization affected slavery, few doubt that it did so in significant ways.

The scholarship produced since the publication of *Slavery and the Peculiar Solution* has further advanced our understanding of the colonization movement and its influence on chattel bondage. In the last few years, researchers have produced excellent studies of the colonization crusade in Virginia, Pennsylvania, Rhode Island, and many other places. They have also shed additional light on the movement during the post-Revolutionary and Civil War years. Finally, they have examined the myriad individuals affected by colonization, from U.S. presidents to the humblest Liberian settlers. Just as *Slavery and the Peculiar Solution* benefited from the literature of the late 1990s and early 2000s, future scholarship will profit from the imaginative, meticulous, and untiring efforts of recent researchers.

Yet much work still needs to be done. First, future scholars need to define the term "colonization" more precisely. For nineteenth-century Americans, colonization as a concept could mean emigration, repatriation, deportation, or missionary work; as a program, it could mean establishing a Christian toehold in Africa, removing free blacks from the United States, or deracinating all black Americans; and colonization, as historian Elizabeth R. Varon has noted, also functioned as a rhetorical device, serving as a metaphor for racial segregation, assimilation, labor protest, psychological thralldom, and slavery itself. In short, researchers need to assess colonization's multiple connotations and better explicate what they themselves mean by the term. Second, scholars should continue to expand colonization's chronological parameters. Third, researchers' geographic scope of inquiry could be widened (the movement was truly a transatlantic enterprise) and narrowed (ACS operations at the community level remain understudied). Finally, scholars ought to situate colonization within the broadest contexts, integrating the movement into the history of the "black Atlantic," for example. In short, we have learned much about colonization recently, and I think *Slavery and the Peculiar Solution* contributed to the burgeoning literature, but the field is still ripe for investigation, and the harvest will be especially good if future scholars define their terms, expand their temporal and geographic boundaries, and view colonization within the widest analytical framework.

Future studies may also be informed by the ACS Database, which I will happily share with other researchers, and which I have enhanced considerably since writing *Slavery and the Peculiar Solution*. Simply put, the ACS Database is now more robust: the original data concerning antebellum emigrants and ACS manumitters have been supplemented with information on postbellum emigrants and the settlers' experiences in Liberia. Although the additional data would not have changed the fundamental conclusions of this book, the enlarged version of the database provides a wealth of research opportunities, especially concerning Liberia, that small, troubled colony-turned-republic that loomed so large in the debates over slavery, race, and freedom. Indeed, the expansion of the ACS Database, along with the continued outpouring of scholarship on colonization and the erudite reviews of *Slavery and the Peculiar Solution*, all suggest that McColley's prophecy has just begun to come to fruition.

Foreword

From the origin of the American republic through the Civil War no issue was more contentious than the question of what to do with freed slaves. Those abolitionists who viewed slavery as a moral evil demanding immediate emancipation advocated equal rights for all. But most white Americans, North and South, opposed such a prospect, regardless of their fears about the dangers slavery posed to civil liberties, prosperity, and republican government. For slaveholders, free black people constituted a dangerous anomaly. For white nonslaveholders, they threatened social and racial order. Like Thomas Jefferson, most white Americans believed that blacks and whites could not live together in harmony if both were free. Therefore, linking black freedom to black migration became a constant theme in discussions of individual manumission and general emancipation. By the late 1820s, black and white abolitionists railed against this idea of tying freedom to migration, insisting that such linkage denied black people their birthright as Americans and denigrated them as unfit for freedom. Abolitionists charged that schemes for colonizing African-Americans were intended to strengthen slavery by eliminating the free black class. However, throughout the antebellum period, some black leaders advocated colonization as the best route out of bondage and toward control of their own communities, free of white interference, and some white reformers regarded colonization as the only way to persuade slaveholders to manumit slaves voluntarily.

Within this complicated setting, the American Colonization Society (ACS) emerged in 1816 as a national organization dedicated to promoting the manumission of slaves and the settlement of free blacks in West Africa, specifically in the colony of Liberia. During the early decades of the nineteenth century, many white southerners believed the ACS promised a way out of the slavery dilemma. However, in reaction to radical northern abolitionism and to Nat Turner's 1831 slave rebellion, increasingly self-conscious white southerners insisted slavery was a "positive good" that should not be held up to even the mildest criticism. To abolitionists, the ACS embodied proslavery influence and arrogance, and they increasingly regarded it as an unmitigated proslavery scheme. Thus, the ACS became suspect in much of the South, to slaveholders and nonslaveholders alike, for its continued interest in freeing slaves. Those few slaveholders who kept up a correspondence with the ACS—especially those who manumitted slaves and supported free black people in Liberia —stood apart as dissenters. Their public willingness to act for manumission and their personal struggles to decide what slavery meant to them and their society are two issues Eric Burin addresses in *Slavery and the Peculiar Solution.*

The historiography of manumission and colonization is as tangled and contentious as its history. Historians have always been aware that the ACS was a multifaceted organization, embracing both proslavery and antislavery tendencies. They have pointed out that colonization would never have ended slavery in the United States because the country's growing slave population was far greater than the few thousands of individuals the ACS was able to transport to Liberia. After the 1960s, most historians accepted the abolitionists' contention that the ACS was essentially proslavery. Slavery, they argued, grew stronger as an institution, in part, because the ACS and its supporters reinforced the notion that African-Americans were incapable of responsible freedom. But, recently, upon closer examination of the dynamics of manumission and black involvement in decisions favoring migration, many historians have arrived at a new perspective. In a series of biographies and local studies, they recast the manumitting slaveholders and colonizationists as a more varied group in motive, interest, and politics than abolitionists and some historians of that movement portray them. In many instances, manumitters challenged the proslavery ideology of the ACS. African-American participation in the manumitting and colonizing process has come more clearly into view. Many black people, slave and free, supported colonization as a means of gaining freedom, cultural autonomy, and economic advancement, and of spreading Christianity in Africa. Until now, however, no comprehensive canvass of slaveholders' interest and involvement in colonization efforts existed to illuminate how particular southern localities and personalities shaped interest in manumission and colonization. Neither was there a substantial profile of the manumitter as a social type.

Burin examines manumission and colonization on two levels. He surveys the movement in its broad compass and probes many individual experiences, magnifying the ways manumission and colonization became "tumultuous affairs" for black and white southerners. To be sure, as Burin indicates, motives of convenience, profit, control, and commerce animated manumitters, as much as humanitarian, ideological, or Christian sensibilities did. Nearly 20 percent of manumissions were implemented by the last will and testament of the slaveholder. By custom, law, and prejudice, slaveholders imposed strict conditions on those who were freed, especially the requirement that they leave the state. But manumission and colonization inherently subverted slaveholders' mastery. By regarding black slaves as something other than chattel, and by arguing that they might build a Christian commonwealth in West Africa, slaveholders who engaged in manumission accentuated the contradictions in human bondage. Slaveholding women who supported colonization societies and freed their slaves threatened the patriarchy of southern society. Manumission and colonization were especially dangerous because they gave slaves agency. Slaves who were promised manumission might insist, for example, that they would go to Liberia only on the condition that their family members also be freed. Slaves witnessing the manumission of others might press for the freedom of all. Newly freed people hired themselves out and accumulated property in preparation for embarkation—activities that put them in competition with whites and gave them a degree of independence. Everywhere manumission and colonization were proposed, social disruption followed. White society responded by tightening laws on manumission and restricting the mobility and employability of free blacks.

Burin points to the limits of dissent in the South, as revealed in the "peculiar solution" of colonization. He also marks the limits of proslavery power in stifling dissent. *Slavery and the Peculiar Solution* reminds us that slaveholders did not speak with one voice on slavery, and all slaves were not silent about their own interests. The persistence of manumission and colonization in the South reflected, and affected, alternative ways of approaching slavery and race that led to freedom for some and hope for many more.

Stanley Harrold and Randall M. Miller
Series Editors

Acknowledgments

Many people helped make this book possible. Credit and blame for my becoming a historian rest heavily with Lester Brooks, who was an inspiring professor during my undergraduate days, an inflexible tormenter during my graduate studies, and a cherished friend both then and now. In like fashion, I will always be grateful to Robert McColley, an otherwise sensible man who agreed to be my graduate advisor when there was no good reason to do so. Professors Vernon Burton and Matt Garcia were also instrumental in the writing of the dissertation, as was Dawn Owens-Nicholson, the quantitative wizard who helped set up the ACS Database.

North Dakota is a fabulous place to write a book, and not just because of its interminable winters. My colleagues at the University of North Dakota have provided an emotional warmth and intellectual stimulation beyond description. Special thanks to the following individuals for reading all or part of the manuscript, answering statistical questions, and providing primary sources: Jim Mochoruk, Kathryn Rand, Paul Sum, Sharon Carson, Richard Beringer, Mark Jendrysik, and the late Walter Ellis. My deepest, most heartfelt appreciation must also be extended to Grand Forks' Lorna and Mike Berg, who every day offer quiet but powerful lessons about humanity, dignity, community, and family. If I knew as much about colonization as they do about life, this book would be much longer and far more enlightening.

Fellowships from Duke University, the Library Company of Philadelphia, the Virginia Historical Society, the North Dakota Humanities Council, and the University of North Dakota facilitated research for this project. With these monies, I visited archives across the country, and I would like to thank all the librarians who helped me over the years. I also want to express my gratitude to my able research assistants, Susie Matejcek, Erik Towne, Joy Greger, Kit

Lim, and Anthony Dutton. Finally, I am much obliged to our departmental secretary, Deneen Marynik, for handling the paperwork and making sure we all got paid.

Some material in this book has been previously published. Small portions of my article "The Strange Career of John Cocke: Contexualizing American Colonization Society Manumissions," *Liberian Studies Journal* 26, no. 2 (2000), are dispersed throughout the work. Parts of chapter 3 come from my essay "Envisioning Africa: American Slaves' Ideas about Liberia," *Liberian Studies Journal* 27, no. 1 (2002). Both pieces are published here with the editor's permission. Chapter 4 is a revised version of my article "Rethinking Northern White Support for the African Colonization Movement: The Pennsylvania Colonization Society as an Agent of Emancipation," *Pennsylvania Magazine of History and Biography* 127, no. 2 (April 2003); it appears here with the permission of the editor.

Other scholars' commentary improved this book immeasurably. The University Press of Florida provided everything an author could want. Editor Meredith Morris-Babb evinced enthusiasm from the start. Series editors Stanley Harrold and Randall Miller gave advice that was nothing short of brilliant. T. Stephen Whitman made equally erudite observations, as did Douglas Egerton. I am also obliged to Kirsten and Ava Fischer, Lisa Norling, James Merrell, Serena Zabin, Jeff Mullins, and the other participants at the Early American History Workshop at the University of Minnesota, and to Jason Digman of the Minnesota Population Center. Finally, Michael Fitzgerald, Ronald Walters, and Frederick Blue all expertly critiqued earlier versions of various chapters. This book's shortcomings are no reflection of these sage and generous scholars.

You can't pick your family. Even if I could, I'd choose the same people. My kin have been loving, supporting, and patient while I wrote this book. I thank every one of you.

But most of all I am indebted to Nikki Berg, my emotional soul mate, my intellectual helpmeet, my everything. This book is for you.

Introduction

American Colonization Society Manumissions and Slavery

Founded in 1816, the American Colonization Society (ACS) hoped to rid the United States of both slavery and black people. Expatriation proposals of this sort first surfaced during the colonial era, and they grew more prevalent over time. By the Revolutionary period, when slavery, race, and freedom dominated the national discourse, such schemes received serious consideration throughout the country. Those ventures fizzled out, but white enthusiasm for black removal ignited once again during the early 1800s. Alarmed by the rapidly growing free black and slave populations, Charles Fenton Mercer, Henry Clay, Daniel Webster, and other notables created the ACS, a group that quickly secured federal funding, rallied an interregional constituency, and established the colony of Liberia as a place for black settlement. As sectional tensions heightened during the antebellum era, colonizationists became more vocal, pleading that only emancipation and deracination could solve the country's troubles. The movement remained powerful during the Civil War, when millions of slaves secured liberty, and during Reconstruction, when Americans disputed the meaning of black freedom. Even in the 1880s and 1890s, thousands of black men and women wanted to reside in Liberia, and the ACS transported some of them there. Simply put, colonization was a prominent force in America from the pre-Revolutionary period through the post-Reconstruction years.

The impact of this long-lived enterprise could be seen everywhere. It influenced national politics, economic debates, gender relations, legal thought, and republican ideology. The present study considers all of these subjects, but it primarily focuses on colonization's relationship with slavery. It investigates the matter from two vantage points. First, it gauges the movement's effect on black bondage by providing a panoramic overview of the colonization crusade; second, it scrutinizes ACS activities as they played out at the local level. From either point of view, colonization tended to undermine slavery.

To argue that the ACS impaired black bondage is to leap into a turbulent historiographic current. From the 1920s through the early 1960s, most historians deemed the ACS a conservative, antislavery organization.[1] Thereafter, scholars grew more critical of the ACS, emphasizing colonizationists' ulterior motives for opposing slavery, the group's rabid racism, and African-Americans' largely negative attitudes toward the enterprise.[2] By the 1990s, many authors no longer considered the ACS an antislavery institution.[3] More recently, however, several researchers have placed the Society (as the ACS was sometimes called) back in the antislavery circle. This work confirms, refines, and extends the latter group's conclusions.[4]

Chapter 1 scans the colonization campaign from grand vistas. It surveys the enterprise from the Revolutionary War through Lincoln's election, interweaving the actions of northern reformers and Upper South residents who ran the ACS, of proslavery enthusiasts and white abolitionists who decried the group, and of black protestors and Liberia-bound emigrants who shaped the organization's fate in both America and Africa. When viewed from lofty heights, one can see that the colonization crusade often subverted proslavery interests.

If chapter 1 gazes upon the colonization movement from afar, the balance of this book zeros in on specific ACS operations. More precisely, the remaining chapters analyze ACS manumissions—that is, instances wherein slaves were freed on the condition that they move to Liberia. Between 1820 and 1860, approximately 560 slaveholders sent, collectively, about 6,000 bondpersons to the ACS's colony.[5] To better understand these episodes, each chapter presents a different viewpoint, with the chapters ordered in such a way that they would follow, generally, the chronology of an individual liberation. Chapter 2 explores the ideas and aspirations of ACS manumitters, while chapter 3 investigates how bondpersons responded to their owners' emancipation proposals. Chapter 4 considers northern colonizationists' financing of ACS liberations. Chapter 5 assesses southern whites' responses to the emancipatory affairs, and chapter 6 analyzes judicial and legislative battles over ACS manumissions. Finally, chapter 7 examines the freedpersons' experiences in Liberia and discusses how their opinions influenced the colonization movement back in America. Though Society officials and southern emancipators expected manumissions to be pacific enterprises, in reality the episodes were often tumultuous affairs that undercut "the peculiar institution."[6]

The tale of Martha Moderwell illuminates many important characteristics of ACS liberations, including their potential to weaken slavery. A resident of Augusta, Georgia, Moderwell sent five bondpersons to Liberia in 1860, making her one of the last ACS emancipators. Like many of her predecessors, Moderwell regarded manumission as a morally sensible, financially sound mechanism of slave control. She had thought so for quite some time. Moderwell's first emancipatory endeavor occurred in 1849, when she sent Disley, a forty-year-old literate laundress, and Disley's ten-year-old son, Charles, to Liberia. A few years later Moderwell permitted George J. Walker to emigrate aboard the *Harp*. In 1860, Moderwell, who was now in her mid-fifties and in ill health, looked to liberate Mary King and her four children. But King was reluctant to leave without her husband, Alfred, whose owner demanded $3,000 for the bondman. Moderwell came up with $2,000, and Alfred's owner dropped the asking price to $2,500. Still $500 short, Moderwell finally succumbed to death. In her will, she granted Mary King the option of going to Liberia. In May 1860, King gathered up her four youngsters, bid a tearful good-bye to her enslaved husband, and boarded the *Mary Caroline Stevens* just as the vessel departed for Liberia. Local sympathizers promised to raise the requisite sums for Alfred's freedom, and King pledged to write her spouse. The fund-raising foundered, as did the couple's correspondence, once the Civil War commenced. As of 1864, Mary King was unsure of her husband's whereabouts, and she implored ACS officials to help her find him.[7]

This short story brings into relief several prominent features of ACS manumissions. Moderwell herself is representative, in many ways, of ACS liberators. Like her counterparts, Moderwell was no antislavery radical. She dispensed freedom at intervals, staggering manumissions in an effort to advance her own pecuniary and psychological interests. Along similar lines, as a female, Moderwell typified those slaveholding women who faced unique "managerial" difficulties and who consequently turned to ACS emancipations in greater numbers, proportionally speaking, than did men. In addition to her approach to manumission and her situation as a female slaveholder-liberator, Moderwell was emblematic of ACS emancipators in other respects. For example, that Moderwell was a Georgian bespeaks how ACS manumissions gradually spread south- and westward as Upper South migrants carried colonizationist ideas into the Lower South. Moreover, by the time she freed Mary King, Moderwell was fifty-six years old—like most ACS liberators, she effected manumissions relatively late in life. Indeed, the last of Moderwell's emancipations came via a testamentary decree, a reflection of the fact that postmortem liberations (and the problems that attended them) were on the rise during the 1840s and 1850s. In short, Moderwell embodies well the objectives and experiences of many white southerners who sent slaves to Liberia.

The Moderwell affair also illustrates bondpersons' perceptions of and impact on ACS manumissions. First, the episode shows how important familial considerations were to would-be freedpersons. From the slaves' perspective, ACS emancipations might sunder kin connections, but they also might protect black families against the vagaries of malicious owners, estate liquidations, and economic fluctuations. Moreover, like Mary and Alfred King, most bondpersons saw their familial struggles as a prolonged battle, one in which leaving for Liberia did not signify an end to the fight but rather a new phase in the protracted engagement. Second, the story highlights freedpersons' participation in the transatlantic communications network. The King's postliberation correspondence was not unusual. Prospective manumittees' requests for information about family, friends, and conditions in Africa resulted in scores of Liberian letters, sojourners, recruiters, and refugees circulating through the South, each reshaping the colonization movement along the way. Third, the tale demonstrates that bondpersons eyed manumission proposals very carefully, accepting, rejecting, and renegotiating the deals based on their perceptions of the likely benefits and potential drawbacks. In this case, Mary King's willingness to emigrate evidently increased once Moderwell passed away. A change in circumstances, it appears, initiated a reassessment of the freedom offer. In the end, virtually all deliberating bondpersons sought to strengthen familial bonds, obtain reliable information about colonization, and work the manumission agreement to their best advantage.

Finally, the Moderwell episode sheds light on the logistical, interregional, social, and legal aspects of ACS liberations. For example, Mary King's attempt to secure her husband's freedom illuminates how slaves' familial demands encouraged "conjunctive emancipations" between neighboring slaveholders (that is, instances wherein two or more slaveholders liberated different members of one slave family). The inability of Martha Moderwell and the Kings to raise the ransom price for Alfred underscores not only how difficult it was to effect conjunctive emancipations but also that the challenge became even greater when, in the mid- to late 1850s, Pennsylvania colonizationists stopped soliciting funds for would-be freedpersons and instead concentrated on the removal of black northerners. In addition, the congeniality evinced by some Augustans makes it clear that many variables factored into white southerners' responses to ACS manumissions, including the location of the enterprise, the magnitude of the undertaking, and the proximity of the observer.[8] Last, that Moderwell freed Mary King by will brings to mind southern jurists' and lawmakers' propensity, over time, to outlaw or circumscribe manumission, a crackdown that included in some states a ban on postmortem emancipations.

Clearly, ACS manumissions were not trifling ventures. The tug-and-pull between slaves, their owners, and other parties rendered the liberations logistically complex, financially troublesome, legally complicated, and, at times, socially disruptive enterprises. To be sure, the number of ACS emancipations was not great. Yet their infrequency was no measure of their import. Each brimmed with social, legal, political, and personal consequences that white colonizationists had not anticipated and could not control. Like pebbles dropped in water, ACS manumissions rippled outward, destabilizing slavery in their wake.

1

⁓ೲ⁓

An Overview
of the African Colonization Movement

Proposals to remove black people from America first circulated during the colonial era. By the Revolutionary period, such schemes were being discussed on a regular basis. The colonization crusade became even more conspicuous during the Early National and antebellum eras as debates over slavery intensified. Even during the Civil War, Reconstruction, and post-Reconstruction years, the campaign to expatriate black Americans churned on. The colonization movement, in other words, was no passing fancy.

The Revolutionary Era through 1815

On the eve of the American Revolution, slavery was spread entirely, if unevenly, across British North America. Two-thirds of the mainland colonies' 469,000 bondpersons dwelled in the Chesapeake region. Another 20 percent resided in Georgia and South Carolina. Approximately 10 percent toiled in the Mid-Atlantic and New England colonies. All totaled, one in five Americans was enslaved at the time of the Revolution.[1]

The War for Independence unleashed forces that challenged slavery in unprecedented ways. Natural rights rhetoric, with its exaltation of human freedom, placed slavery's proponents on the defensive, as did the egalitarianism of evangelical Christianity. Wartime resistance from bondpersons also undercut

[handwritten: 1776 slavery was uncertain]

the institution. Economic shifts—urbanization, commercialization, and the transition to mixed farming in the Chesapeake especially—likewise tested slavery's viability. In a word, bondage's future in America was uncertain.[2]

[handwritten margin note: northern states VT MA NH CN RI]

The aforementioned ideological, economic, and social forces slowly disintegrated slavery in the northern states. Chattel bondage collapsed first in New England, where it was weakest. Vermont abolished slavery by constitutional fiat in 1777. Shortly thereafter, judicial and legal processes, though somewhat ambiguous in nature, signaled the end of unfree labor in Massachusetts and New Hampshire. Connecticut, which had more bondpersons than any other New England state, and Rhode Island, which was deeply involved in the Atlantic slave trade, passed gradual abolition laws in the early 1780s. Dismantling slavery proved more difficult in the Mid-Atlantic states, where 33,000 African-Americans were held in bondage in 1770. Pennsylvania's gradual emancipation act of 1780 liberated only those slaves born after the statute's date of enactment, and even these would-be freedpersons did not escape thralldom until their twenty-eighth birthday. New York and New Jersey passed similar statutes, but not until 1799 and 1804, respectively. Still, by the early nineteenth century, all of the northern states had embarked on the road to abolition, though several did not expect to reach their final destination for quite a long time.[3]

[handwritten margin note: PA NY NJ]

Northern slaveholders and their allies littered the path to freedom with numerous obstacles. In many respects, the first and most coherent defenses of slavery were developed by northerners during the late eighteenth and early nineteenth centuries. The institution's supporters claimed that economic necessity, private property rights, and the Bible itself justified the continuation of chattel bondage. Southern apologists would later employ all of these arguments. So, too, would they utilize another contention of northern opponents of abolition: that liberated, propertyless, black men and women would become a burden on society.[4]

[handwritten margin note: 1/4]

This was not a new idea. As early as 1714, one New Jersey resident suggested that slaves "be set free . . . [and] sent to their own Country." Neither emancipation nor colonization materialized at that early juncture, but the mistrust of freedpersons remained. In the early eighteenth century, every northern colony except New Hampshire enacted statutes that were designed to prevent manumittees from becoming public charges. The dawning of northern abolition magnified long-standing anxieties about freedpersons exponentially. Some commentators consequently suggested that liberated blacks be transported to distant lands. In 1768, for example, an antislavery article in a Philadelphia newspaper urged that a "Negro colony" be established "to the southward." In the early 1770s, both Anthony Benezet and Thomas Paine proposed settling black people beyond the Allegheny Mountains. In 1776, Rhode Island clergyman Samuel Hopkins, building on his previous missionary scheme, proclaimed that American slaves should be sent to Africa. During the "first emancipation," in other words, many prominent figures hoped to conjoin deportation to abolition.[5]

All of these expatriation proposals came to naught. They foundered for several reasons. Some observers, noting that not a single state required the removal of manumittees, regarded the compulsory expulsion of freedpersons too radical a measure. Along similar lines, powerful organizations like the Pennsylvania Abolition Society called relocation plans morally repugnant and contrary to the humanitarian principles of the antislavery movement. Other detractors objected on pragmatic grounds, dismissing deportation schemes as impractical. Still others claimed that, feasibility aside, northern governments that had rejected compensated emancipation programs would never fund an expatriation venture. Finally, some opponents insisted that the whole matter was moot. The northern black population was too small to threaten whites' interests, they averred. Moreover, with the institutionalization of new forms of black dependency, the removal of African-Americans might not even be desirable. Liberalism, pragmatism, and self-interest thus undermined colonization in the Revolutionary-era North.[6]

So, too, did African-American opposition. As Gary Nash has observed, northern slaves "did not regard their requests for freedom as appeals to a merciful master class but as a demand for the restoration of inherent rights unlawfully wrested from them." Confident bondpersons who considered liberty their birthright bristled at the thought of relocation being a condition for emancipation. Indeed, the establishment of black churches and benevolent societies served notice that African-Americans had every intention of staying in the United States, where they would labor to secure equality for themselves and freedom for those still in chains.[7]

Most black northerners opposed colonization, but some expressed interest in the idea. In 1773, four Massachusetts slaves petitioned for public monies to help found a settlement in Africa. Similar proposals surfaced among black people in Newport, Rhode Island, in 1780 and in Boston, Massachusetts, in 1787. These projects differed from those espoused by white promoters, however. For many black Americans, colonization was imbued with a nascent sense of pan-Africanism. Although thousands of slaves had been imported into New York, Pennsylvania, and other northern colonies during the mid-1700s, by the

close of the century, the divisions between Igbos, Coromantees, and other cultural groups had receded. For the most part, black northerners now saw each
other simply as people of a generalized African ancestry living in the United
States. With notions of a universal African identity awhirl, little wonder that
some individuals favored colonization. Even so, the vast majority of black
northerners intended to remain in America.[8]

Thwarted during the war years, the northern colonization movement
gained strength in the late eighteenth and early nineteenth centuries. Massachusetts lexicographer Noah Webster, along with fellow Bay State politician
James Sullivan, British philanthropist William Thornton, Philadelphians John
Parrish and Thomas Branagan, and an anonymous New Hampshire pamphleteer, all advocated, with varying degrees of enthusiasm, black relocation programs. Some of these turn-of-the-century northern colonizationists pitched
expatriation as a means of ending southern slavery; others, reflecting a conservative retreat from the social environmentalism and egalitarian republicanism
of the Revolutionary days, simply wished to banish free blacks from the North.
Southern intransigence and northern timidity frustrated the former; African-
American opposition impeded the latter. Yet the colonizationists did not despair. The trends of the times suggested that their day would come. White hostility toward black northerners grew daily; southern slavery appeared more
problematic than ever. Both dilemmas demanded solutions. In the early 1800s,
northern colonizationists were certain they had the answers.[9]

The solvents that eroded northern slavery failed to dissolve bondage in the
Chesapeake region. As Ira Berlin has reminded us, westward expansion, natural population growth, and the continued importation of African bondpersons all meant that far more black people were enslaved in the United States at
the end of the Age of Revolution than at the beginning. Yet slavery did not
advance uncontested. Natural rights ideology, evangelical equalitarianism,
economic uncertainty, and African-American resistance all slowed its proliferation. Thousands of southern slaves secured liberty during this period, and
in some areas, such as Maryland's Eastern Shore, black bondage was withering
noticeably. In short, both slavery and freedom expanded in the Chesapeake
states following the Revolution.[10]

It was within this context that Thomas Jefferson wrote *Notes on the State of
Virginia* (1787), a book that offered the most elaborate disquisition on colonization to date. Slavery, lamented Jefferson, was politically divisive, economically inefficient, and morally unsound. It was also horrifyingly dangerous, warned the Virginian, for bondpersons would eventually revolt. Yet it was

unwise to free slaves unconditionally, he cautioned. In explaining himself, Jefferson offered two somewhat contradictory reasons for his position. On one hand, he claimed that unrestricted emancipation would beget miscegenation, that freedpersons would end up "staining the blood" of white Americans. On the other hand, Jefferson asserted that instinctive racial antipathy would result in a war between ex-slaves and their former owners. Unconditional emancipation, fretted Jefferson, would surely and tragically culminate in either blood-letting or blood mixing.[11]

Jefferson suggested solutions for the nation's predicament. The first step, he argued, was to bottleneck slavery by banning the importation of African bondpersons and preventing bondage's westward advance. Once circumscribed, slavery could be whittled away with a post-*nati* emancipation and colonization program. Bondpersons born after a certain date, contended Jefferson, should be apprenticed "according to their geniuses" and then, as young adults, be properly outfitted and sent "to such place as the circumstances of the time should render most proper." Jefferson thought that white southerners were ready for such an antislavery experiment. "I think a change is already perceptible, since the origin of the present revolution," he wrote optimistically. Ready or not, a "total emancipation" was inevitable, averred Jefferson. The only question was whether it would come "with the consent of the masters, rather than by their expiration."[12]

Other southerners concurred with Jefferson's analysis, though their colonization proposals varied in the particulars. In 1788, James Madison advocated the establishment of an African colony to encourage manumissions. The same year, Baltimore resident "Othello," writing in the political and literary magazine *American Museum*, called for a program of gradual abolition and expatriation. Virginia magistrate William Craighead argued that slaves should be slowly liberated and sent to the Old Northwest, where they would occupy a position analogous to that of native tribes. Fellow Virginian Ferdinando Fairfax designed a federal emancipation and removal program in 1790. Six years later, another well-known resident of the Old Dominion, St. George Tucker, unveiled a gradual emancipation scheme in which freedpersons would be denied virtually all civil rights and thereby encouraged to "seek those privileges in some other climate." In the late 1780s and 1790s, antislavery advocates in the Chesapeake region rarely spoke of emancipation without mentioning expatriation.[13]

These proposals fell victim to northern indifference and southern antipathy. Although Fairfax and Tucker had hoped to enlist the support of northern reformers and lawmakers by publishing their works in Philadelphia, which was the seat of the U.S. government at the time, their pleas went unheeded. The schemes fared no better among southerners. In the Virginia legislature, for example, Tidewater politicians brushed aside Tucker's work. A disappointed Tucker reflected in 1796 that "Actual suffering will one day, perhaps, open the oppressors' eyes. Till that happens, they will shut their ears against argument." Four years later, when Virginian slave Gabriel organized a slave conspiracy in Richmond, white Virginians were listening attentively. The message they heard, however, differed from the one Tucker had anticipated.[14]

Gabriel's insurrectionary plot moved the Virginia General Assembly to secretly request that the state's governor, James Monroe, communicate with the United States president, Thomas Jefferson, concerning "whither persons obnoxious to the laws or dangerous to the peace of society may be removed." Like Jefferson, Monroe favored colonization in light of its emancipatory possibilities. The president, after reading the Virginia resolution, asked the lawmakers to clarify their intentions. In 1802, the legislators, again deliberating behind closed doors, responded that they originally had wanted to colonize rebels, insurgents, and others who had conspired with Gabriel. But having just learned of a second slave conspiracy, they now intended to include among the potential deportees free blacks, whose numbers had increased rapidly over the last two decades, and new manumittees, who were presently not required to leave the state. Unlike Jefferson, Monroe, and others who saw colonization as a means to end slavery, many Virginia lawmakers—and especially those from the black-belt Tidewater areas—regarded it as way to protect the institution. The former wanted to expatriate all black people; the latter aimed to remove individuals who were thought to endanger bondage. That the resolutions were passed unanimously suggests that the older, emancipation-oriented colonizationists voted with the newer, proslavery ones. A fragile alliance between two former political foes had been born.[15]

In the meantime, Jefferson learned that the most likely site for black relocation, Sierra Leone, was in dire straits. Founded in 1787, Sierra Leone was a floundering English colony in West Africa for "recaptured" African slaves and British freedpersons. Transporting any African-Americans there was simply out of the question. The coalition of Virginia colonizationists was not deterred. After the Louisiana Purchase in 1803, antislavery colonizationists like St. George Tucker eyed the West as a place for a black settlement. Proslavery colonizationists in the Virginia legislature were thinking along the same lines and consequently passed resolutions in 1804 and 1805 urging the state's congressmen to secure a portion of the Louisiana Territory for the purpose of colonizing free blacks and future manumittees. Like their predecessors, these westward-looking colonization proposals went nowhere.[16]

Stymied in their attempts to obtain a colony, proslavery Virginians sought to safeguard bondage by other means. Hoping to stem the growth of the free black population, in 1806 Tidewater and Piedmont planters secured a state-wide ban on domestic emancipations—that is, liberations wherein freedpersons were allowed to remain in the state. Hereafter, slaves, if emancipated, could not stay in Virginia. The legislators also circumscribed free blacks' rights, hoping the latter would leave voluntarily. From the lawmakers' perspective, where manumittees and free blacks went was less important than that they actually left the Old Dominion.[17]

At this juncture, proslavery Virginians had to decide whether they would continue to champion colonization. There were good reasons for carrying on the cause. A narrowly defined version of colonization could politically unite rural planters and urban white artisans for the latter often resented competition from free black labor. Such a program could also weed out any remaining Gabriels. Despite the prohibition on domestic emancipations, many newly liberated African-Americans remained in the state. Nor had the onslaught of repressive legislation produced a free black exodus. Under such circumstances, some proslavery persons favored the establishment of a state agency that could guarantee the removal of manumittees and perhaps cajole free blacks into departing, as well. Simply put, colonization still appealed to slavery's defenders.[18]

Yet proslavery Virginians also understood the dangers of being committed to colonization. It took little imagination to envision antislavery crusaders taking over the project and implementing their more radical version of the scheme. Preventing such a coup would be difficult enough with a state-run program; keeping emancipationists' hands off a federally administered enterprise would be an even greater challenge. Proslavery Virginians thus faced difficult decisions concerning colonization. As they were contemplating the matter, America became entangled in a series of international conflicts that culminated in the War of 1812. The planters' decisions—indeed, the whole colonization campaign—hung in a state of suspense for nearly a decade. Once the war with England ended in 1815, the colonization issue burst forth once again.

Between the Revolutionary era and the early nineteenth century, colonization shaped the discourse on slavery and race. Initially, black expatriation proposals represented a form of antislavery conservatism, and many supporters continued to regard it as such. In the late eighteenth century, though, some white northerners stripped colonization of its emancipationist aspects and regarded it as a mechanism for ridding their region of black people. A similar turn of events occurred in the Chesapeake region during the early 1800s, when proslavery individuals co-opted the scheme. Most African-Americans rejected colonization all along, but some saw it as a means of promoting black nationalism. In 1816, this conglomeration of colonizationists gave rise to the ACS.

1816–1830

ACS

"Its origin is not a little curious," remarked Charles Fenton Mercer of the ACS. The events preceding the Society's founding were indeed curious, and Mercer had been in the middle of it. In February 1816, Mercer and fellow Virginia politicians Dabney Minor and Philip Doddridge were drinking heavily when the Federalist Doddridge exclaimed that Thomas Jefferson was "a consummate hypocrite." Minor, a Jeffersonian Republican, demanded to hear Doddridge's proof. Doddridge replied that Jefferson had advocated black deportation in *Notes on the State of Virginia,* but when the Virginia legislature repeatedly passed procolonization resolutions in the early 1800s, Jefferson, as president, had "coldly evaded the application." The young Mercer sat astonished. Over the next few weeks, he investigated the matter further. Fascinated and inspired, Mercer began laying the groundwork for the establishment of the ACS.[19]

Men like Mercer added a new and important constituency to the colonization coalition: southern modernizers who wished to replace the slave-based agrarian economy with a free-labor, commercial-industrial one. Such individuals believed, however, that a remade South would have its own problems. For starters, a boisterous working class would be created, one whose discontent and passions could be manipulated "to the most destructive purposes." The haughty Mercer figured that an anesthetizing educational system and an upward-looking middle class would keep the rabble in line. Yet the opiate of instruction and optimism would not work on ex-slaves. Since nature or God had made races antagonistic, reasoned Mercer, black people could never ascend in society. With no carrot of hope to follow, freedpersons would sink into vice, burst into rebellion, or both. The only remedy was to send them to Africa. There, black colonists would destroy the slave trade, Christianize "heathens," and establish commercial relations with the slave-free South. Colonization's benefits, mused Mercer, were all-encompassing.[20]

Mercer committed himself to founding a colonization society. During the summer of 1816, he traveled throughout the Chesapeake and Mid-Atlantic regions, telling everyone who would listen about his scheme. Three of Mercer's associates, Baltimore lawyer Francis Scott Key, Supreme Court clerk Elias B. Caldwell, and New Jersey clergyman Robert Finley, canvassed Washington, D.C. The coterie rejoiced when Bushrod Washington, a nephew of George Washington and a Supreme Court justice, agreed to serve as the proposed organization's president. On 21 December 1816, Washington, along with the other men that Caldwell, Key, Finley, and Mercer had contacted, met to establish their new group. Mercer himself was not present, but many prominent political figures were in attendance, including Henry Clay, Daniel Webster, William Crawford, Ferdinando Fairfax, John Taylor of Caroline, and John Randolph of Roanoke.[21]

During the charter meeting, the thorny subject of slavery came up. Robert Finley, the New Jersey minister, had previously stated that colonization would extinguish slavery. Conversely, John Randolph now opined that the Society, by deporting free blacks, would strengthen the institution. In between Finley and Randolph were men like Henry Clay, who, like Mercer, thought slavery obstructed southern progress, but, as a Border State politician, avoided public proclamations on the issue. Indeed, Clay, eyeing the mishmash of proslavery planters, Piedmont vacillators, southern modernizers, and northern evangelicals in attendance, told the ACS's founding members that the new organization should sidestep the "delicate question" of slavery altogether. Most attendees agreed. One week after Clay offered his advice, they created the discreetly titled "American Society for Colonizing the Free People of Color of the United States."[22]

ACS leaders immediately attempted to tap the national coffers. A fortnight after the Society's founding, John Randolph introduced a resolution in the House of Representatives begging federal aid for the ACS's program, but the Slave Trade Committee rejected the initiative as too expensive. Momentarily rebuffed, Representative Mercer led the counterattack. Knowing that in 1808 the United States had outlawed the importation of African slaves, Mercer asked what was to be done with African bondpersons who were illegally smuggled into the country. Mercer's Slave Trade Act of 1819 authorized the federal government to transport these so-called recaptured Africans back across the Atlantic. Debates immediately arose over whether the law allowed the president to purchase land in Africa. Although most of Monroe's cabinet expressed skepticism, ACS officials badgered Attorney General William Wirt into offering a favorable opinion. Monroe accepted Wirt's interpretation of the

statue. Shortly thereafter, U.S. naval officer Robert Stockton sailed to West Africa, where he negotiated for land with a pen in one hand and a drawn pistol in
the other. Stockton signed the ensuing contract on behalf of the Society, which
administered the land, soon to be named Liberia, as a private colony. In the
meantime, Monroe began allocating funds to the ACS, ostensibly so that the
organization would make Liberia a congenial place for recaptured Africans.
Thus began a tenuous but vital relationship between the national government
and the ACS.[23]

The ACS's joy at securing federal support was short-lived, for the Missouri Crisis of 1819–21 changed the terrain of antislavery politics. During the
debates, a number of Upper South congressmen abandoned the old notion
that restricting slavery would hasten the institution's demise and instead contended that the best way to eliminate bondage from their region was to spread
it across the continent. By funneling enslaved African-Americans westward,
the argument went, Maryland, Virginia, and similarly situated states could
reduce their black-to-white ratios and thereby achieve the preconditions for
abolishing slavery altogether. This "diffusion" theory portended problems for
the ACS, for it showed how Upper South states could become free-labor, lily-
white bastions without the pragmatic and political difficulties of colonization.[24]

The Missouri Crisis created a second dilemma for the ACS, one that concerned southern perceptions of antislavery northerners. According to some
southern congressmen, northerners who wished to ban bondage in Missouri
conceptualized slavery as a sectional cancer that Congress ought to circumscribe. Proslavery politicians naturally resented such highhandedness, but so
too did many antislavery leaders in the Upper South. The latter hoped to use
federal power to achieve emancipation, but that power, they insisted, must be
exercised at the request of the South. Such an invitation would never come if
northerners continued moralizing and chest-thumping. Within this context,
the ACS, already despised by Lower South officials, became a source of doubt
among some Upper South ones. They wondered whether the Society intended
to succor or strong arm antislavery southerners.[25]

As the Missouri Crisis rancor suggests, the ACS was struggling to forge a
nationwide constituency. Proslavery and abolitionist opposition, along with
competition from other black emigration schemes, undermined colonizationists' efforts to build an interregional coalition, and the ACS's own policies
simply worsened the problem. Many Society officials worked only part-time
on colonization; when the officers did labor on the movement's behalf, they es-

chewed local-level organizing and instead sought endorsements from famous individuals whose sponsorship could be parlayed into federal cash. Once the ACS named Connecticut native Ralph R. Gurley corresponding secretary in 1825, however, the organization began cultivating grassroots support and exhibiting administrative savvy. Following Gurley's suggestions, the ACS board of managers employed traveling agents who created auxiliary societies, collected donations, lobbied legislators, and convinced ministers to devote their Independence Day sermons to colonization. Gurley's recommendations invigorated the movement. As one board member boasted in 1828, "we have united in our ranks men of all capacities, all places, all dominations."[26]

The ACS's growth had profound consequences for black northerners. Numbering nearly 100,000 in 1820, African-Americans in the North were divided by class and cultural distinctions, with the "respectable" middle class and the "coarse" poorer folk eyeing one another with mutual suspicion. But as the racial climate worsened, black northerners came together in new ways. Questioning white Americans' commitment to equality and their own faith in the gospel of individual uplift, the region's black leaders began articulating a race consciousness. For some individuals, such as John Russwurm, coeditor of the first black newspaper, *Freedom's Journal,* departing for Liberia offered a solution to black people's predicament. But for most, including abolitionist stalwarts Lewis Woodson, Samuel Cornish, Peter Williams, and Maria W. Stewart, the answer lay not in emigration but rather in increasingly militant protests against slavery, racism, and colonization. As a result, between 1820 and 1830, only 154 black northerners moved to Liberia.[27] The few who left endured the condemnation of those who stayed. "Those who are ignorant enough to go to Africa, the coloured people ought to be glad to have them go," declared the abolitionist David Walker in 1829, "for if they are ignorant enough to let the whites *fool* them off to Africa, they would be no small injury to us if they reside in this country."[28]

Like their counterparts in the North, most southern free blacks opposed the ACS. This was especially true in Baltimore, where William Watkins, William Douglass, Jacob Greener, and others harassed Society agents, disrupted emigrant expeditions, and encouraged a young William Lloyd Garrison to forsake colonization. Even so, several southern free black leaders embraced the ACS's program. Worried about their deteriorating economic, social, and legal conditions, 720 southern free blacks went to Liberia between 1820 and 1830. Led by Joseph Jenkins Roberts, Lott Cary, Daniel Coker, and other prominent figures, many of these early emigrants represented the elite ranks of the southern free black community. Over two-fifths of those over age sixteen could read or write. Only 33 percent had jobs related to agriculture. Politically wise and economically astute, southern free black emigrants would go on to dominate Liberian society.[29]

Meanwhile, the ACS did virtually nothing in the realm of manumissions. Between 1820 and 1825, the Society sent just six freedpersons to Liberia. Small wonder abolitionists insisted that colonization was an artifice designed to remove free blacks so that slavery would be more secure. Then, in 1826, the Rev. John Paxton of Virginia arranged for the emancipation and emigration of twelve slaves, claiming, "I owed it to God . . . and to my conscience and peace of mind." The number of ACS manumissions slowly climbed thereafter. By 1830, several dozen slaveholders had freed, collectively, 479 bondpersons on the condition that the latter move to Liberia. Impressed with the course of events, one giddy northern colonizationist claimed, "one hundred thousand slaves are ready to be given up if means can be found for sending them to Africa."[30]

Liberia could scarcely receive one hundred bondpersons, much less one hundred thousand. The colony was a death trap. Between 1820 and 1830, 1,670 emigrants went to the ACS's settlement, but malaria and other diseases felled 29 percent of them. The survivors offered mixed opinions about their new home. The destitute and forlorn sent back disparaging reports. The well-situated, benefiting from their minor government posts and economic advantages, informed black Americans that they were "grateful to God and our American patrons for the happy change which has taken place in our situation." For their part, ACS officials insisted that imprudence had caused the death of many in the colony and that the settlers' situation was better than the conditions experienced by the Jamestown and Plymouth pioneers. "That, in its progress, [Liberia] has met with obstacles and experienced discouragements, is most true," remarked Henry Clay in 1829, who then asked, "What great human undertaking was ever exempt from them?" The timetable for African colonization "may appear to us mortals of long duration," he reminded his listeners, but "in the eyes of Providence . . . [it] is short and fleeting."[31]

Sanguine about colonization's prospects at home and abroad, ACS leaders pressed the federal government for additional support. Upon assuming the presidency, John Quincy Adams, though deeming colonization a "day-dream," had continued Monroe's policy of funding the Society. By the mid-1820s, many ACS supporters assumed that colonization was an integral component of the American System, a program of national economic development that included a protective tariff, a national bank, and federally funded roads, canals, and other "internal improvements." Others colonizationists went even further, asserting that the publicly financed ACS was, in effect, a branch of the U.S. government. Emboldened, in 1824 Ohio and several other northern states called for a federally administered plan of emancipation and expatriation. The next year, Senator Rufus King of New York proposed that western land sales be used to fund an abolition and removal venture. The ACS itself sought more federal subsidies in 1827, and Representative Mercer submitted a colonization bill to Congress in 1830. Colonizationists were upping the ante. They paid dearly for their daring.[32]

Colonizationists' ever-bolder moves generated shrill opposition from proslavery southerners. Four Lower South legislatures denounced the Ohio resolution, while South Carolina senator Robert Y. Hayne, Georgia governor George M. Troup, and many others execrated King's 1825 proposal. The ACS's 1827 memorial to Congress fared no better. South Carolinian Robert Turnbull warned that colonizationists were as deceptive and dangerous as English abolitionists, a group that had begun with minor measures but now was on the verge of toppling slavery in the British West Indies. Fearing that a similar course of events would unfold in the South, Turnbull bellowed that the "Colonization Society must be then driven out of the Halls of Congress, and driven out with disgrace." Mercer's 1830 bill aroused still more fury. The *Charleston Mercury* thought the proposed legislation worse than the Tariff of Abominations, calling it "the climax of indignity to the South." The House immediately tabled the bill, while proslavery men like James Henry Hammond questioned Mercer's regional loyalties, calling the Virginian a southern "bastard."[33]

The proslavery backlash prompted the Jackson administration to investigate the government's dealings with the Society. In the late fall of 1830, Navy Secretary John Branch discovered that the ACS had received $264,000 from the national government over the previous eleven years. Only a fraction of the emigrants transported to Liberia by the Society, he noticed, had been illegally imported "recaptured" Africans. In Branch's mind, the 1819 Slave Trade Act did not authorize the president to finance a colony or send black Americans to Africa. Adopting a narrow interpretation of the law, the Jackson administration ceased making payments to the ACS. The gargantuan program of colonization would now have to be financed exclusively by private charity and state appropriations.[34]

The ACS's first fifteen years had been eventful ones. Established in 1816 by a hodgepodge of southern modernizers, Jeffersonian vacillators, northern evangelicals, and even a few proslavery planters, the Society forged an interregional constituency, secured federal funding, and founded Liberia during the 1820s. Along the way, however, the ACS incurred the ire of most African-Americans, North and South. Black opposition, in turn, was prompting some white anti-slavery advocates to reconsider colonization. Moreover, proslavery partisans were straining to close the door on colonization, howling that a breach, no matter how small, could not be tolerated, especially with covert emancipationists like Henry Clay shoving on the other side. By 1830, the battle lines between colonizationists, black Americans, white reformers, and proslavery crusaders had been fairly well drawn. Then Nat Turner's 1831 slave revolt radically reconfigured the contest over slavery, race, and colonization.

1831–1847

Emigration to Liberia surged in the aftermath of Nat Turner's Rebellion. The upswing came partly because southern free blacks were fleeing vengeful whites. Three months after Turner's revolt, the ACS outfitted the *James Perkins*, a ship that carried to Africa 326 free blacks from panic-stricken Southampton County, Virginia, and adjacent counties in North Carolina. In 1832, another 392 southern free blacks moved to Liberia, 35 percent of whom were from the insurrection-anxious city of Charleston, South Carolina. The increase in Liberian emigration also occurred because ACS emancipations continued to multiply, with nearly 600 manumittees journeying to Liberia in 1832 and 1833. Some of these new freedpersons had cajoled their owners into letting them emigrate with their beleaguered free black kin. Others had used the jittery state of affairs to press their claims for liberty. Still others had finally completed their owners' multiyear manumission programs. All totaled, over 1,300 black southerners went to Liberia between late 1831 and 1833, leading one ACS official to describe Turner's uprising and the backlash that followed as "a loud call of Providence" that alerted black people to the "opportunity of escaping to the land of their Fathers."[35]

Turner's Rebellion also prompted Upper South lawmakers to contemplate once again the colonization or "diffusion" of black Americans elsewhere. During the famed Virginia legislative debates of 1831–32, many speakers favored ending slavery in the Old Dominion, though they disputed whether the institution should be dissolved through the interstate slave trade or some colonization scheme. In the end, Virginia's lawmakers simply endorsed the principle of deporting free blacks while postponing the question of slave expatriation, a compromise that the measure's sponsor, Archibald Bryce, deemed an "entering wedge" to abolition. The legislators then argued over whether free blacks should be forcibly relocated. This debate was not resolved until the following year, when the assembly appropriated $18,000 for five years for the noncoercible deportation of free blacks. Similar disputes erupted during the Tennessee Constitutional Convention of 1834, with western planters thwarting eastern proposals for an emancipation-oriented colonization program. As had been the case in Virginia, Tennessee lawmakers settled their differences by appropriating funds for the expatriation of free blacks. In Maryland, however, state lawmakers earmarked $200,000 for the colonization of both free blacks *and* new manumittees. In the Old Line State, the emancipatory breach had been crossed.[36]

As the colonization movement gained momentum, William and Mary professor Thomas R. Dew wrote *Review of the Debate in the Virginia Legislature of 1831 and 1832* (1832). In his famous treatise, Dew vacillated over slavery's propriety. While black bondage might thrive in the torrid Lower South, he argued, temperate Virginia was "too far North" for the institution. Natural geographic and economic forces, when coupled with state-funded internal improvements, Dew hoped, would siphon slaves out of the Old Dominion. To a great extent, Dew shared Charles Fenton Mercer's vision of a commercial-industrial Upper South, but he scoffed at the latter's means of modernization, calling the ACS's program expensive and infeasible. After examining logistical and financial aspects of the scheme, Dew declared, "[T]he whole plan is utterly impracticable, requiring an expense and sacrifice of property far beyond the entire resources of the state and federal governments."[37]

Was Dew correct? Was colonization unachievable? ACS officials insisted that their program was viable, but most modern scholars have expressed skepticism, describing the venture as an escapist fantasy. In the mid-1990s, however, William Freehling suggested that perhaps colonization was not so fanciful. The nineteenth century, Freehling noted, was an age of mass migrations. At the time, the transport of two or three million African-Americans to Liberia did not seem ludicrous, especially if the federal government got into the act, as it had with American Indians. Freehling also maintained that colonization's "practicality" was not dependent upon moving every black American overseas. Colonizationists were powerful in the Upper South, he explained, and they would have grown stronger as the patronage-offering Republicans rose to power. What would have happened, asked Freehling, if colonizationists had finally succeeded in the Upper South? Lower South planters pondered this question incessantly, and the answer was always the same: the Deep South would have been encircled by free states, and in time slavery would have been strangled out of existence. In placing colonization within the context of mass migrations and geopolitics, Freehling showed why ACS leaders believed their program could work, and why proslavery partisans regarded the colonizationists' confidence as no mere bluster.[38]

Freehling's analysis errs in one critical respect, though: he ignored how ACS activities played out at the local level. Colonization did not function like an abacus, with black people being moved effortlessly from one side of the Atlantic to the other. Rather, Society enterprises were halting and complicated affairs, for ACS emancipators, would-be manumittees, free blacks, neighboring whites, southern jurists, and many others labored to make colonization serve their interests. Consider slaves' influence on Society operations. Slaves refused offers of freedom in Africa; they demanded information about Liberia (preferably from a black person); they importuned nearby slaveholders to emancipate their kin; they changed their minds on their way to port; they returned from Liberia, sometimes at the behest of ACS leaders, sometimes uninvited, and usually to the displeasure of proslavery whites. More often than not, ACS endeavors were messy. In failing to distinguish between theory and practice, Freehling overlooked one reason why colonization may not have been so feasible.

One man who disregarded such logistical questions was William Lloyd Garrison. Garrison had once championed the ACS, but by 1830, the Boston reformer had forsaken colonization and vowed to discredit the Society. Garrison denounced the ACS in his newspaper, the *Liberator*, and in his book *Thoughts on African Colonization* (1832). In the book, Garrison admitted his former affinity for colonization. "It is true," Garrison remarked of his previous association with the ACS, "—but whereas I was then blind, I now see." What Garrison saw was a group that safeguarded slavery and rationalized racism. The colonizationist idea that prejudice was indomitable, proclaimed Garrison, was itself unchristian and un-American. "As long as there remains among us a single copy of the Declaration of Independence, or of the New Testament," he wrote, "I will not despair of the social and political elevation of my sable countrymen." In effect, Garrison demanded that white Americans conquer the mountains of racial intolerance that ACS advocates had judged unassailable. Garrison's critique of the Society—a critique that prompted well-known activists like Elizur Wright Jr., Amos A. Phelps, and Theodore Dwight Weld to quit the ACS—was astute in many respects. These antislavery radicals correctly argued that the colonizationist creed reinforced racism by assuming that

ACS
+ but
a racist
ideology
an

prejudice was an immutable law of nature or an inviolable decree of God. Simply put, colonization was a racist ideology.[39]

But it was not necessarily a proslavery one. One of the few things upon which disparate northern and southern colonizationists concurred was the notion that black men and women had a capacity for improvement. According to one colonization publication:

> There is nothing in the physical, or moral nature of the African, which condemns him to a state of ignorance and degradation. Extraneous causes press him to the earth. Light and liberty, can, and do, under fair circumstances, raise him to the rank of a virtuous and intelligent being.[40]

Colonizationists disputed the nascent proslavery argument that black people were hopelessly "degraded" and therefore naturally suited to be slaves. Once black men and women settled in Africa, ACS leaders argued, once they were outside the canopy of prejudice, their innate abilities would blossom. The colony of Liberia thus assumed tremendous symbolic significance for both colonizationist and proslavery spokespersons, for the fledging settlement was the physical manifestation of the two camps' ideological differences.[41]

Those distinctions were also evident in Washington, D.C., where proslavery politicians repeatedly blocked colonizationists' stratagems to obtain federal support. Whereas Representative Mercer's ill-fated 1830 bill had proposed that the federal government give the ACS twenty-five dollars for every emigrant sent to Liberia, in January 1832 the Virginia congressman suggested that western land sales be used to finance the emigration of only free blacks. The initiative was shot down, but four months later, Mercer, revising his tactics, presented a memorial on behalf of British subjects praying aid for the Society. That effort failed as well, with South Carolina representative James Blair calling Mercer "a recreant to the cause" and warning that the matter might ultimately be settled on the battlefield. Shortly thereafter, Henry Clay introduced his Distribution Bill in the Senate. The act proposed that the national government allocate funds to the states with the hope that the latter would give "special consideration" toward spending the monies on emancipation and colonization. Clement Clay of Alabama announced that if anything was going to destroy the Republic, it was this bill. The measure passed both houses, only to be pocket vetoed by President Jackson. Disappointed once again, ACS supporters regrouped and planned for another assault.[42]

new bills
vetoed by
Pres. Jackson

Colonization lurked behind the era's great debates. For example, during the Nullification Crisis of 1832–33, when South Carolina declared federal protective tariffs null and void in the state, South Carolina governor James Hamilton Jr. fumed that if the Constitution's "general welfare" clause permitted these kinds of tariffs, the same provision would allow the national government to establish "colonization offices in our State, to give bounties for emancipation here, and transportation to Liberia afterwards." After the Nullification conflict passed, John C. Calhoun predicted that colonization would rise again. When that moment came, he warned, the slaveholding states would have to resist "at any hazards."[43]

Colonizationists disagreed over how to appease their proslavery detractors. During the Gag Rule controversy, when Congress debated what to do with the thousands of antislavery petitions it received each year, Henry Clay contested a plan to reject all such petitions and instead urged that the documents be sent to a committee, which would hopefully decide "against granting the prayer." This compromise, thought Clay, would placate proslavery leaders while still retaining the possibility that emancipation and deportation might be effected in the future. A career politician, Clay was forever leaving the antislavery door ajar. But as Lower South legislators turned up the pressure, some colonizationists began to buckle. William Cost Johnson, a Whig from northern Maryland and advocate of state-sponsored emancipation-expatriation programs, called for an ultrastrict gag rule so that "outsiders" could not interfere with slavery. With colonizationists like Johnson informing Clay that the antislavery door had to be shut still further, ACS leaders had yet another reason to despair for their movement.[44]

Indeed, during the 1830s the ACS was in the throes of an institutional crisis. For several years, a rift had been growing between the Upper South men who dominated the powerful board of managers, and the northerners who filled many important positions in the organization. The groups differed on two issues.

One involved the Society's public image. Northerners espoused a strongly emancipationist vision of colonization, while the more conservative southern leaders, many of whom were pragmatic politicians, wanted to muffle their brethrens' bold talk of slavery's downfall. ACS front men glossed over the internal squabbles by offering vague and paradoxical messages about their enterprise. Yet the northerners may have had the upper hand in this respect, for Ralph R. Gurley of Connecticut edited the organization's monthly, the *African Repository*. The northern faction pressed their advantage at the Society's yearly meeting in January 1833. As was the custom, Gurley read the annual report in a bland manner, and the attendees approved the document in an equally listless fashion. Unwittingly, the body had just voted to remove five southern board members, including slaveholders Francis Scott Key and Walter Jones, and to replace them with northerners. The deposed objected, but the decision stood.[45]

The second dispute among ACS insiders concerned fiscal management. After Jackson ended federal funding for colonization in 1830, the Society was largely dependent on private donations, and most contributions came from white northerners. During the early 1830s, northern colonizationists repeatedly warned the managers that the Garrisonian assault had undermined the ACS's fund-raising efforts in the free states. The managers, seizing on the post-Turner interest in colonization and believing that emigrant expeditions generated still more excitement, spent money with abandon anyway. Even after northerners wrested some power in January 1833, monetary problems dogged the Society. Although the ACS collected $19,000 in late 1833, at the January 1834 meeting the managers admitted that the organization was still $45,000 in debt. The group vowed to exercise financial restraint, pledging, among other things, to circumscribe emigration to Liberia. With bankruptcy looming, the ACS beseeched its auxiliary societies for "their aid and influence in freeing it from pecuniary difficulty."[46]

Such assistance was not forthcoming. Disagreements over how to handle abolitionist and proslavery foes, when combined with the Society's financial woes, threatened to tear the colonization movement apart. The Maryland society opted for complete independence in 1833; the next year, the New York and Pennsylvania auxiliaries began nearly autonomous operations, a course that lead them to establish their own settlement in Africa; in 1836, Mississippi colonizationists announced their intention to do the same; two years later, their counterparts in Louisiana followed suit. Longtime ACS leaders bewailed the balkanization, but the centrifugal forces appeared unstoppable. Finally, in 1838, a compromise was reached. The ACS adopted a new constitution, one in which the organization became a federation of state auxiliaries. Under the new arrangement, the board of managers was replaced with a board of directors, with each state's representation being proportional to its financial contributions and the size of its settlement in Liberia. For all practical purposes, northerners now controlled the Society. They named as board president Buffalo businessman Samuel Wilkeson, whose no-nonsense managerial style helped replenish the ACS's treasury. Teetering throughout the 1830s, the Society slowly righted itself thereafter.[47]

By the time Wilkeson assumed power, the U.S. black population stood at 2.9

million. This figure represented a 63 percent increase since 1820, when the ACS launched its first vessel, and a 518 percent increase since 1770, when colonization proposals first began to circulate regularly. Meanwhile, the Society had transported just 3,963 emigrants to Liberia. Die-hard colonizationists dismissed the organization's paltry totals, claiming, as always, that the enterprise must proceed at a judicious pace. Nevertheless, for antislavery advocates, the ACS's emigration record was hardly inspiring. The simple truth was that, given the nature of its enterprise, the Society needed extensive government assistance. One of its best opportunities for securing federal aid came in 1844 when Henry Clay ran for U.S. president on the Whig Party ticket.[48]

paltry results

1844

Many thought Clay would win in a landslide. A longtime statesman, five-time presidential contender, and (after 1836) president of the ACS, Clay was one of the most well known figures of the day. The Democrats initially planned on running Martin Van Buren, but his candidacy was cut short by proslavery obduracy and northern pliability, with the result being that the expansionist James K. Polk received the party's nomination. Polk defeated Clay by a very narrow margin. Had Clay received 5,107 more votes in New York (out of 485,000 cast), he would have won the presidency. As historian Gary Kornblith observed, "the outcome of the 1844 presidential election seems more arbitrary than inevitable." With that twist of fate, colonizationists experienced disappointment once again.[49]

Barred from the public purse, the Society trudged on. Over the years, ACS emigration patterns changed in several respects. First, the northern leaders' penny-pinching contributed to a 40 percent decline in overall emigration figures. Second, a greater proportion of ACS emigrants were manumittees. Third, the character of ACS emancipations was changing. For example, a larger number of them were occurring in the Lower South, mostly because Upper South slaveholders had migrated to that subregion over the course of their lives.[50] Also, testamentary liberations became much more common as slaveholders who had been reared in the Revolutionary and Early National periods passed away.[51] ACS leaders assured their followers that the manumitters were well intentioned. "It has been said that where slaves are liberated to be sent to the colony, their masters are governed by selfish purposes; that none are set free unless they are old and worthless, or young and vicious, and then, only to get clear of the trouble and expense of keeping them," remarked Society officials. But if such skeptics actually witnessed an ACS embarkation, they would understand "the benevolent and philanthropic feelings of those southerners who are seeking the removal to Africa of the colored race!" For Society spokespersons, the rise in ACS liberations suggested that the desire for interregional antislavery cooperation was alive and growing.[52]

Free black interest in colonization, on the other hand, was at a standstill. Although over seven hundred southern free blacks journeyed to Liberia after Nat Turner's 1831 rebellion, by the mid-1830s free African-Americans in the South were almost uniformly opposed to the ACS. Despite a general deterioration in their living standards and legal privileges, several factors led most southern free blacks to reject colonization, including negative reports from previous emigrants, a dissipation in the post-Turner hysteria, kinship ties with enslaved African-Americans, and improving economic conditions for some individuals. Between 1834 and 1847, only 158 southern free blacks moved to the ACS's colony. Vexed Society leaders projected their own disappointment onto the African-Americans themselves. "There may be those among the colored population," they complained, "who are incapable of fully appreciating the blessings of colonization."[53]

The ACS was faring even worse among African-Americans in the North. The 1830s and 1840s were decades of growing militancy among black northerners. Wearied by white abolitionists' own racism, frustrated by their white counterparts' narrow goals and tactics, and troubled by an onslaught of disfranchisement, economic displacement, race riots, and segregation, black northerners embarked on their own antislavery course during the late 1830s. In linking northern prejudice with the fate of slaves, they embraced an agenda that was more expansive than that espoused by most white abolitionists. And in advocating political and social activism, their tactics were more experiential and confrontational than those adopted by their white allies. The stridency of African-American abolitionism guaranteed that the ACS's efforts to deport black northerners would be futile. Between 1834 and 1847, only fifty-six black northerners went to Liberia. Philadelphian Sarah L. Forten described African-Americans' attitudes toward the ACS well: "I despise the aim of that Institution most heartily—and have never yet met one man or woman of Color who thought better of it than I do."[54]

The few free blacks who went to Liberia during the late 1830s and 1840s, along with the hundreds of manumittees who journeyed there, usually described the colony as "a hard country." Mere survival was no easy feat. Of the 2,887 emigrants transported to Liberia between 1831 and 1843, 42 percent died from encounters with disease, indigenous peoples, and the sundry dangers of settler life. Another 12 percent abandoned the colony before death could run them down. The remaining settlers tried their hand at farming and petty trade, though few prospered like the southern free blacks who had arrived in the 1820s and continued to dominate the colony. Despite the poverty and mortality, however, many settlers contended that Liberia offered African-Americans freedoms that were unavailable in the United States. This sentiment flourished in 1847, when Liberia declared its national independence, a move that was encouraged by the money-conscious ACS. During the 1850s, when southern states considered expelling or enslaving free black people, when northern states further circumscribed African-Americans' rights, and when Congress passed the Fugitive Slave Law and the Supreme Court issued the *Dred Scott* verdict, many black Americans would take a second look at the republic of Liberia.[55]

For colonizationists, the 1831–47 period was filled with peaks and valleys. On one hand, they cheered the post-Turner upswing in emigration, took solace in the near miss with Clay's Distribution Bill, celebrated the proliferation of ACS manumissions, and rejoiced at Liberia's independence. On the other hand, they bemoaned proslavery and abolitionist assaults; bickered over organizational goals, publicity, and finances; decried free blacks' growing militancy; and lamented Clay's defeat in the 1844 presidential election. The ups and downs had fatigued the organization. But the ACS was far from dead. During the "decade of crisis," colonizationists would be as active as ever.

1848–1860

In the late 1840s and 1850s, the South's white antislavery activists worried the region's proslavery leaders. In Kentucky, for example, the united strength of colonizationists, diffusionists, and abolitionists portended the possibility of state-sponsored emancipation and prompted one proslavery man to remark in 1848 that "many . . . regard the crisis as at the door." In 1849, Kentucky senator Henry Clay once again championed a federal emancipation and colonization venture. The heresies of Virginia's Beverly Tucker were especially disturbing to slavery's supporters. The son of the late eighteenth-century expatriation advocate St. George Tucker, Beverly was a secessionist with a twist. With the establishment of a southern confederacy, Tucker declared in 1850, slavery could fulfill its destiny: the intellectual and moral elevation of Africans, with black Americans serving as their educators and missionaries. In a southern nation, Tucker explained, gifted bondpersons would first be sent to normal schools in the Gulf South, and thence to Africa, where they would edify that continent's inhabitants. As for slavery in the confederacy, it would only "endure until it shall have accomplished that to which it was appointed."[56]

Proslavery perpetualists heard still more Upper South blasphemies during the Compromise of 1850 debates. The Pratt amendment to the Fugitive Slave Law, in particular, alarmed Deep South politicians. Moved by Maryland senator Thomas Pratt, the measure stipulated that the national government recompense slaveholders that "lost" runaway bondpersons because of northern noncompliance with the Fugitive Slave Law. Pratt's amendment miffed both antislavery northerners and proslavery southerners. The former balked at the idea of rewarding slaveholders for a runaway's mettle; the latter claimed that the Pratt amendment would become a federal emancipation and compensation program. Upper South slaveholders, predicted several Lower South senators, would let their bondpersons flee, conspire with northerners to ignore the absconders, and then pocket federal cash for their "losses." By these means, the region would end bondage, attract white migrants, and profit in the process. When the vote came, Lower South senators joined forces with their northern counterparts to defeat Pratt's proposal.[57]

Even without the Pratt amendment, the Fugitive Slave Law aroused controversy, and these disputes changed the course of the colonization movement. Among other things, the statute inspired Harriet Beecher Stowe to write *Uncle Tom's Cabin* (1852), a novel in which the protagonist George Harris, a mulatto runaway and Christian convert, emigrates to Liberia. "We have *more* than the rights of common men," Harris contends. "We have the claim of an injured race for reparation. But, then, *I do not want it*; I want a country, a nation, of my own." Abolitionists denounced the passage as an "evil influence." Colonizationists applauded Stowe's apparent endorsement of Liberia and used the literary tribute to expand their movement.[58]

As always, the ACS sought federal aid. In 1851, Society leaders asked Congress for postal subsidies for Africa-bound mail, fully expecting that a government contract would allow them to launch a line of steamships to Liberia. The measure failed, but ACS officials took comfort in the fact that they still had powerful friends in Washington. Influential politicians like Daniel Webster, Edward Everett, Henry Clay, Stephen Douglas, and Millard Fillmore all attended the Society's meetings. Nor were these men mute on the matter. In March 1850, Webster called for federal funding for African colonization. A year later, Secretary of State Everett publicly lauded the ACS. President Fillmore intended to propose a colonization venture in his December 1852 State of the Union Address, but his advisors convinced him to exorcise the passage. For proslavery leaders, such episodes in Washington seemed so threatening because Border South bondage seemed so insecure.[59]

From the perspective of the Lower South, Upper South slavery was in tatters. In the region's northernmost tier, manumissions, slave escapes, and interstate sales had contributed to a decline in the bonded population. In Washington, D.C., abolitionists operated intrepidly. In Virginia, western non-slaveholders exacted concessions from eastern planters at the Constitutional Convention of 1850–51. In Maryland, Kentucky, Missouri, Virginia, and Tennessee, lawmakers implemented colonization programs (though disputes over objectives, enforcement, and funding mitigated the programs' impact). There appeared to be no end to the unraveling. Northern farmers were "invading" the Upper South, and southern reformers were pleading for more commercial and industrial development. Chagrined by slavery's frayed condition in the region, South Carolina secessionist James L. Orr remarked that his state had "no hope" of securing Upper South support for disunion.[60]

ACS emigration figures confirmed such conclusions. When judged by the number of ACS emancipations effected, the late 1840s and 1850s were the Society's "golden age." More slaveholders sent more bondpersons to Liberia between 1848 and 1860 than in the previous thirty years combined. Manumission trends that had begun in the 1830s and 1840s became even more pronounced during the 1850s. For example, testamentary liberations rose to the point where 56 percent of all ACS manumittees obtained freedom upon their owners' demise. Lower South liberations also continued to increase, with nearly one-third of ACS freedpersons coming from that subregion. Colonization officials took pride in their emancipatory record. Noting that since 1820 the Society had sent 6,000 manumittees to Liberia, they asked, "Is not this practically *anti-slavery?*"[61]

ACS leaders mollified proslavery apprehensions by pointing out that southern free blacks were also going to Liberia in unprecedented numbers. During the 1850s, southern lawmakers debated various means of diminishing the free black population, be it through voluntary colonization, forcible deportation, or mandatory enslavement. These efforts failed, but the unremitting hostility prompted over 1,500 southern free blacks to depart for Liberia between 1848 and 1860. The sojourners were a diverse lot. Two-thirds were from the Upper South; one-third from the Lower South. Five-eighths were from rural areas; three-eighths from urban locales. Among the adults, 25 percent had some degree of literacy. The emigrants' heterogeneity testifies to the pervasiveness of the 1850s reign of terror. As one Savannah emigrant remarked, only in Liberia could free black people expect "delivernce fr the present Bond-age an degredation they ear labering ounder."[62]

African-Americans in the North also sought a refuge from racism. The Fu-gitive Slave Law, when combined with discriminatory state statutes, induced many black northerners to embrace emigration. For such individuals, the es-tablishment of a black nation would function in the same way that "personal uplift" had during earlier times: namely, to demonstrate that condition, not color, fostered prejudice. A black sovereignty, like middle-class respectability, would refute racist arguments. With such notions gaining popularity among black abolitionists, the 1850s witnessed what may have been the largest expa-triation movement in American history. Although emigrationists such as Mar-tin Delany, Henry Highland Garnet, and James T. Holly advocated an exodus to Africa or the Caribbean, most departing African-Americans went to En-gland or Canada, which is where Samuel Ringgold Ward, Henry Bibb, Henry "Box" Brown, and other prominent fugitives-turned-abolitionists went. But some black northerners opted for Liberia. Between 1850 and 1855, an average of 61 northern African-Americans went to Liberia each year. Emigration figures temporarily dipped for this group thereafter, but they rose again following the *Dred Scott* verdict in 1857. All totaled, between 1848 and 1860, 649 black north-erners went to Africa under the auspices of the ACS, two and half times as many as had gone during the previous thirty years combined.[63]

The 1848–60 upsurge in ACS operations had profound ramifications for Liberia. Since the 1820s, southern free black emigrants had dominated the former colony. But the influx of new settlers, and especially of manumittees, changed the social and political dynamics of the African republic. The late-arriving freedpersons complained that the entrenched elite used legal and ille-gal means to advance their own interests at the expense of others. Brewing tension between the two groups finally boiled over in the late 1860s and early 1870s. In 1869, Edward J. Roye, a dark-skinned man, won the presidency over James Spriggs Payne, a light-skinned leader in Liberia. Hoping to extend the presidential term from two to four years, Roye declared martial law after two years in office and appealed to freedpersons, recaptives, and others to resist the traditional elite. He also secured an unfavorable loan from the British. With the nation verging on civil war, Roye was deposed. His subsequent death be-came a source of mystery and controversy for many questioned the official story that he drowned while escaping from prison. Meanwhile, Roye's ill-advised loan became a financial millstone that would eventually plunge Li-beria into economic dependency and jeopardize its sovereignty.[64]

If the 1850s upswing in ACS emigration ultimately created political and economic strife in Liberia, it demonstrated to proslavery southerners that colonizationists could not be counted out, that antislavery threats loomed within the South itself. Such anxieties were evident during the Kansas-Nebraska debates, an imbroglio initiated by Missouri's proslavery senator David Atchison. With only 13 percent of its population enslaved, the Show Me State teemed with individuals like Frank Blair Jr., who was an outspoken colonizationist, and Thomas Hart Benton, who figured that sidestepping slavery issues was the best way to attract white migrants and concomitantly expel black bondpersons. Moreover, Missouri was bordered by the free states of Illinois and Iowa. If Kansas joined the Union without slavery, thought Atchison, bondage would surely perish in Missouri. Unfortunately for Atchison, the Missouri Compromise of 1820 had banned slavery in the Louisiana Territory north of 36°30' latitude. Nevertheless, Atchison and his southern allies persuaded Illinois Democratic senator Stephen Douglas to sponsor a bill that would repeal the long-standing agreement. The proposed legislation stipulated that slavery's status in the Kansas and Nebraska territories would be determined on the basis of popular sovereignty (that is, the territories' voters would decide whether to permit slavery). The bill passed, largely because Douglas convinced just enough northern Democrats to vote for the measure. It proved a costly victory for proslavery forces.[65]

The Kansas-Nebraska Act's political repercussions were momentous. The legislation contributed to the Whig Party's collapse. Northern Whigs had voted unanimously against the Kansas-Nebraska bill. Their Lower South counterparts, embarrassed by their colleagues' obstinacy, had looked soft on slavery. Unable to find a middle road, northern and southern Whigs went their separate ways. In the meantime, the Democratic Party, while showing more cohesiveness than the disintegrating Whigs, suffered the defection of northerners who had tired of appeasing proslavery southerners. The North's ex-Democrats and ex-Whigs, along with former Free-Soilers, political abolitionists, and some nativists, soon established the Republican Party.[66]

Many Republicans championed colonization. In the North, argued the scheme's proponents, colonization could attract antislavery conservatives in key states like Indiana, Illinois, and Pennsylvania. In the Border South, it could woo the nonslaveholding majority. The colonizationist campaign within the Republican Party faced two obstacles, however. First, the colonizationists themselves disagreed on program specifics—whether black people should be sent to Latin America or Africa, whether emigration would be voluntary or compulsory, and whether the enterprise should be overtly emancipationist. Second, intraparty detractors contended that colonization contradicted Republican ideas about marketplace freedom, that black Americans' economic rights were equal to those of white Americans. The colonizationists remained confident nonetheless. Program details could be worked out; opponents conceded that freedpersons might squander their economic liberty, or that racism would render that liberty meaningless. As time passed, colonizationists became more vocal within the party.[67]

Concerned about the Republican ascendancy in the North and antislavery agitation in the Upper South, proslavery partisans circled the wagons. Southern intellectuals offered increasingly bold arguments, hoping to convince white waverers of bondage's virtues. The institution's defenders also tried to reopen the Atlantic slave trade, believing that the renewed traffic would decrease the Lower South's dependency on the interstate sales and thereby compel Upper South slaveholders, who would be unable to vend their human chattel southward, to defend bondage more vigilantly. Proslavery forces likewise hailed the Supreme Court's 1857 *Dred Scott* verdict, wherein the justices held that bondage could not be outlawed in the territories. Whether wrangling over fugitive bondpersons, the Atlantic slave trade, Kansas, or the lands farther west, proslavery southerners were determined to protect the perimeters.[68]

The late 1850s brought them no relief. In 1857, North Carolinian Hinton Rowan Helper wrote *The Impending Crisis,* a book that savaged slavery for its economic inefficiency and called for the deportation of black people. In 1858, when Kansas' proslavery Lecompton Constitution came before Congress, six ex-Whigs from the Upper South cast the deciding votes to defeat the measure. And all the while, the ACS grew stronger. The organization's income skyrocketed, thanks to munificent legacies left by southerners like John Stevens of Maryland and John McDonogh of Louisiana. Moreover, the Society finally obtained federal funding when President Buchanan agreed to pay the group fifty dollars to transport recaptive Africans to Liberia and one hundred dollars for their maintenance there. Flush with money, the ACS built a new headquarters building on Pennsylvania Avenue, just blocks from where Abraham Lincoln would soon reside.[69]

An admirer of Henry Clay, the up-and-coming Lincoln occasionally expressed interest in colonization. If given the power, declared Lincoln, "my first impulse would be to free all the slaves, and send them to Liberia—to their own native land." But such an undertaking, he admitted, was logistically impossible. Even so, Lincoln wistfully hoped that black people could be sent to Latin America, and many of his fellow Republicans harbored similar sentiments. Frank Blair Jr. lobbied to have colonization incorporated into the party's 1860 platform, but his opponents squashed the campaign, arguing that long-standing disagreements over the matter would undermine party unity. Despite the setback, colonizationists took solace in the fact that both Lincoln and his running mate Hannibal Hamlin had intimated some affinity for colonization.[70]

So too had the other parties' presidential candidates. Northern Democrat Stephen Douglas regularly attended Society meetings. Constitutional Unionist John Bell of Tennessee likewise dabbled in colonization. Even southern Democratic candidate John C. Breckinridge had once commended the movement. But Lincoln was the most receptive to colonization, and he was the one who captured the presidency. Ninety years after American Revolutionaries began contemplating the expatriation of freedpersons and forty-five years after the ACS's establishment, a colonizationist sympathizer occupied the White House.

From the Revolution onward, the African colonization movement occupied a central place in debates on slavery and race. The enterprise's longevity and salience partly stemmed from its malleability: the venture certainly meant different things to different people. For most ACS members, though, colonization was a way to slowly rid America of both bondage and black people. Reviled by abolitionists for their gradualism and racism, Society supporters also angered proslavery partisans who decried the colonizationists' plans to dissolve the South's "peculiar institution." ACS devotees had remained undeterred, claiming that their emancipatory record proved the viability and wisdom of their program. The remainder of this book examines these "ACS manumissions" and their effect on slavery.

2

ACS Manumitters

Their Ideology and Intentions

In the mid-1820s, Margaret Mercer of Maryland was wrestling with a dilemma. A slaveholder herself, Mercer regarded human bondage as an evil institution. Though she abhorred slavery, Mercer shuddered at the thought of unconditional emancipation. "I would rather die with every member of my family than live in a community mixed up of black & white," she proclaimed. Mercer concluded that the only solution to her quandary was to educate apt and compliant bondpersons and send them to Liberia, where they would escape the ravages of racism and enlighten indigenous Africans. Such notions, thought Mercer, would gain wider acceptance if presented in the form of a novel. As she began to formulate her own manumission plans, Mercer implored a friend to write a pro-ACS book that would demonstrate "the advantages . . . Christianity invests in the savage." The story should begin, Mercer explained, with an African boy and girl "dancing under every palm tree" and "rolling . . . cocoa-nuts" suddenly being sold into slavery by the girl's mother. After surviving the Middle Passage and Caribbean bondage, the young protagonists would be emancipated by Quakers. The saga should conclude, Mercer suggested, with them "going home good Christians in the [Liberian] colony's vessels." Mercer insisted that the yarn was "an o'ver true tale" and expected that her own ventures would unfold along the same lines.[1]

Mercer was not unique in entertaining fanciful ideas about colonization. Many ACS supporters considered it the only remedy for, as one planter termed it, "the cancer of slavery."[2] Human bondage, they argued, was an inherently flawed institution. Inexorable economic and social forces made a mockery of proslavery platitudes concerning the reciprocal duties of masters and slaves. The uncontrollable yet commonplace vagaries of life—a drop in crop prices, the demands of creditors, the death of an owner—all sliced through the worn and frayed threads of paternalism that proslavery intellectuals claimed tethered slaveholders and bondpersons. Something more was needed to tie these parties together, contended the colonizationists, and manumission would provide that magical bond. The expectation of liberty, they declared, would arouse in slaves industry, dependability, and loyalty; and the prospect of hard-working, reliable, and filial bondpersons, they continued, would compel slaveholders to keep their promises of freedom. Thus when ACS liberators mused about manumission, they deemed it an absolutely necessary, morally upright, and financially astute mechanism of slave management.

ACS Manumitters, 1820–1840

Born during the Revolutionary era and reared amid the Second Great Awakening, most would-be ACS manumitters regarded slavery as both a secular and moral problem. Though troubled by black bondage, few liberators freed their slaves gratis. Instead, they concocted time-consuming manumission programs. The incipient emancipators announced that these schemes would prepare slaves for freedom in Liberia, but they also assumed that the projects would serve their own interests, that the lure of freedom would coax obedience and loyalty from bondpersons while simultaneously molding them into devout, temperate, and literate emigrants. ACS liberators saw themselves not as radical visionaries but as enlightened moderates, and they regarded their endeavors not as reckless risk-taking but as cautious trials in emancipatory experimentalism.

Upper South Manumitters and Their Thoughts on Slavery

ACS emigration patterns changed over time. Between 1820 and 1822, the ACS did not transport a single bondperson to Liberia. All of the emigrants during that time were free blacks. In 1823, however, Daniel Murray of Maryland manumitted James Fuller, a twenty-four-year-old wheelwright, on the condition that Fuller go to Liberia. The number of ACS emancipations grew thereafter. By 1834, 1,251 freedpersons had been sent to Liberia. Free black emigration also increased during the late 1820s and early 1830s, but it declined dramatically by the mid-1830s. The totals for manumitted emigrants, conversely, continued to keep pace. Between 1835 and 1840, 666 ex-slaves hazarded the transatlantic journey to Liberia. By then, freedpersons outnumbered free blacks among ACS emigrants.[3]

The vast majority of ACS manumissions during this early period took place in the Upper South. Between 1820 and 1840, 85 percent of ACS emancipators were from this region. Virginia and Maryland alone could claim 59 percent of the manumitters. Nor were these individuals strangers to one another. Many were members of an interconnected group of prominent families that included the Blackford, Page, Randolph, Cocke, Custis, and Mercer clans. Yet consanguinity was not the only thing linking these persons together. Equally important was their shared outlook on slavery and mutual interest in manumission. An affective "colonizationist community" emerged as ACS liberators penned letters to one another, offering advice and encouragement as they designed their emancipation programs.[4]

The communications mostly flowed through a corridor that stretched from South Central Virginia northward along the Allegheny Mountains and then across the Potomac River into Maryland. This geographic setting made ACS liberations distinctive in two respects. First, they were a rural phenomenon. Studies by T. Stephen Whitman, Judith Kelleher Schafer, and other historians have shown that manumissions traditionally occurred in metropolitan areas. But urban slaves, unwilling to forsake the autonomy and opportunities of city life, expressed little interest in emigrating to Liberia, and their disinclination helped push ACS operations into the countryside. In the plantation districts, the comparative disadvantages of rural living made bondpersons more amenable to offers of freedom in Liberia, while white antipathy toward free blacks increased the likelihood that manumittees would in fact move overseas. Second, the bucolic character of ACS liberations meant that the manumitters were exceptionally large slaveholders, at least compared to the urban emancipators examined by previous scholars. In short, the landed aristocrats of Central Virginia and Maryland were pivotal figures during the early years of the colonization movement.[5]

So too were North Carolina Quakers. For decades, Friends in the Tar Heel State had expressed their distaste for slaveholding, but the group had failed to act boldly on the issue, an indecisiveness born of their decentralized, consensus-oriented system of governance and North Carolina's prescriptive manumission laws. Many of the state's Quakers simply gave their bondpersons to the sect itself. By the 1820s, the Society of Friends in North Carolina owned hundreds of slaves. The body attempted to settle some bondpersons in Haiti, but after one disastrous expedition to the Caribbean nation, the group turned its attention to Liberia. Between 1825 and 1830, 398 North Carolina blacks emigrated to Liberia, the majority of whom were sent by Friends. Quaker activity of this sort was short-lived, however. A large number of North Carolina Friends washed their hands of the whole situation and migrated to the Midwest. Those who remained discovered that the African-Americans still under their charge, upon learning about the sorrowful fate of their friends and kin in Liberia, balked at the idea of moving to the African colony. By the early 1830s, the era of Quaker-initiated ACS manumissions was over.[6]

Most ACS emancipators came of age during the late Revolutionary period. As youngsters they absorbed that era's liberal ideologies, and as adults they shouldered the burden of making those ideas reality. Eradicating slavery was among their most important charges. Yet by the early nineteenth century, when this generation reached maturity, these sons and daughters of the Revolution had failed to fulfill their forebears' wishes of delivering the nation from black bondage. In fact, the institution was expanding and, judging from Gabriel's Rebellion, the 1811 New Orleans slave conspiracy, the Missouri Crisis, Demark Vesey's insurrectionary plot, and other tension-filled affairs, its perpetuation and growth were jeopardizing the Republic.[7]

The religious teachings of the day further agitated emancipators' anxiousness over slavery. The Second Great Awakening gave an ethical urgency to what had become a shoulder-shrugging, head-scratching political and philosophical question. Many, perhaps most, southern evangelicals channeled their Christian zeal into a worldview that glorified a hierarchical, organic social order founded on reciprocal obligations. Mutual responsibilities, the argument went, bound together all of society's members, including slaveholders and slaves. Kindly and conscientious masters provided for the material and spiritual well-being of bondpersons who returned the favor with fidelity, gratitude, and industry. Proslavery theorists admitted that some unscrupulous slaveholders might take advantage of their authoritative position, but the institution's defenders nevertheless insisted that it was the abuses of slaveholding power, not the power itself, that were condemnatory.[8]

ACS manumitters were intrigued by such arguments. Levelers they were not. As men and women who sat atop southern society, ACS emancipators had no interest in inviting the bottom-dwellers up to their lofty status, nor did they intend to clamber down and muck about with their social inferiors. "A learned man should not be interrupted in his intellectual labors by the necessity for cooking his own dinner, nor cleaning his own boots," announced Margaret Mercer. But Mercer, who was the daughter of former Maryland governor John Francis Mercer and the cousin of ACS founder Congressman Charles Fenton Mercer, went on to explain that scholars must respect the work of cooks and bootblacks, for "all the foundations of society rest upon the basis of reciprocal duty."[9] The problem, insisted manumitters like Mercer, was that slavery, as a system, militated against the establishment of mutually satisfying relationships. The inherent nature of the institution prevented bondpersons from identifying with their owners.

The traffic in slaves, in particular, drove home the inevitable injustice of bondage. For example, after Ann R. Page's husband died in 1826, the settlement of his debts required the sale of over one hundred bondpersons, a flesh-mongering operation that exemplified in Page's view the evils of an indefensible system.[10] Many Upper South slaveholders rationalized the selling of slaves, blaming the unseemly business on inescapable debt, uncontrollable circumstances, or, better still, the slaves themselves. Some ACS manumitters, however, were evidently incapable of such ethical sidestepping.[11]

Economic fluctuations likewise eroded any semblance of partnership between slaveholders and bondpersons. Echoing the criticisms of slavery voiced by colonizationists like Henry Clay and Henry Speed, many manumitters regarded the South's system of bonded labor as an unviable and ultimately dangerous labor arrangement. John Hartwell Cocke contended that as tobacco profits dried up, slaveholders neglected their bondpersons, who in turn grew "more idle and more vicious." William Blackford also speculated that labor competition would engender levels of racial hostility that would culminate in the annihilation of African-Americans. John McDonogh similarly declared that economic forces would prompt slaveholders to free their slaves and "drive them away." The unpredictable churnings of the market economy, in other words, promised to dash paternalist benevolence to pieces.[12]

Manumitters had plenty of reasons to ponder the relationship between socioeconomic instability and plantation management during the Early National period. To many, slavery was unraveling in the Upper South. Urbanization, advances in transportation and communications, the growth of the southern free black population, bondage's demise in the North, and the advent of abolitionism all weakened slaveholders' grip over bondpersons. Moreover, soil depletion had rendered traditional crops like tobacco less profitable than before. Many Upper South slaveholders responded to these conditions by selling bondpersons to the Lower South. Others switched to mixed agriculture or began hiring out their slaves. For scores of colonizationists, manumission was the means by which they would reestablish their rule.[13]

The emancipators' dealings with blacks further impressed upon their minds the precariousness of paternalism and the certainty of slave resistance. Disobedience was inevitable because bondage was unnatural. "[T]hey are like other men," asserted one liberator, "flesh and blood, like you and myself." Blacks instinctively despised their enslavement and expressed their discontent in everyday acts of insubordination. Thus the Virginia planter Nathaniel Hooe was displeased but not surprised when a bondman whom he had hired out complained about his situation, that another was being tried for burglary, and that his carpenters would "do but little if not well attended to." Insolent hirelings, petty thieves, and shirking laborers irritated ACS manumitters, but it was the thought of a slave revolt that kept them awake at night. Recall that most ACS emancipators were Virginians and consequently were all too familiar with Nat Turner's Rebellion. "[T]he white race or the Black race shall cut the others [sic] throat," observed one manumitter after the affair; "there is no alternative."[14]

Proslavery theorists assumed too much of slaveholder beneficence and too little of slave recalcitrance, argued the emancipators. Inculcation alone could never cement the two parties. The solvents of estate liquidations, economic unpredictability, and personal freedom were just too corrosive and common. Something else was needed—something that established real interdependence and promoted the uplift of bondpersons and slaveholders alike.

Abolitionism was not the answer. Having batted around proslavery theories, ACS manumitters took off the kid gloves in preparation for pummeling abolitionist arguments. Some opened with haymakers. Mary Blackford charged that northern immediatists who vilified southerners did not appreciate the sacrifices of slaveholders or the delicacy of manumission. Mary Custis Lee likewise railed against the publication of William Lloyd Garrison's *The Liberator* and the New England fanaticism that she believed it represented. Margaret Mercer despaired when her friend Gerrit Smith took up the Garrisonian cause, claiming that he had banded with a man who would "throw the firebrand into the powder magazine" and then stand "at a *distance* to see the mangled victims of his barbarous fury." After this initial flurry of scorn, ACS manumitters settled in and threw more precise punches, contending that the critical shortcoming in the abolitionist position was that unconditional emancipation generated even less social cohesion than did slavery.[15]

Instinctive, inscrutable antipathy would forever stand between blacks and whites, opined the colonizationists. Abolition would therefore unleash the worst in both races. As heirs of the Enlightenment, the liberators contended that physical and cultural conditions dictated human behavior and consequently regarded the United States, where racism seemed ubiquitous and indomitable, as a degenerative place for blacks. Manumittees who remained in America, they declared, would be political, economic, and social outcasts. "[W]hether as slaves or . . . free people," one emancipator explained to two bondpersons, "you have felt and witnessed the degradation of your colour in this country." African-Americans who were released from slavery, the liberators warned, would suffer if exposed to the withering torridness of American racism. Ex-slaves would need a refuge beyond the nation's borders.[16]

And Africa would be the freedpersons' sanctuary. While some whites contended that the West and the Caribbean were likely sites for black relocation, ACS advocates favored Liberia. Emancipators envisioned the African colony as a place with bountiful resources waiting to be exploited, countless "heathens" longing to be saved, and a despicable slave trade needing to be extinguished. Most of all, in Africa freedpersons would escape racism. One couple who sent slaves to Liberia summed up this perspective succinctly: "[T]aking all things into view, we thought their prospects for doing well, permanently, were better at Liberia than in this country, either in the free or the slaveholding States."[17]

Ideologically, ACS manumitters occupied the middle ground in the debates over slavery. They disagreed with northern abolitionists who called for immediate emancipation and racial equality. At the same time, they believed that proslavery arguments about reciprocal duties and organic interdependence, while delightful in theory, were poppycock in practice. There were too many large-scale forces that prevented the realization of the paternalist ideal, contended the liberators. At bottom, ACS emancipators were not militant dissenters from the slave system but rather ambivalent participants in it. They looked to bring harmony and stability to an institution that was, by nature, disharmonious and unstable. Thus they turned to manumission.

ACS emancipators' approach to manumission would be conservative—conservative not only in the sense that they abstained from abolitionism but also in the sense that they intended to retain their profits, power, and sense of being "good" slaveholders. In short, their manumission schemes were designed to put one's finances in order, one's slaves in their place, and one's conscience at ease.

Manumission Programs

ACS liberators conceived of manumission as a well-regulated, protracted experiment. They imagined the venture beginning with a small number of slaves participating in "training programs" that prepared bondpersons for freedom and rendered them more tractable. After completing the programs, the slaves would promptly depart for Liberia. The manumitters further envisioned the bondpersons-turned-freedpersons penning reports concerning their progress in Africa. The liberators then pictured themselves evaluating the enterprise and deciding whether they would continue with their emancipatory endeavors. Having conceptualized the entire breadth of the undertaking, the incipient manumitters pinpointed the initial training programs as the key to success. This is where they would devote their time, energy, and intellect. No two emancipators devised identical schemes, but most plans entailed subjecting carefully selected bondpersons to unspecified amounts of religious indoctrination, educational instruction, and occupational training.

Evangelicals themselves, many manumitters wanted to bring their version of Christianity to the slave quarters. Some emancipators hired clergymen to preach to their bondpersons; others took upon themselves the responsibility for proselytizing on the plantation. The message proffered stressed devotion to God, duty to one's owner, and defiance of temptation. Slaves who internalized these principles, thought the liberators, would stand out for their piety, loyalty, and industry. While the emancipators believed that religious instruction would aid in the moral uplift of bondpersons, they also assumed that slaves who took their teachings to heart would be more manageable. Properly sermonized bondpersons would take for granted that their owners' wishes matched those of Providence, or so the manumitters hoped.[18]

ACS liberators also made schooling a vital component of their manumission programs. Emancipators had many reasons for emphasizing education. As evangelicals, they saw a direct relationship between one's commitment to Christianity and one's ability to read the Bible. As racial liberals, they wanted to demonstrate blacks' capacity for intellectual advancement. As members of the colonizationist network, they appreciated the benefits of literacy. Yet these were not the only reasons why ACS manumitters schooled would-be freedpersons.[19]

The emancipators also hoped that the lure of literacy would help them exercise greater control over their bondpersons. As ACS manumitter John McDonogh bluntly asserted, he enticed slaves with education and freedom in order to "to make my will and interest, after Divine will, the study and rule of their lives." Slaveholders like McDonogh knew that bondpersons coveted the ability to read and write, and they aimed to take advantage of this yearning for learning. If nothing else, by making literacy a prerequisite for freedom, emancipators slowed the pace of manumission. In fact, slaveholders could postpone the date of emancipation almost indefinitely, for their definitions of literacy were inherently arbitrary and often impermanent. Nevertheless, the liberators remained confident that bondpersons would comply with even the most time-consuming and ill-defined literacy requirements, so great was the slaves' desire for education and freedom.[20]

Teaching slaves how to read and write would pay additional dividends after the bondpersons went to Liberia. Despite the manipulative aspects of their manumission programs, many liberators were genuinely concerned about their slaves' welfare, and they recognized that exchanging letters was the only practical means by which they could learn about freedpersons' fate in Africa. Along similar lines, the liberators expected to use emigrant missives when assessing their emancipatory experiments and deciding whether they would send additional parties overseas. Lastly, the ex-slaves' epistles would give the emancipators a means of motivating their remaining bondpersons. ACS supporters correctly predicted that prospective freedpersons would take great interest in letters from Liberia. So when they devised their manumission schemes, emancipators anticipated getting a letter like the one John McDonogh received from the freedwoman Nancy Smith McDonogh, who wrote: "Please read this in the presence of all your servants. . . .[A]ll you servants pay attention to your master, and go to school and learn. If such should not be obeyed, I think a little punishing would not be wrong." Whether or not such missives produced the effect that emancipators envisioned is discussed in chapter 3. For now, it suffices to note that when ACS liberators ruminated on manumission, they believed that, for both humanitarian and utilitarian reasons, emigrant epistles would constitute an enormous return on a small investment in slave literacy.[21]

Emancipators were less certain about the role that vocational training would play in their manumission programs. As slaveholders in Baltimore and elsewhere had discovered, instructing slaves in the ways of, say, masonry, could make for good business. Occupational training of this sort evidently rendered slaves more compliant and allowed emancipators to profit from specialized labor. Still, ACS manumitters wondered whether such vocational skills would be useful in Africa. Most liberators believed that freedpersons would be best served by farming in Liberia and therefore reckoned that their slaves merely needed to know how to build a house, mend a fence, and construct the sundry items associated with agricultural life. Conflicted about what to do in regard to vocational training, most emancipators did little. Their labors in this realm certainly paled in comparison with their efforts concerning religious and educational instruction.[22]

Having formulated their manumission programs, the emancipators selected bondpersons whom they thought worthy of liberty. In most slaveholding societies, male manumitters tended to free their illicit offspring, a practice that was common in colonial America and, to an extent, was still prevalent in cities such as Charleston, Mobile, and New Orleans right up to the Civil War. However, the custom of emancipators favoring their "illegitimate" children appears to have died out among nineteenth-century colonizationists. There is very little evidence to suggest that paternity played a role in the selection of would-be freedpersons. The emancipators apparently had other criteria in mind when identifying candidates for freedom.[23]

Sex and age were the most important factors. ACS liberators almost always selected adult bondmen to head their manumission programs. The emancipators justified their decisions by contending that full-grown males would fare best in Liberia, and they were generally right. ACS officials usually applauded the liberators' choices, partly because Liberia needed adult men and partly because the Society's leaders thought that the emancipators were praiseworthy humanitarians. Since bondmen usually fetched higher prices than bondwomen, argued the Society's spokespersons, ACS liberators were magnanimously giving their most valuable slaves a shot at freedom. Thus when one manumitter turned down $650 for a bondman and instead sent him to Liberia, the *African Repository* declared that, once again, an altruistic colonizationist had provided "an example for Abolitionists."[24]

ACS officials exaggerated the extent of the emancipators' generosity. They failed to note that liberators allowed only select slaves to participate in their manumission programs, and that the programs themselves were partially designed to profit the owner. The Society's leaders also neglected to mention the economic advantages of offering freedom to adult bondmen. Slaveholders incurred fewer long-term losses by liberating men. Manumitting a male meant sacrificing at most the market price and future labor of the individual freed. Liberating a woman entailed the same costs, as well as foregoing any profit-producing progeny she might later bear. From the emancipators' perspective, manumitting men was a better bargain, at least in the long run. In a like manner, there were pecuniary reasons for freeing adults. Financially speaking, a slaveholder "broke even" by the time a bondman reached his mid-twenties. In identifying adults—especially adult men—as candidates for freedom, and in subjecting them to extended training programs, manumitters hedged against economic losses.[25]

Emancipators also claimed that they considered their bondpersons' virtues when deciding whom to manumit. The liberators maintained that they were searching for devout, industrious, perceptive, and resolute individuals. This was only a half-truth. What they really wanted were slaves who possessed such characteristics *and* who employed them on their owners' behalf. The bond-man George Skipwith was one of the most ambitious and strong-willed persons John Hartwell Cocke ever encountered, and the Virginia planter tabbed him as a likely prospect for manumission. But Skipwith devoted his remarkable energy and considerable intellect to procuring alcohol, seducing women, and bullying others. Cocke gave up on him as a candidate for colonization, complaining that Skipwith had turned his school of emancipation into "a plantation brothel." From the liberators' standpoint, the best-qualified candidates for freedom were not just the most pious, intelligent, and sedulous slaves. They were also the most obedient ones.[26]

ACS emancipators usually did not specify how long it would take slaves to complete their training programs. John McDonogh was atypical in that he declared that his slaves would toil for fifteen years before they could secure their freedom. Yet most emancipators left the matter open-ended, an ambiguity that was supposed to play to their advantage.[27]

The liberators were also vague about when, if ever, they would end their ventures in colonization. Most manumitters conceptualized their programs as ongoing experiments. These were long-term projects that, if properly executed, would involve successive acts of manumission of increasingly eager bondpersons. "How blessed it would be to let the best go [to Liberia]," asserted Ann R. Page, "and draw on the rest . . . if they improved in moral development." As Page's statement suggests, manumitters hoped that the allure of freedom would continuously rally bondpersons to assiduity, probity, and fidelity.[28]

The emancipators' desire to control slaves even shaped their thinking about the virtues of sending manumittees abroad. The liberators sincerely believed that freedpersons would suffer under American racism. But they also knew that maintaining their power over their former slaves would be easier if the individuals freed were located in Liberia. For one thing, emancipators would be able to rely on ACS officials and the colonizationist network to keep tabs on ex-bondpersons. "I cannot set you free here [in the United States]," one manumitter told her bondpersons; "you would be in obscure places where I should never know whether you were doing well or ill." In the Old South, control and concern often went hand-in-hand.[29]

Emancipators trembled when contemplating what their former bondpersons might do if left to their own devices in America. They were not just worried that freedpersons would fall into a state of relapse. They harbored still greater fears. Even a cursory glance at the activities of free blacks in Baltimore, Richmond, Washington, and other cities suggested that ex-slaves might unite with antislavery radicals. Indeed, several manumitters would later stand aghast when their former slaves eschewed going to Liberia and instead went to the North, where they joined ranks with the abolitionists. From the emancipators' viewpoint, complete black independence meant not backsliding but backstabbing.[30]

Skeptical of both abolitionist and proslavery arguments, ACS liberators created manumission programs that promised to stabilize slavery. Judicious emancipatory experiments, they declared, would shore up the system. The key was caution; these would be deliberate undertakings. For many, dilatoriness became inertia. As time passed, there emerged an aging cohort of colonizationists, experts in the art of temporizing and rationalizing. In the two decades before the Civil War, some of them finally effected ACS manumissions.

ACS Manumitters, 1841–1860 ＞ 1820 - 1840

There were over twice as many ACS manumissions between 1841 and 1860 as there had been in the 1820–40 period. This upsurge was partly due to new legislative and judicial policies: most southern states required the removal of newly liberated blacks, while northern states discouraged the settlement of African-Americans in their territories. Slaveholders who might have previously allowed ex-slaves to remain close by, or who might have taken them to free states, may have now figured they had no alternative but to convey manumittees to Africa. Yet the passing of laws was not the only reason for the rise in ACS liberations. The passing of elderly colonizationists was equally important. Many of the emancipators of the 1841–60 period were the aged, affluent, and scattered remainders of a bygone era, and they effected manumissions as death summoned them.[31]

Early converts to colonization powered the late revival of the movement. The individuals who sent slaves to Liberia during the 1850s were well along in life. Nearly three out of five had been born during the eighteenth century, and one out of five had been alive before the signing of the Treaty of Paris in 1783. On average, these individuals were fifty-nine years old when they liberated their bondpersons. When they reminisced about their formative years, ACS emancipators recalled the late 1700s and early 1800s.[32]

Youthful days in the Upper South, in particular, came to mind. Seventy-five percent of the individuals who effected ACS manumissions during the 1850s were Upper South natives. Virginia led the way (43 percent of the emancipators had been born there), with Kentucky (13.5 percent) and North Carolina (11.5 percent) placing a distant second and third. A handful of liberators were either from the North (7.4 percent) or foreign lands (3.4 percent). Just 11 percent had been born in the Lower South, and most of these were from Georgia. "If any scheme of policy is thoroughly Virginian," wrote the Rev. Philip Slaughter in 1855, "it is the scheme of African Colonization." As far as the birthplaces of ACS emancipators were concerned, Slaughter was more or less correct. Virginia (and the Upper South generally) was the seedbed of colonization.[33]

Most of these individuals stayed close to home, effecting manumissions in their native region. Nearly one-third (32 percent) of ACS emancipations during the 1841–60 period took place in Virginia. Kentucky, with its numerous colonization advocates, accounted for one-fifth (20 percent) of such liberations, while Tennessee, with its unusually permissive manumission code, was the site of one-eighth (12 percent) of the emancipations. All totaled, 75 percent of ACS manumissions during the 1841–60 period transpired in the Upper South.[34]

Yet this represented a decline from the 1820–40 era, when 93 percent of ACS liberations had occurred there. Despite increasingly proscriptive manumission laws and a suffocating social climate, during the 1841–60 period, one in four emancipations took place in the Lower South. Colonization was hardly a South-wide movement, but it was spreading.

Georgians and Upper South migrants were largely responsible for the rise in Lower South manumissions. Back in the 1810s and 1820s, some Georgians had voiced their support for colonization. The state's ACS advocates had been silenced but not vanquished. In the 1850s, a handful of Georgia slaveholders, now aged and facing death, sent slaves to Liberia. A few Georgians who had left their home state and moved farther south pursued a similar course. But beyond the borders of the Peach State, ACS recruitment efforts failed abysmally. Georgians notwithstanding, very few slaveholders who had been born in the Lower South effected ACS manumissions.[35]

Along with the Georgians, migrants from the Upper South abetted the rise in Lower South liberations. Thirty-seven percent of the Deep South emancipators were originally from outside the region, with most having come from Virginia or North Carolina. Not surprisingly, the majority moved to Georgia (the Lower South state most amenable to colonization), but a small number ended up in the Gulf States. The experiences of these sojourners is a valuable reminder about migration in the nineteenth century: although scholars have focused on the exploits of Edward Coles, the Grimké sisters, and others who moved north, most southern whites, when they relocated, went farther south. Along with their families, slaves, and material possessions, they sometimes brought an affinity for colonization.[36]

Isaac Disheroon was typical of such persons. Born in Delaware during the American Revolution, by the middle of the nineteenth century Disheroon was living in Whitfield County, Georgia, the owner of nine bondpersons and $8,000 in real estate. Despite being a slaveholder, Disheroon had qualms about keeping blacks in perpetual servitude. "I have for a long time been strongly impressed with an aversion to the institution of slavery, and [have] an ardent desire for the emancipation of the African race from bondage," averred Disheroon in February 1852. Disheroon could support himself without the aid of slave labor, and consequently permitted his bondpersons to live, in his words, "virtually free." Yet the seventy-four-year-old Disheroon knew that his death was imminent and that the fate of his slaves was uncertain. "As I can not expect to live long it would be a comfort to me to know that they were wholly discharged from the shackles of slavery. I wish them sent back to the continent from which their forefathers came," he wrote to the ACS. Disheroon sold his farm and secured provisions for the would-be freedpersons, but one dubious observer noted that the slaveholder's heirs and other interested parties were going to "trouble him" and prevent the emancipation. Disheroon staved off his detractors and three months later, in May 1852, liberated his slaves on the condition that they go to Africa.[37]

Like Disheroon, most Lower South emancipators who had been born outside the region were in the twilight of their lives. The migration south- and westward, it appears, further delayed the already glacial pace of manumission. The average age of such liberators was sixty-eight. Nearly half a century after they had reached adulthood, these transplants from another place and seemingly another time finally sent bondpersons to Liberia.

By the time ACS manumitters got around to freeing their slaves, they had accumulated a considerable amount of wealth. Half of the individuals who transported bondpersons to Liberia during the 1850s owned seventeen or more slaves. They claimed an impressive amount of real estate as well, with the median value of their land holdings coming in at $7,850. Not surprisingly, male liberators had more resources than did their female counterparts (twice as much real estate and a third more slaves, on average), but neither group was threatened by destitution.

Outside sources of income provided further financial security, at least for the male manumitters. Approximately 30 percent of male emancipators listed something other than farmer or planter as their occupation. The most common nonagricultural trades were merchant, physician, lawyer, and preacher. The emancipators' vocations, along with their land assets and slaveholdings, provided a sizable buffer from penury.

Nor did emancipators intend to leave their children penniless. If generational turnover occurs every twenty-five years, then the typical emancipator's child would have been thirty-four years old—that is, a full-grown adult with resources of his or her own. Indeed, nearly 50 percent of all ACS emancipators lived either by themselves or with just one other person (enslaved African-Americans notwithstanding). ACS propagandists claimed that manumitters put their slaves' liberty before their heirs' interests, but the statistical evidence suggests that the emancipators' offspring had already ventured off to establish their fortunes.[38]

Between 1841 and 1860, then, most ACS manumitters were old-time throwbacks of a long-gone era. Many could recall the heady days of the Revolution; even more could remember the evangelical fervor that had swept through the Upper South in the early 1800s; and all could recollect the instability that seemed to have beset slavery during the first decades of the nineteenth century. But those times had passed, and many manumitters reckoned that their days were numbered, too. They had changed some over the years, of course. Many were now sizable slaveholders, and a large minority had moved to the Deep South. But they were still ACS advocates, and as such they retained their life-long interest in manumission and colonization.

Slaveholders like Anne Rice of Virginia continued the tradition of "experimentalist" manumissions. Rice was a deeply religious, sixty-two-year-old widow. She bemoaned the nation's troubled times and "felt great anxiety about the immortal souls committed to my charge," presumably referring to her seventeen slaves. In December 1847, the distressed Rice looked into sending some of her bondpersons to Liberia. At the center of her investigation stood Anderson Brown. Thirty-nine years old, Brown had worked at a female boarding school, where both the proprietor and the patrons testified to the bondman's impeccable integrity. Rice, too, thought Brown "remarkable for truth & honesty," and regarded him as a prime candidate for freedom. Rice subsequently endeavored to "prepare" Brown for freedom. In fretting over slavery, employing selective manumissions, "readying" bondpersons for emigration, anticipating freedpersons' reports, and (later) sending additional companies to Liberia, Anne Rice was a quintessential experimentalist.[39]

For some aging manumitters, the time for experimentation had passed. With their own demise near at hand, such persons arranged for the transport of their slaves to Africa. Elizabeth Holderness is a case in point. Born in North Carolina in 1790, Holderness was one of those Upper South migrants who had surreptitiously carried the colonization cause to the Lower South. In 1850, Holderness was living in Columbus, Mississippi, the owner of $21,000 in real estate and seventeen bondpersons. A slaveholding opponent of slavery, the sexagenarian mistress coped with the incongruity in predictable fashion, claiming that she treated her servants with exceptional kindness. "They have never been abused[,] never rushed & never worked too much either in hot or rainy weather. They know nothing of the rigors of slavery," she declared. Holderness had often considered letting her bondpersons go to Liberia but had repeatedly put off the decision. Having reached the age of sixty-five, however, Holderness believed the matter could be delayed no longer. "I am now getting old & it is necessary for me to take some action," she informed ACS official William McLain in March 1855.[40]

Holderness wondered whether sending her slaves to Liberia was the right thing to do. "I do not wish to free them merely for the sake of freedom, when they will probably be rendered more miserable & unhappy by the change," she explained. "Nor do I wish them to remain in slavery if freeing them will prove a benefit[,] an advantage[,] a blessing to them." Holderness agonized over the decision. "I think a great deal about it. My mind is in conflict doubt & distraction." As she pondered her next move, Holderness concealed the anguish within, refusing to inform her neighbors, kin, and, oddly enough, even her slaves about her interest in colonization.[41]

Holderness's and Rice's emancipatory efforts highlight an intriguing feature of ACS liberations: females were overrepresented among the manumitters. Approximately 10 percent of all slaveholders were women, yet 21 percent of ACS emancipators were females. Why did women effect ACS manumissions at a greater rate, proportionally speaking, than men? The short answer is that female slaveholders were particularly eager to safeguard their investments in slavery, but southern gender norms sensitized them to some of the institution's injustices and left them vulnerable to sex-specific forms of servile resistance. As a result, they turned to ACS manumissions as a means of protecting their profits, salving their conscience, and appeasing their slaves.

Planter-class females aimed to perpetuate slavery generally and to exercise control over their own bondpersons specifically. If anything, such women were more dependent on slave-generated revenue than were their male counterparts, who enjoyed the benefits, flexibility, and security that came with having more vocational choices and material wealth. Simply put, elite women's financial well-being rested heavily on the backs of bondpersons, and they wanted their slaves to shoulder that burden diligently, faithfully, and without complaint.[42]

Yet female slaveholders needed to exact obedience and labor from bondpersons without transcending southern gender norms, which declared white women to be naturally pious, humble, and submissive beings. As numerous historians have noted, southern white women were bombarded with messages from kin, ministers, authors, and regional leaders about the virtues of feminine domesticity, morality, and meekness. Inculcated from birth, most southern white females accepted the prescriptive gender standards.[43]

Plantation mistresses' moral sensitivity was sometimes heightened by their close contact with bondpersons, especially domestic workers. In directing household affairs, nursing the sick, and providing religious instruction, elite white women routinely interacted with slaves. For some, these everyday dealings may have engendered an emotional intimacy with their bondpersons; for most, they simply provided an up-close picture of some of slavery's inequities. To be sure, plantation mistresses never understood the pain, sorrow, and rage of enslaved African-Americans. Yet compared to southern white men, they had more opportunities for glimpsing slavery's atrocities, and for those women who internalized southern gender ideals, they were apt to be disturbed by what they saw.[44]

Those images could cause female slaveholders to doubt whether they were being sufficiently pious, and this uncertainly haunted women who knew that death was always nearby. Rampant diseases, along with the dangers of childbirth, made life a tenuous thing for females in the South. Consequently, many southern white women were, in the words of historian Catherine Clinton, "preoccupied with their souls."[45]

Designated as the moral gatekeepers of the South and fearful for their own salvation, plantation mistresses could be repulsed by some of slavery's injustices. The buying and selling of bondpersons, in particular, could chafe the conscience of elite white women. Observing blacks' agony on the auction block certainly pained ACS advocate Mary Blackford, who could see the activities of local slave traders from her house. The daily tragedies prompted Blackford to keep a journal entitled "Notes Illustrative of the Wrongs of Slavery." In her journal, Blackford detailed how her cook's husband was accosted by slave dealers, tossed into jail, sold to the highest bidder, and forever separated from his wife. Witnessing such incidents caused Blackford to predict, "the time will come when we shall look back and wonder how Christians could sanction slavery."[46]

Enslaved African-Americans were aware of the expectations that southern society placed on white women, and bondpersons used those gender norms to advance their own interests. Southern notions of womanhood, in other words, made female slaveholders the targets of distinct forms of resistance. For example, African-Americans knew about white women's putative concern for their familial needs, and thus bondpersons' pleas against the slave trade could hit female slaveholders with particular force. The aforementioned Blackford may have disliked the selling of slaves, but it seems reasonable to assume that bondpersons' implorations agitated her conscience even further.

Slaves' sex-specific methods of resistance could both flatter and confuse their owners. Margaret Mercer's bondpersons, for instance, utilized southern gender mores to gull their mistress. Mercer had planned on sending some of her slaves to Liberia, but to her surprise, many of them had reservations about moving to the African colony. "My people are not altogether reconciled to going," Mercer observed, "they say *if I will* go with them they should like it." Mercer's slaves, knowing that their mistress was expected to have a special affinity for her black "charges," effectively masked their indignation with avowals of filial devotion.[47]

To summarize, female slaveholders found themselves in an awkward position. As whites, they had myriad reasons for supporting slavery. As people with comparatively few occupational options, they had economic incentives to defend the institution. But as women, they were supposed to abide by gender norms that demanded from them piety, gentility, humility, and submissiveness, all qualities that complicated their efforts to uphold slavery. Moreover, those same norms provided African-Americans with unique opportunities to resist their thralldom. To extricate themselves from this dilemma, elite white women looked for a system of plantation management that would protect their stake in slavery, allow them to act in conventionally feminine ways, and vitiate their slaves' opposition. ACS manumissions, with their emphasis on religious and educational instruction, fit the bill perfectly.

mostly women Quantitative evidence further illustrates slaveholding women's affinity for ACS emancipations. As previously indicated, female slaveholders, responding to the southern notions of womanhood and their slaves' manipulation of those norms, were more likely than their male counterparts to send their bondpersons to Liberia. They were also more prone to engage in multiple acts of manumission—nearly one-third of "recidivist" emancipators were females, even though only 21 percent of ACS liberators were women. Female manumitters also freed a greater proportion of their slaves (39 percent, compared to 29 percent for male liberators). Of course, manumission was not the only means by which southern mistresses managed plantations. But the statistical evidence indicates that they were particularly fond of ACS emancipations as an administrative tool.

This was especially true for widows, who, by the 1850s, constituted one-eighth of all ACS manumitters.[48] As women who inherited part or all of their husbands' estates, and who regained control over property that they had brought into the marriage, these widows had at their disposal a substantial amount of wealth. Almost all of them owned real estate, and the median value of their holdings was a tidy $5,200. Equally dramatic, they owned, on average, eighteen slaves. The widows were well off. Yet their affluence did not make them more generous.

Having come into wealth, widows were dead set on keeping it. Their dilemma lay in managing large numbers of bondpersons without violating normative gender ideals. ACS manumissions were well suited to the widows' predicament. Determined to preserve their assets, these individuals did not effect manumissions wantonly. They freed some slaves, but they retained three-quarters of their bonded laborers. If "managerial" difficulties explain why so many widows effected ACS manumissions, carefully planned parsimony elucidates why they freed so few slaves.

Widows were not always the instigators of emancipations. In some instances, widows may have received "credit" for manumissions wherein they were carrying out the testamentary requests of their deceased husbands. Decades could pass between the demise of one's spouse and the embarkation of bondpersons, and under these circumstances the misidentification of the manumitter was bound to occur. Yet clerical errors might also have been made because widows exercised considerable control over these postmortem manumissions. They purchased outfits for the emigrants, sent the party to port, attended to legal matters, haggled with ACS officials, and sometimes even determined who would be freed and who would be left behind. Such activities came dangerously close to breaching the boundaries of "proper" behavior, but widows were safeguarded under the cloak of "wifely obligation." Few southern men dared obstruct a mourning woman who sought to fulfill the last wishes of her departed husband, even when her "duties" necessitated that she traverse into traditionally masculine realms. In light of the widows' wide-ranging and self-assured actions, it is little wonder ACS record keepers sometimes mistook them for the "real" manumitters.[49]

With the aging of ACS emancipators came an increase in testamentary manumissions. Liberations of this sort had always been a part of the colonization program. Even in the 1820s a few ACS supporters had freed their slaves by will. As time passed, postmortem manumissions became more numerous. By the 1850s, 29 percent of all ACS manumissions were of the testamentary variety. The men and women who ordered them were the wealthiest members of a well-heeled group: they owned, on average, twenty-two slaves. They did not engage in wholesale liberations—even in death, manumitters played favorites. But they did free more individuals (thirteen typically) than their nontestamentary counterparts (who manumitted just two persons, on average). A significant change in the nature of ACS operations, these postmortem affairs compelled colonization officials to spend many hours in cemeteries and courthouses.[50]

Southern jurists were among the first to notice the rise in postmortem emancipations, a realization that prompted some of them to adjudge the testamentary liberators' sanity. In 1842, for example, the Tennessee Supreme Court opined that John Gass had been "an eccentric man" who had held "peculiar opinions" but concluded that his emancipatory provisos did not constitute evidence of dementia. The same year, the Mississippi high court heard arguments concerning religious "fanatics" who warned slaveholders about "the peril in which their souls stand if they do not disinherit their offspring by emancipating their slaves!" Two years later, Virginia justices assessed the mental lucidity of testamentary emancipator William Ragland. South Carolina chancellor Job Johnston also inveighed against the growth in postmortem liberations and the moral cowardice he believed they represented. "This is another of those cases," fumed Johnston in *Gordon v. Blackman* (S.C., 1844), "multiplying of late with a fearful rapidity, in which the superstitious weakness of dying men, proceeding from an astonishing ignorance of the solid moral and scriptural foundations upon which the institution of slavery rests, and from a total inattention to the shock which their conduct is calculated to give to the whole frame of our social policy, induces them, in their last moments, to emancipate their slaves." Thus Johnston and other proslavery apostles raged when testamentary emancipations—those embarrassing and unsightly vestiges of colonization sentiment—cropped up like weeds in an immaculate southern garden.[51]

Many posthumous emancipators would have been startled by such denunciatory outbursts. They figured that disappointed heirs might speak ill of their testamentary decisions, but on the whole they believed that the enterprises would enhance their postmortem reputations. Eulogists and former bondpersons, they reckoned, would surely praise their memory. Even more important, a person's soon-to-be-met Maker might look favorably on testamentary liberations. When James Crawford drew up his will, for example, he assumed that there was a connection between one's last acts in this world and one's fate in the next. After providing for the emancipation of a dozen slaves, Crawford wrote, "I bequeath my Soul to God," no doubt expecting that the divine legatee would accept the bequest in light of the slaveholder's postmortem beneficence.[52]

In the meantime, testamentary liberators concentrated on the here and now, which above all meant procuring profits and controlling bondpersons. In the emancipators' view, a well-worded will could help one achieve earthly objectives and otherworldly ambitions. Even more than experimentalist manumissions, testamentary emancipations delayed slaves' day of liberation. Many years could come and go before bondpersons escaped thralldom. Postmortem manumitters bet that the grandeur of freedom would narcotize slaves' rebelliousness all the while. In this sense, testamentary manumissions were like desert mirages, forever beckoning their beholders forward, always promising to relieve them of their burdens. The bondpersons' determined trek toward liberty, of course, was calculated to profit the emancipators handsomely.

Slaves' journey to freedom could be a long one. It should come as no surprise that emancipators who used testamentary decrees were older than those who did not. The average age of postmortem liberators during the 1850s was sixty-four years old. Moreover, bondpersons were not always freed immediately upon their owners' demise. Many male testators deferred liberation until after their wives either died or remarried. Others requested that their bondpersons be hired out to cover the costs of colonization. Still others ordered that slaves reach a certain age before emigrating. From the blacks' perspective, the barrens of bondage appeared endless.[53]

Even the most morally troubled emancipators used testamentary devices and thereby squeezed additional years of toil from their bondpersons. Anna J. Banks of Tennessee professed to have "long entertained conscientious and religious scruples upon the subject of slavery," but she did not liberate her slaves during her own lifetime. Nor did she emancipate her slaves upon her death. Rather, Banks's slaves were eligible for freedom only after their mistress's sister passed away. Another distraught slaveholder, Sarah Freeman of North Carolina, temporized in a like fashion. As a Quaker, Freeman disliked slavery, but she repeatedly postponed manumitting her bondpersons. To assuage her conscience, Freeman penned a will that provided for their liberation and transport to either a free state or Liberia (she preferred the latter). Still moral demons haunted her. At one point, Freeman summoned her agent and told him to make the necessary arrangements for sending the slaves out of state. Not long afterward, however, she rescinded her instructions, pleading that she was old and infirm, and that she could not survive without her slaves' labor. Only after Freeman's death did her bondpersons secure their long-awaited liberty.[54]

Postmortem liberations not only wrung more labor from bondpersons, but they theoretically improved the quality of work extracted. Some emancipators were quite frank about how they expected their testamentary devices to elicit diligence from slaves. When Edward Poindexter penned his will in 1835, for example, he insisted that his bondpersons work for his wife and then, upon her demise, be given the option of emigrating to Liberia. "If any of the servants loaned to my wife should be refractory or hard to manage," Poindexter added, "I wish my executor to dispose of such at public sale." For over twenty years, Poindexter's slaves plodded toward freedom, the horrors of the auction block never far from view. Several died during this extended period. When freedom finally came within their grasp, the Virginia Supreme Court, reflecting a growing judicial hostility toward the ACS, ruled Poindexter's will invalid, arguing that bondpersons who chose between liberty in Africa and bondage in America enjoyed the power of self-emancipation. In some instances, slaves, like sand-dune wanderers, never arrived at an oasis of relief.[55]

Poindexter had not anticipated this obstacle to emancipation, and he was not alone in this regard. Many ACS manumitters failed to foresee how much "outside forces" like the courts would affect their undertakings. From their slaves, the manumitters simply expected obedience and earnestness; from colonization officials, accurate intelligence about Liberia and useful information about logistical matters; from northerners, occasional financial assistance; from their neighbors, forbearance while their manumission projects unfolded and the acumen to see the efficacious results. In short, the emancipators were a somewhat myopic lot who never imagined the shockwaves that their endeavors sometimes unleashed.

3

—⁓ↄ◌ↄ⁓—

Slaves

Negotiating for Freedom

In August 1855, Elijah McLean of Washington, Missouri, was getting ready to transport a slave family to Liberia. McLean assumed that the bondpersons "were entirely willing to go." To his surprise, several of the slaves decided against emigrating. McLean identified two reasons for the bondpersons' demurral. First, familial considerations weighed heavily on their minds. As the details of the plan took shape, the two eldest children balked. The siblings' refusal had a domino effect. Other family members did not want to be separated from these two and consequently opted to stay put. McLean also discerned a second reason for the slaves' recalcitrance: the ACS's opponents. "I have no doubt but they have been badly consulted by some enemy to Colonization," he reported. McLean thought it "improper and unwise" to force the slaves to emigrate, but he intended to keep encouraging them to go. The owner of various ACS publications, McLean believed that providing the bondpersons with information about Liberia would initiate a reversal of opinion among them. Still, he did not know if bondpersons would ever leave. He simply hoped that they would depart "at some future period."[1]

As McLean's experiences suggest, convincing slaves to move to Liberia was a critical and challenging task for Society supporters. Most ACS manumitters, believing that emigration should be a voluntary endeavor and that blacks were capable of self-government, allowed their bondpersons to choose between freedom in Liberia and enslavement in America. The final decision on emigration, in other words, was normally the slaves' alone.

Bondpersons' thoughts and actions were informed by the context of the times. Their choice was not between peril in Africa and monotony in America. Rather, slaves selected from several unpalatable, volatile scenarios. Instability always harried bondpersons. The death of an owner—to take a familiar example—had the potential to wreak havoc on slaves' lives. The precariousness that always tormented bondpersons became even more pronounced during the antebellum era. With cotton's westward expansion, Upper South slaves were forcibly moved to the Lower South with their owners or, even more likely, were sucked into the abyss of the interstate slave trade. So whatever doubts slaves harbored about Liberia, they could be equally unsure about their future in America.[2]

An almost endless series of questions ran through the minds of bondpersons who contemplated emigrating to Liberia. How exacting were the terms of manumission? Could the stipulations be completed before one's owner passed away? Were other avenues to freedom available? Suppose one went to Liberia—would suitable outfits be available for the journey? Would emigration be a familial endeavor? Could one return to America if unsatisfied in Africa? Since each bondperson faced a unique set of circumstances, there were no universal answers to these questions. Generalizations about slaves' thoughts on colonization must be hazarded with caution.

Even so, it is evident that slaves, like their owners, attempted to maximize the material, social, and psychological benefits of manumission while minimizing its potential downsides. They did not blindly accept their owners' offers. Bondpersons haggled over the requirements for freedom, sought reliable intelligence about Liberia, and looked to secure family ties. ACS liberations were not instances of complaisant slaves dutifully working toward freedom, as white colonizationists had originally expected. Rather, they were the product of tenacious negotiations that fundamentally recast slaveholders' manumission plans.[3]

Assessing the Terms of Manumission

Slaves' appraisal of manumission depended in part on the nature of their owners' propositions. Many slaveholders demanded that their bondpersons complete "training programs." Others required their slaves to purchase their lib-

erty. Then there were the ones who presented freedom via a postmortem decree. In each instance, bondpersons carefully studied the terms of manumission, looking for ways to exploit the offers to their best advantage.

From the mid-1820s through the mid-1840s, most ACS liberations were of
the nontestamentary, "experimentalist" variety. During this period, many ACS
manumitters demanded that their slaves complete "training regimens" and, in
some instances, pay for their liberty. The bondpersons generally welcomed the
chance to obtain freedom. This was true even for the individuals who had to
recompense their owners. Such persons were usually allowed to hire themselves out, a labor arrangement that afforded bondpersons economic opportunity and social autonomy. For the enslaved, all roads to freedom, no matter
how daunting, merited some investigation.[4]

Bondpersons' general interest in manumission was further boosted by the
fact that the majority of ACS emancipators resided in rural areas, where slave
liberations were uncommon events. Not only were manumissions rare in the
countryside, but also the ramifications of refusing freedom were grimmer for
plantation slaves than for their urban counterparts. A bondman from, say,
Richmond, Virginia, who declined going to Liberia could still take advantage
of the anonymity and opportunities that southern cities offered African-
Americans. His similarly disinclined counterpart in the hinterland, conversely,
would carry on in a less hospitable milieu. For most slaves, foregoing freedom
meant remaining rural, and remaining rural often meant braving an uncertain
and unenviable future.[5]

Specific aspects of emancipators' training programs also intrigued bondpersons. For example, many emancipators offered prospective manumittees
educational instruction. Among other things, the emancipators had hoped
that slaves would become less refractory as they doggedly pursued the bait of
literacy. Most bondpersons were, in fact, eager to learn their letters. For them,
literacy promised power for the aspiring, biblical study for the devout, and
self-actualization for the downtrodden. Later, in Liberia, it would offer a
means for the homesick and the destitute to communicate with Americans.
Thus, between 1820 and 1840, when "experimentalist" manumissions were
most common, at least 15 percent of freedpersons over the age of sixteen were
literate. In the realm of education, the interests of slaves and manumitters temporarily "articulated"—that is, both parties shared the same goal, albeit for
different reasons.[6]

Bondpersons and their owners once again went their separate ways over the
issue of religious instruction. A liberal dose of sermonizing, the emancipators

had anticipated, would instill in slaves a healthy respect of their earthly and heavenly masters. Yet the proselytizing had not gone as planned. Bondpersons' piety had not led to unthinking docility. When one manumittee recalled her owner's religious cudgeling, she commented, "I thought the Sabbath was one of the most burdensome days I ever wished to see." Although this individual eventually obtained a passage to Liberia, other bondpersons decided that their owners' terms for freedom were so excessive that they did not merit further pursuit.[7]

From the start, there were slaves who opted out of manumission projects. Many emancipators from the 1820–40 era, including Mary Blackford, Margaret Mercer, Ann R. Page, Edward Brett Randolph, Richard Bibb, and Emily Tubman, confronted bondpersons who were unwilling to move overseas. And the passage of time only brought more instances of intransigence on the slaves' part. ACS records are replete with examples of bondpersons who refused to go along with their owners' manumission schemes. We will never know how many slaves fell into this category, but enough did to demonstrate that bondpersons scrutinized proposals for freedom with care and caution.[8]

Emancipators' responses to their slaves' "contrariness" ranged from equanimity to outrage. Consider the reactions of Henry B. Goodwin and John D. Parkham, two Maryland brothers-in-law who discovered that most of their slaves had decided against emigrating to Africa. At first, Parkham was quite calm about the matter. His patience soon expired, though, and he requested that the sheriff transport his ex-slaves out of the state, as the law required. Goodwin took the affair in stride. He seriously pondered why so many of his bondpersons had rejected his offer of freedom in Africa. For generations, he thought, blacks had been disappointed by the broken promises of self-proclaimed white philanthropists. From the blacks' perspective, Goodwin speculated, white altruism must have seemed like a contradiction in terms. No wonder they declined going to Liberia. Goodwin held out the hope that those who did emigrate would send back positive reports and thereby induce the doubters to reconsider their positions. In the meantime, he hired his former bondpersons and learned that they were more productive as free laborers than as slaves.[9]

Other emancipators exhibited a similar range of reactions. Some interpreted their slaves' reservations about Africa as evidence of fidelity. Others were startled by their slaves' decisions against colonization. For example, John McDonogh was exasperated when one of his slaves received a medical education in the North and then refused to emigrate to Liberia. Still other manumitters reworked their entire philosophy on freedom and slavery. Thirty years of frustration with colonization turned John Hartwell Cocke into a proslavery advocate. A slave society headed by patriarchal masters represented "the highest state of human existence," argued the disenchanted Cocke, who added that it was a "monstrous absurdity to be regarded otherwise." The experiences of Cocke, McDonogh, and Mercer were repeated again and again as slaves rejected the opportunity to go to Africa.[10]

By the mid-1840s, however, a growing number of slaveholders never learned of their bondpersons' decisions, for these would-be emancipators offered their slaves freedom via a testamentary decree. These postmortem proposals presented bondpersons with extraordinary dilemmas. The ramifications of refusing a testamentary bequest of freedom were especially grave. For slaves whose owners were still alive, the consequences of foregoing freedom were comparatively predictable: the bondperson would probably continue to serve the same master or mistress under somewhat familiar circumstances. For those slaves whose owners had passed away, the future was far less certain. In all likelihood, the bondpersons would be parceled out like the testator's other property. Postmortem manumissions, in other words, wedged slaves between the dangers of Liberia and those of an estate liquidation.

Most bondpersons who were offered freedom by postmortem decree eventually went to Liberia. Among the voluminous ACS records, one finds few instances in which large numbers of slaves refused testamentary offers of freedom. In fact, some bondpersons went to great lengths to ensure that outside parties did not subvert their owners' postmortem wishes. Testamentary bequests of freedom were not always successfully effected, but enraged heirs, insistent creditors, and hostile judges, not obdurate slaves, usually prevented their execution.[11]

Some slaves declined postmortem gifts of liberty, though. For example, upon the demise of William Smart of Gloucester County, Virginia, in 1840, one observer remarked that his best servants had decided to remain in America. A few years later, Capt. J. Early willed that his slaves have the option of going to Africa—and most seized the opportunity to do so—but one bondman ran away rather than emigrate, while one bondwoman feigned illness in order to stay in Virginia. When Sidney B. Clay of Bourbon County, Kentucky, passed away, five of his bondpersons accepted his postmortem gift of freedom in Liberia, but two individuals refused, claiming they would rather drown themselves than move overseas. For slaves, turning down a testamentary bequest of freedom often meant stepping into a foggy future, one where estate divisions, public auctions, and the interstate slave trade all loomed in the shadows, but some bondpersons strode into this daunting unknown anyway, preferring such perils to those that lurked in the Liberian darkness.[12]

Testators intended to give slaves a simple, clear-cut choice between thralldom in America and freedom in Liberia, but the slaves saw other options. Between the black-and-white offers they identified much gray area. When James Bradley of Georgia passed away, for example, he willed that his bondpersons could go to Liberia if they wanted (and most did emigrate), and that one prospective manumittee, Peter Jordan, should receive a medical education in Philadelphia before his departing for Africa. In Pennsylvania, Jordan fell in with abolitionists and subsequently refused to emigrate. The severing of traditional lines of authority thus provided bondpersons with the opportunity to press their ideas about manumission.[13]

Slaves exercised their prerogatives in ways and at times that flabbergasted white colonizationists. Consider the deeds of Peter Fisher's bondpersons. In 1827, Fisher died and left a will that called for the emancipation of his slaves. Heirs contested the will, but in 1834 the Tennessee Supreme Court ruled that the bondpersons should be sent to Liberia. Two years after the court decision, Fisher's slaves headed east toward the embarkation port of New York. Upon reaching Pittsburgh, the entire party fled. Neither the state Supreme Court nor Peter Fisher had imagined that the slaves would end up living in the North, largely because both the jurists and Fisher had failed to foresee that the bondpersons would imprint their own aspirations on the testamentary bequest of freedom.[14]

If Fisher's slaves wanted no part of Liberia, other bondpersons who were freed by will expressed more interest in the colony. These individuals also molded manumissions in ways that white colonizationists had not anticipated. Such was the case with Moore Worrell, who had been emancipated upon the demise of his owner and who insisted on visiting Liberia before deciding whether he would reside there permanently. Worrell departed in 1848, returned to America shortly thereafter, and then left for Africa once again in 1850, this time with his wife and children. Although ACS supporters had envisioned testamentary liberations as rigid and stable enterprises—bondpersons would either stay or emigrate—the truth was that slaves rendered them alterable and unpredictable affairs.[15]

Slaves' responses to manumission plans were as varied as the plans themselves. Some bondpersons complied with the terms for freedom; others fulfilled only some conditions; still others added their own provisos; and a number rejected the deals altogether. Yet if slaves' decisions were diverse, their goals were uniform: to augment the advantages of the emancipation while downsizing its drawbacks.

Slaves' Ideas about Liberia

ACS manumitters insisted that their slaves, if freed, move to Liberia. So in addition to assessing the other aspects of their owners' plans, bondpersons needed to formulate opinions about the African colony. Slaves consulted three sources when doing so. First, they conferred with American informants (for example, their owners, ACS agents, and colonization's opponents). Second, they queried returnees from Liberia. Finally, they examined letters from Liberia. As they pondered the question of emigration, then, slaves had at their disposal a fair amount of impressionistic, prejudicial, and contradictory information. Yet the individuals who held the highest opinions of Liberia had more resources than did the colony's critics. As a result, deliberating bondpersons, while cognizant of Liberia's flaws, tended to be excessively optimistic about what life would be like in Africa.

American Sources of Information

Bondpersons had several ways of learning about Liberia. They could start with their own families and communities. As Sterling Stuckey and others have argued, the retention of African cultural characteristics among slaves was extensive. Additionally, bondpersons might have consulted actual Africans. Despite an 1808 federal law that banned slave importations, some bondpersons were illegally smuggled into the United States every year. Yet the African influence should not be overstated. General impressions about Africa were not the same thing as precise information about Liberia. More specific intelligence would have to come from other sources.[16]

Candid slaveholders alerted their bondpersons to Liberia's attributes and shortcomings. As Ann R. Page of Virginia readied her slaves for emigration, for example, she told them to expect adversity in Africa. Another Virginian, John Hartwell Cocke, offered his bondpersons similar advice, as did John McDonogh of Louisiana. Mississippian Edward Brett Randolph likewise warned his slaves that sickness and poverty pervaded Liberia. Although abolitionists alleged that colonizationists cast unprofitable and unwary bondpersons to the wilds of Africa, few ACS emancipators acted so malevolently. To the best of their knowledge, they told their slaves about Liberia's imperfections. Most freedpersons suffered anyway, but their misfortunes cannot be ascribed to malicious intentions or cunning deceptions on their former owners' part.[17]

Slaves also asked ACS agents about Liberia. Potential emigrants turned to these traveling spokespersons from the earliest days of the colonization movement and continued to do so throughout the antebellum period. The officials' information about the colony was less than perfect, but they knew more than most people, and the facts were downright disturbing. ACS agents were presumably familiar with a medical report written by a Dr. Henderson and presented to the ACS board of managers in May 1832. According to the report, malaria alone was killing one out of six emigrants. Henderson analyzed the matter thoroughly. He calculated the safest seasons for emigration embarkations and compared how persons from different regions of America fared in Liberia. So when ACS representatives conversed with slaves, they knew what they were talking about. Whether they spoke forthrightly with would-be emigrants is another matter.[18]

ACS leaders may not have flat-out lied to slaves and their owners, but they seldom committed acts of full disclosure either. In 1828 and 1829, for example, the ACS sent 319 black Americans to Liberia. Twenty-six percent of them died before 1830. Nevertheless, ACS officer Ralph R. Gurley informed one supporter whose mother had sent bondpersons to Liberia that "the intelligence from the Colony is of a very encouraging character." In 1832, Gurley was again playing a shell game with the facts of colonization and, by extension, the lives of emigrants. By then, another 833 African-Americans had gone to Liberia (18 percent of whom had perished), and Henderson's medical report had come out, yet Gurley wrote a Virginia slaveholder who was about to send slaves to Liberia that the latest word out of the colony was heartening. No doubt ACS leaders did receive positive reports from some prosperous colonists. Yet their overreliance on such materials may have left bondpersons with misconceptions about Liberia.[19]

Colonization leaders denied that they suppressed unfavorable intelligence. "Our managers are exceedingly anxious to know the truth concerning the colony," professed Gurley, who then added, "even should it be distressing." To the extent that ACS agents conceded Liberia's problems, they had ready explanations for the setbacks. Pointing to America's own early history, they asserted that colonization was an indelicate business. "You must expect disappointments, and difficulties, and troubles in every place," they warned future settlers in 1840, "and it is only by perseverance that any body succeeds." Those who practiced prudence would be spared in Africa: "Foolish and unnecessary exposure to the dew and night air, and the indulgence of their appetites," they asserted, "have caused the death of many emigrants before they had become accustomed to the climate." For all intents and purposes, the ACS assumed that most downcast colonists had brought hardship upon themselves.[20]

Bondpersons nonetheless continued to rely on Society officials for information about Liberia. Occasionally, slaves themselves wrote the ACS. One Missouri bondman asked the organization for additional volumes of the *African Repository*, explaining, "I am a poor slave but . . . I Expects to goe to Liberia before long and would like to know all about It." In 1855, two bondpersons wrote the ACS that they had heard "the negroes in Liberia was killing one another and Eating [the victims]." The epistlers themselves were undeterred, but when other members of their party learned of the terrible tales, it "fritened some of them almost to death." Through correspondence and conversation, slaves tried to tap ACS officials' knowledge about Liberia.[21]

To the consternation of colonization leaders, slaves also learned about Liberia from the ACS's opponents. Whether northern abolitionists' diatribes against the ACS reached the slave quarters is uncertain, though David Walker's *Appeal* (1829), with its blistering attack on colonization, definitely circulated in the South. But even if northern remonstrations did not reach slaves' ears, there was still plenty of anti-ACS squabbling in the South.[22]

Free blacks became a topic of endless complaint among southern white colonizationists. Free black protests against the ACS occurred in Washington, D.C., and Baltimore, while other cities such as Charleston and Richmond witnessed heated debates on the topic. Not surprisingly, these disputes gave pause to black Americans who considered going to Liberia. ACS advocate William H. Bayne of Fayetteville, North Carolina, gave one self-purchased man a copy of the *African Repository* but griped, "there are those here, I believe free negroes, who are trying to dissuade him" from emigrating. Samuel Lewis likewise noted that in Petersburg, Virginia, free blacks terrified would-be emigrants with woeful tales about Africa. Although over three thousand southern free blacks moved to Liberia, the caste generally detested colonization, and their opposition unquestionably undermined ACS operations among deliberating slaves.[23]

Perhaps most disheartening, from the colonizationists' perspective, was the fact that white southerners also joined the anti-Liberian refrain. Such detractors often had personal reasons for lambasting Liberia. Individuals who expected to inherit bondpersons, for example, could be especially critical of the colony. As one colonization agent pointed out, slaves who had been freed by will sometimes declined going to Africa because the testator's kin—who were the heirs at law and would be entitled to the slaves who refused to emigrate—would disingenuously tell bondpersons that death and deprivation awaited them in Africa. Even if slaves recognized the heirs' wile, the warnings, especially if corroborated by other sources, had to be taken seriously.[24]

Slaves who desired a clear picture of Liberia had to sift through a puzzle of incongruous pieces. The information offered by American sources (that is, their owners, colonization officials, interested onlookers, ACS opponents, and the occasional African slave) simply did not fit together. ACS leaders knew that bondpersons would discard their accounts first. In 1818, before the ACS had sent a single person to Africa, colonizationist Robert G. Harper offered an easy answer to this credibility question. "However distrustful of whites, they will confide in the reports made to them by the people of their own color and class," he wrote. Harper was thinking about free blacks at the time, but his remarks applied equally to slaves. For bondpersons who were considering emigration, African-Americans who had visited Liberia provided the most reliable intelligence about the colony.[25]

Returnees from Liberia

Many settlers were eager to leave Liberia. Between 1820 and 1843, 22 percent of all emigrants quit the colony.[26] Yet getting back to the United States was a very difficult task. Most southern states did not permit the immigration of free blacks, and even if they had, financial obstacles made a journey to America nearly impossible for most Liberians. As one former bondman, John M. Page Sr., complained, a voyage from Monrovia to Baltimore cost about forty or fifty dollars. Then there were additional expenditures for housing, meals, and transportation to one's final destination. Obviously, individuals who lacked sufficient food and clothing were in no pecuniary position to go to America. As a result, just one in five colonists who left Liberia managed to return to the United States. The others mostly went to Sierra Leone or Cape Palmas, the latter being a comparatively well-run settlement established by the independently operated Maryland Colonization Society.[27]

Despite the impediments, between 1820 and 1843, at least 113 emigrants returned to the United States. Nearly 80 percent of them were originally residents of the South, and over half of these were manumittees. Not surprisingly, the freedpersons who came back had more resources to draw on than other ex-slaves in Liberia. For example, whereas 15 percent of adult manumittees during this time period could read or write, 39 percent of the liberated returnees boasted some degree of literacy. In a like manner, women were underrepresented in this reverse migration. During the first two decades of Liberian colonization, 45 percent of the emancipated emigrants were females. Yet women constituted only 16 percent of manumitted returnees. Had females and illiterate emigrants—two groups that sometimes struggled in Liberia—been better represented among the returnees, the African colony's reputation would have been worse among black Americans.

Not that Liberia's standing was particularly good. Many of the freedpersons who made it to America told stories about wild beasts and harrowing conditions in the settlement. When a Mr. Peele of Northampton County, North Carolina, sent forty-five slaves to Liberia in 1828, he was the largest emancipator to date. After eight of his former bondpersons died within their first year in Africa, two of the remaining emigrants, William and Sandy Peele, rushed back to America with tales of tragedy, death, and despair. Two of Margaret Mercer's ex-slaves quit Liberia for the same reasons in 1830. The same year, Franklin Anderson sent six bondpersons to the African colony. Five of them were dead by year's end, and the sole survivor, thirty-year-old Charity Claget, returned to America in 1831. To be sure, not all of the returning freedpersons defamed Liberia. Some admired the colony and sojourned to America only to secure their kin's liberty. From the ACS's perspective, though, such affairs were rarities. Most of the returning freedpersons had found Liberia disappointing, and they broadcast their discontent widely.[28]

Like the manumitted returnees, the southern free blacks who came back to America were disproportionately skilled, literate males, and, like their ex-slave counterparts, some of them praised Liberia. Frederick James emigrated in 1820, and on a subsequent visit to the United States, he told free blacks in both the North and the South about Liberia's virtues. George McPherson was another Liberian devotee who crisscrossed the ocean several times, spreading the good word on each trip. Richmond free blacks heard positive reports from several of their former neighbors. None outdid Lott Cary. A tobacconist who emigrated in 1821, Cary did not return to America, but in letters and articles he contested inimical rumors about Liberia and encouraged blacks to emigrate there. "You will never know, w[h]ether you are men or monkies so long as you remain in America," taunted Cary in 1827. "I shall believe you to be men[,] when I see you conducting the affairs of your own Government," he continued, "and not before."[29]

These free black partisans were weak voices straining to overcome a chorus of anti-Liberia invective. Even in Richmond, African-Americans grew skeptical. Cary himself died preparing for battle in 1828, an untimely demise that caused many blacks to question the sagacity of colonization. To worsen matters, the following year, Gilbert Hunt, a quarrelsome man who had purchased his freedom and then moved to Liberia, returned to Richmond thoroughly disgusted with the colony. Along with him came three other dissatisfied persons. Richmond free blacks' interest in colonization declined precipitously thereafter. One dejected ACS official knew exactly why the city's African-Americans had turned their backs on Liberia, noting simply, "I fear they have received unfavorable accounts."[30]

Perhaps the most devastating attack came from Thomas C. Brown. In 1833, Brown emigrated from Charleston, a city that, like Richmond, had witnessed a fair amount of free black interest in colonization. After fourteen frustrating, sorrowful months in Liberia, Brown returned to America, where his disillusionment became grist for anti-ACS forces. Brown claimed that the ACS had deceived him. "My expectations had been raised by the Colonization Society," he explained, insisting that his disappointment was not unusual. Bemoaning the infirm economy, political oligarchy, and high mortality, Brown asserted that "Great numbers would like to come back, and had rather suffer slavery than stay in that country and starve." Brown added that this sentiment was not confined to the poorest colonists. "Some who appear to be doing well are anxious to remove from that country," he maintained. ACS officials disputed Brown's testimony but without success. For African-Americans, the scale of truth always tipped in favor of blacks' accounts of Liberia.[31]

Colonization officials hoped to minimize the influence that disgruntled men like Brown were having on their movement. In addition to denigrating displeased returnees, they invited carefully selected colonists to promote their program among African-Americans. For example, in 1833 the Maryland Colonization Society (MCS), worried about the unfavorable reports coming out of the colony, asked Jacob Prout to talk with blacks about the enterprise and to head the upcoming expedition of the *Lafayette*. Prout, a twenty-nine-year-old, literate free black from Baltimore, had sailed to Liberia aboard the *Indian Chief* in 1826. He was visiting America when the MCS made its offer, and, after a moment's reflection, he agreed to the bargain. When nearly 150 blacks sailed to Africa shortly thereafter, colonization leaders were convinced that Prout's efforts had been instrumental in making the expedition a success.[32]

Other recruiters followed in Prout's footsteps. The ACS preferred to bring back free blacks who had previously resided in urban areas. Such selections were a calculated risk on the colonizationists' part. The danger was that proslavery whites would protest the return of free blacks to their neighborhoods. The potential benefits were numerous, though. Free black spokespersons would have the best things to say about Liberia, were most likely to have the personal skills and community connections to recruit effectively, and might mollify southern whites' fears by convincing other free blacks to emigrate to Liberia. As it turned out, the gamble never quite paid off for the ACS. White southerners remained suspicious of the recruiters, and African-Americans were even more distrustful. White peevishness and black incredulity made for odds that the ACS could never beat.

The recruiters themselves were often the wager's big winners. Blacks who toured America at the behest of colonization officials were not unwitting dupes. They profited from the arrangements. Jacob Prout's position as leader of the *Lafayette* party gave him power—power that he abused by plundering the ship's provisions. Another spokesperson, Alexander Hance, obtained his children's liberty. His counterpart, Sion Harris, visited his friends and family while in America and made a little money along the way. ACS leaders had to make these kinds of concessions to their recruiters, for they were certain that such men were needed to advance the movement. Even when southern whites complained and skeptical blacks scoffed, colonization officials felt they had little choice but to stick with the black boosters.[33]

ACS leaders were equally chagrined by the investigative parties that some-times traveled to Liberia. The Society's leaders figured that African-Americans might embrace colonization if prominent and trusted blacks were to visit Liberia and come back with upbeat accounts. Unfortunately for the ACS, these envoys did not always return with recommendations for emigration. Even when they did praise Liberia, local blacks still resisted heading overseas. As one colonization publication complained, "[I]n many cases ... where an agent has been selected by the colored people themselves, to visit Liberia, and make a report of the condition of affairs there, such Report, when made on their re-turn, has been disregarded and disbelieved." Blacks who visited Liberia may have been slaves' most credible source of information about the colony, but no individual's testimony was above suspicion.[34]

During the nineteenth century, one could witness a transoceanic merry-go-round as ACS emigrants repeatedly crisscrossed the Atlantic. The individuals who sailed between America and Africa held different opinions about Liberia and had different reasons for journeying back and forth. Some were fleeing hardship in Liberia; others came back to obtain their family's freedom; still others traveled at the request of ACS officials; and a handful were returning to

their communities with their assessment of Liberia. These sojourners profoundly affected the colonization movement in America for their opinions
influenced slaves who had the opportunity to go to Liberia. Yet the returnees'
accounts, like those offered by slaves' "American sources," were subject to thor-
ough examinations. Would-be freedpersons carefully appraised these reports
and compared them with statements given by other persons, including epistlers in Liberia.

Letters from Liberia

Slaves who could not converse with a returnee sought the next best thing—a
letter from Liberia. Prospective freedpersons made it clear that they wanted
intelligence straight from the colony. John Calloway's slaves were perfectly
frank about the matter. Calloway had sent sixteen manumittees to Liberia, but
his remaining bondpersons expressed unease about joining the others. "Those
that I intend sending are desirous to know more about the country," observed
Calloway, "and to hear it from their fellow servants that I sent to Liberia." As
Calloway's comments indicate, letters from Liberia played a critical role in the
colonization movement.[35]

Emancipators' manumission schemes often turned on information provided by former bondpersons. After receiving distressing reports from the fifty
freedpersons he had sent to Liberia, William Kennedy of Tennessee permitted
his few remaining slaves to have the final say on whether they would emigrate.
"It makes me seem somewhat fickle in my purposes," he admitted, "but I leave
it entirely to themselves to stay with me as long as they please and to go when
they please." When contemplating the matter, Kennedy's bondpersons wanted
the best information available, and, according to their owner, that meant
intelligence provided by their compatriots in Liberia. Indeed, Kennedy himself questioned the credibility of the ACS's reports, suggesting that the organization's officials were misinformed about conditions in the African republic. "I
fear you are deceived by your agents at Greenville [Liberia]," Kennedy wrote
one colonization leader. His former slaves living there, he explained, had complained that the needs of new emigrants were not being met. "[A]t least some
of my people write so to me," the planter-emancipator concluded, "and say you
ought to have the thing looked into." In effect, the chain of command had been
reversed. Instead of a top-down model where ACS officers called the shots, ex-
slaves remonstrated to their former owners, who in turn suggested that the
Society investigate the grievances.[36]

Colonization leaders recognized the influence that letters from Liberia were having on their program, and they made every effort to showcase approbatory missives. Just as ACS officials employed black recruiters to dispute displeased returnees, so too did they use laudatory letters to blunt disparaging epistles. Publishing correspondence in the *African Repository* was a favorite tactic in this regard. The Society's monthly journal was filled with glowing reports from previous emigrants. The paper's white readers studied the testimonials with great interest and even sent in communiqués of their own. For example, Mary Custis Lee delighted in the news that she received from her former slaves in Liberia and believed that others would be equally impressed. According to Lee's cousin (who edited the letters before forwarding them to the ACS), Lee thought that the Society would publish the pieces because "they may prove an encouragement to those who are interested in the great and good cause of African Colonization." Lee was correct—the ACS's letter-publishing strategy heartened embattled white colonizationists in the South. Yet it seems doubtful that the organization's policy had any direct bearing on bondpersons' thinking about Liberia.[37]

The *African Repository*'s contents were outside most slaves' pale of knowledge. Perhaps a few literate bondpersons perused the periodical and the dispatches therein; some slaves probably asked other blacks to read the serial's epistles to them; and a number of bondpersons must have learned about the letters in the *African Repository* from their owners. In the final analysis, though, most deliberating slaves were either unaware of the journal's missives or unimpressed by them.

White colonizationists occasionally admitted that the reprinting of letters did not influence blacks' attitudes toward Liberia. "They are not satisfied with second hand news published at Washington," wrote one supporter from Louisville, Kentucky. "They want the *Liberian Herald* sent direct from Africa." The *Maryland Colonization Journal* likewise admitted that African-Americans ignored the correspondence that filled the periodical's columns. "Such being the case, we almost tire of publishing and republishing letters of this kind," wrote the editor, "—we tire of piping when they not only refuse to dance, but like the deaf adder stop their ears to the music." Although the letters that appeared in colonization journals did not greatly affect slaves' decisions concerning emigration, other missives did influence bondpersons' thoughts about Liberia.[38]

Nobody better understood the impact that letters from Liberia had on the colonization movement than the ACS's own field agents. Positive reports, they averred, could work wonders. ACS representative John Bruner attributed the procolonization sentiment he found in one Tennessee county to "the labors and influence of E. L. Mathes, Esq., and from the good reports sent back by the emigrants whom he has heretofore sent to Liberia." Bruner's colleague R. W. Bailey in Virginia was equally aware of the effects of favorable intelligence, remarking that ACS opponents who were trying to dissuade one man from emigrating would soon be changing their tune. "If he gives a good report of the country," predicted Bailey, "others will follow from this section."[39] To ACS agents, it was perfectly obvious that encouraging letters immeasurably enhanced the Society's prospects.

It was equally manifest that negative reports undercut the colonization movement. The melancholy missives penned by the ex-slave Samuel Harris, for example, pained ACS spokesman William Ruffner, who canvassed Harris's old neighborhood in Rockbridge County, Virginia. "Sam'l Harris . . . has written back within the last month or two such doleful accounts of Liberia, that he has scared nearly all my emigrants," complained Ruffner. The ACS official dismissed Harris as a "weak-minded man who never knew what it was to have to support a family before he went out there" but conceded that the freedman's transatlantic communications were exercising a powerful influence on the colonization cause in America. "I still believe that *some* will go this fall from here," he wrote in May 1848, "but how many will depend principally on Harris's next letter."[40]

As should be evident, there was no consensus about Liberia among emigrant epistlers. In fact, the disputes between letter-writers themselves were often acerbic. Quarrels between members of the same emigrant party could be especially cantankerous. The row between James Patterson and Titus Glover, two men who were liberated by William Rice of Louisiana, was typical. Patterson did not fare well in Liberia. "[W]e did not find the country as we exspected [sic]," he explained to his former owner's brother. Already disillusioned, Patterson suffered a leg injury that required medical attention that was unavailable in Liberia. In addition, he could not obtain basic supplies. "My pervisions is scarce and my money is scarce & my clothing is geting scarce," wrote Patterson. Titus Glover, who had a much better go of it in Liberia, retorted, "dont listen to every tales others persons will say about our Republic because it is fine place." Patterson's and Glover's epistolary rivalry was by no means unusual, for many freedpersons engaged in this sort of literary jousting.[41]

Contravening the reports of returnees represented an even greater challenge for letter-writers. As previously noted, returnees were African-Americans' most trusted source of information about Liberia. Even so, some epistlers contested the claims of persons who went back to the United States. When the freedmen James and William Watson departed for America after a month's stay in Liberia, for example, the ex-slave James W. Wilson was ready to dispute any criticism that the two men might utter against the African republic. Wilson himself had resided in Liberia for seven months and consequently believed that he could judge the country more accurately than a couple of excursionists who had stayed for just forty days and who had not even walked about the settlement. "I do not know What William & James Watson return for unlest it Was for the Whipe," announced Wilson. Statements that the Watsons made about Liberia, he cautioned, reflected more about themselves than the African nation.[42]

Despite Wilson's concern that the Watsons would tarnish Liberia's image, it appears that the republic's advocates bellowed louder than its critics. ACS officials, prosperous emigrants, paid recruiters, and others who championed colonization disseminated their message more effectively than did the impoverished and forlorn settlers who offered less Pollyannaish proclamations. Indeed, as discussed in chapter 7, freedpersons were often crestfallen upon landing in Liberia. The manumittees' preemigration intelligence, in other words, turned out to be imperfect. Yet their quest for information about Liberia had far-reaching ramifications. Bondpersons' inquiries compelled Society leaders to refute disappointed emigrants, hire black promoters, publish optimistic letters, and constantly trumpet Liberia's virtues, real or imagined. In short, slaves' information-gathering had a considerable impact on the colonization movement. As shall be seen, the same can be said about slaves' familial maneuverings.

How Slaves' Familial Bonds Affected ACS Manumissions

Slaves' familial universe was immense. It was filled with spouses, siblings, and children, as well as grandparents, cousins, and fiancées. Fictive kin loomed as large as "real" relatives, and all exerted a force upon bondpersons who contemplated colonization, pulling the deliberators to and fro. Even persons who were rarely seen, or who dwelt in faraway places, made their presence felt. The power of slaves' familial affinities sent ACS emancipations careening in every direction, radically transforming projects that manumitters had originally envisioned as self-contained, closely regulated experiments.

Bondpersons' free black kin influenced ACS liberations in several respects.

Colonization officials grumbled that free black relatives dissuaded slaves from going to Liberia. Free black women, in particular, became the object of the colonizationists' contempt. The tale of Daniel Brown, they asserted, illustrated the pernicious influence that free black females had on ACS operations. Brown was a slave who had scraped together enough money to purchase his freedom. Hoping to circumvent a Virginia law that required new manumittees to leave the state, Brown convinced his owner to sell him to his free wife, Ann Brown. Later, when Daniel decided that he wanted to go to Liberia, Ann objected. The two quarreled until Ann reminded her husband that she still held title to him, and that the Virginia Colonization Society could not transport him overseas without her consent. Ultimately, Ann allowed Daniel to move to Liberia. The freedman then tried to convince his incredulous wife to join him in Africa. Ann Brown does not appear among the ACS ship registers, and judging from the Society's own records, many other free black females also held colonization in low esteem: "*woman* will not go," "she proved to be the *better half*," "Mrs. J. . . . has more fears about [Liberia than her husband]" and so on. One Virginia colonizationist became so frustrated with such affairs that he urged the state legislature to enslave free black women who refused to emigrate to Africa. In short, free black family members quashed many ACS manumissions.[43]

Yet the kinship between enslaved and free African-Americans also cut the other way, with ACS liberations prompting free blacks to depart for Liberia. Even free black females pushed aside their misgivings about colonization when confronted with the imminent departure of their soon-to-be-freed spouses. For example, Eliza Andrews of Riceboro, Georgia, assembled her four children and set sail for Africa once her husband, Ephraim Andrews, secured his freedom. Another Georgian, twenty-year-old seamstress Catherine Harris, did likewise when her spouse Jack Harris obtained his liberty. Charity Carney of Virginia and her six children followed suit upon the manumission of Mingo Carney. In this fashion, ACS emancipations encouraged free black emigration.[44]

Many of the free blacks who hoped to move to Liberia with their newly emancipated kin were far from ideal settlers, at least in the ACS's estimation. Although Society officials were reluctant to give passage to older, poorer individuals, they often let the aged and destitute journey to Liberia nonetheless. As ACS agent Thomas C. Benning admitted, "[W]hen they are connected with a family, I do not feel at liberty to decline taking them." In the process of gathering emigrants, colonizationists traversed the boundary that separated the bonded from the free.[45]

Quantitative data show how frequently that line was crossed. Approximately 25 percent of the time, when a group of emigrants left a southern county, the party consisted of some combination of free blacks, manumittees, or "purchased" emigrants.[46] In such cases, the party's members were often related by blood or marriage. Given that many southern colonization leaders were purposefully vague about the movement's relationship with slavery, the simultaneous departure of free black and manumitted emigrants tended to further muddle the ACS's murky relationship with bondage.

Just as bondpersons' familial ties with free blacks affected ACS manumissions, so too did their kin connections with other slaves. Uncertainty among just one or two family members could scotch an entire emancipatory enterprise. For example, in 1848 the Rev. J. Packard intended to send his cook to Liberia, assuming "that the whole matter was settled." But the cook's husband, who was owned by another individual and who had also planned on emigrating, began to have doubts. As Packard flatly remarked, "Of course, this has changed the aspect of things as to my cook." A similar turn of events occurred a few years later in Georgia, when apprehension spread through the ranks of Francis Gideon's slaves. One of their number, Washington, announced that he would "stay or go with the old ones." Sarah likewise said that she would "either stay or go as the rest do." Dennis concluded that, "If the rest stay, I will stay—if they go, I will go." Slaves' emotional closeness to their kin meant that embers of disinclination could conflagrate into a roaring rejection of colonization.[47]

If dissension among bondpersons represented a serious problem for colonizationists, slaves' interplantation familial ties constituted a challenge of equal magnitude. Such bonds necessitated "conjunctive emancipations"— that is, instances wherein different slaveholders liberated various members of one black family. The issue can be studied statistically by calculating how often two or more manumitters freed bondpersons at the same time and in the same county.[48] The resulting figures do not perfectly measure the extent of collaboration between emancipators, nor do they reveal every nuance in blacks' struggle to emigrate with their kin. Sometimes local slaveholders manumitted bondpersons simultaneously simply because it was convenient to do so. Conversely, there were occasions when slaveholders in distant counties worked together, each liberating different members of a black family. Conjunctive emancipation statistics fail to account for these scenarios, and thus should be seen only as a general estimate of cooperation among ACS advocates.

Even with these shortcomings in mind, the frequency of conjunctive emancipations suggests that slaves' familial maneuverings expanded the realm of

ACS operations. On seventy-nine separate occasions, multiple slaveholders freed bondpersons at the same time and in the same county. Most of these conjunctive emancipations involved just two slaveholders, though there were several cases wherein five or more took part. All totaled, 221 manumitters (that is, 39 percent of all manumitters) participated in conjunctive emancipations. Southerners who freed bondpersons may have endured "the cold stare and angry words of their neighbors," as historian Ira Berlin once contended. But for a sizable minority of ACS liberators, a fellow traveler was nearby to offer words of consolation and encouragement.

Most conjunctive manumitters simply got caught up in the emancipatory endeavors of others. M. L. Anderson of Virginia found himself so ensnared. In the early 1850s, Anderson's aunt, Mildred M. Lewis, died. Lewis willed that two of her slaves, the brothers Jack and John Barnet, could go to Liberia with their respective families. Lewis then bequeathed to Anderson the bondmens' parents, Jack and Ellen, assuming that the two oldsters were unfit for sailing the Atlantic and pioneering in Liberia. Yet Lewis had underestimated her slaves' familial affinities. Jack and Ellen despaired at the thought of their sons' departure. Not having any other offspring, the elderly couple asked their new owner if they could accompany their children and grandchildren to Liberia. "I have consented that they may do so," wrote Anderson to an ACS official, "but [I] do not feel able to give them up and pay for their passage also."[49] Colonization leaders agreed to cover the costs of transporting Jack and Ellen overseas, and on 31 December 1851 the entire party left for Liberia. Thus did Anderson, who still owned eighteen bondpersons and was evidently untroubled by this fact, enter the historical record as an ACS emancipator.

Anderson's liberation of Jack and Ellen illustrates an important aspect about conjunctive emancipations: a growth in the number of manumitters did not result in a proportional increase in the number of slaves freed. The typical emancipator, when working alone, liberated five bondpersons. When another slaveholder joined the enterprise, the two emancipators collectively manumitted an average of just seven bondpersons. Conjunctive emancipators like Anderson, in other words, typically freed just one or two slaves.

The possibility of conjunctive emancipations benefited ACS manumitters in a variety of ways. There were financial rewards: emancipators profited from additional slave labor while their bondpersons engaged in protracted and far-flung familial deliberations. There also were managerial advantages: a liberator who promised to ask another slaveholder to free, say, a bondman's wife, no doubt expected that the gesture would pacify the bondman himself. And then there were psychological perks: manumitters who tried but failed to effect conjunctive emancipations could pass the blame for breaking up slave families on to others. In short, would-be liberators could countenance time-consuming dialogues between distant bondpersons and exhibit a passing interest in conjunctive emancipations and remain certain that they were meeting, as one manumitter put it, the "responsibility resting on me to do the best I can for them."[50]

Slaveholders who refused to engage in conjunctive emancipations sometimes took the opportunity to cut deals with hard-pressed colonizationists and desperate bondpersons. Thomas Mallard, for example, looked to cash in on colonization. Mallard owned Harry Bacon, whose family had been liberated by the Hon. C. Hines of Georgia. Mallard claimed that Bacon was worth $1,500 but said he would sell the bondman for $1,000. ACS officials thought Mallard a bit avaricious, yet the slaveholder claimed that he was being as charitable as his circumstances would permit. "I have a large family to provide for," he protested, "and it would not be doing justice to them to give Harry away because he wants his freedom." Mallard nevertheless agreed to drop the price for Bacon another one hundred dollars. With the help of special donations, colonization officials managed to purchase the bondman, who sailed with his family for Liberia in January 1855. One senses that ACS leaders had been through this sort of thing before. Shortly after buying Bacon, William McLain expressed relief that Mallard was unaware that the funds were being raised by emergency contributions. If Mallard had known, McLain speculated, "he would have stuck us for another hundred dollars."[51]

That the ACS would have difficulties securing the liberty of freedpersons' kin is not surprising. What is instructive is that ACS manumissions prompted individuals like M. L. Anderson to effect conjunctive emancipations, and that they enticed slaveholders like Thomas Mallard to approach the bargaining table. Bondpersons' familial demands drew in slaveholders who were otherwise indifferent—or even hostile—toward colonization.

Although southern colonizationists and would-be freedpersons managed to prod, beg, and flatter scores of slaveholders into effecting conjunctive emancipations, they were not always successful in this regard. When they failed, bondpersons had to choose between their kin and colonization. And as the size of the proposed emancipation grew, so too did the number of slaves confronting that horrible dilemma. For example, Edward Poindexter's will called for the liberation and emigration of dozens of bondpersons, but one observer noted that many of the slaves, if they chose to go to Liberia, would have to leave their spouses behind. One especially vexed bondman actually had enough money to purchase his wife, but he did not have the means to pay for her transport to Liberia, and consequently he too he faced the prospect of spousal separation. For countless manumittees, embarking for Liberia necessitated leaving loved ones.[52]

Yet many freedpersons did not regard the voyage to Africa as the final act in their familial drama. Instead, they departed with the expectation that they would secure the liberty of their bonded kin at a later date. This was certainly the intention of the freedman Alexander Hance, who wept over the fact that his children remained enslaved in Maryland. "I Cannot bear the idea of Staying heare without them," Hance wrote from Africa. "For if it is ten or twelve years to com I will go Back Again to them." Hance eventually orchestrated the liberation of his offspring, and he was not the only manumittee to pull relatives out of slavery. Indeed, for slaves who worried about estate sales, planter debts, capricious owners, and economic instability, emigration to Liberia might have represented their best chance at keeping their families intact. Colonization thus had a paradoxical effect on African-American families: it could both sunder them apart and seal them together.[53]

Kin considerations were central to bondpersons' decisions regarding emigration. This concern affected the ACS in several important ways. Slaves' familial demands impaired ACS efforts to send blacks to Africa; they also aided the organization by prompting conjunctive manumissions; finally, they obfuscated the ACS's relationship with slavery, for related free black and manumitted emigrants sailed to Liberia together. In short, African-Americans' kin networks fundamentally altered the character of ACS manumissions.

When ACS emancipators initially drew up their manumission programs, they had envisioned grateful bondpersons eagerly embracing the schemes. Their slaves, however, quickly dispelled such fantasies. The lure of freedom, it turned out, did not render bondpersons infinitely tractable. Instead, slaves bargained hard with their owners. They manipulated the terms of emancipation, sought intelligence from Liberia, and consulted with their kin. In doing so, they changed the entire nature of ACS operations. Along the way, some slaves opted against emigrating to Liberia. But others intended to pursue the matter further. For these individuals, the emancipatory enterprise was far from finished.

4

—◦◦ᴐ◦—

The Pennsylvania Colonization Society
as a Facilitator of Manumission

In January 1848, Thomas C. Benning, a Society agent working in Savannah, Georgia, was busy organizing an ACS expedition. Benning had just learned that thirty-seven new manumittees were interested in going to Liberia. "I think it will be a very valuable company," remarked Benning, who then noted ominously, "though they be poor." The group was so destitute, he reported regretfully, they could not afford a passage to Liberia. And therein lay a reoccurring problem for the ACS. The organization often lacked the financial means to cover the costs of colonization. The expenses associated with slave emancipations were especially numerous and troublesome. Manumitters sometimes refused to pay for freedpersons' conveyance to Liberia; testamentary liberators frequently failed to set aside funds to carry ex-slaves overseas; neighborhood slaveholders demanded compensation for liberating the bonded kin of prospective emigrants. Considerable sums had to be raised, in other words, and seasoned colonizationists like Benning knew that it was pointless and perhaps dangerous to solicit donations in many southern locales. "With regard to money, the prospect is gloomy . . . in this region," Benning wrote to ACS secretary William McLain, "and I am afraid all the expense will have to be borne by your New England friends."[1]

As Benning's comments suggest, financial considerations made ACS manumissions interregional enterprises. Indeed, many Society supporters in the South were perfectly blunt about the pecuniary aid that they expected from their northern counterparts. "Can not the friends of emancipation in the noisy North raise that sum [$1,800] to relieve 28 slaves from Bondage?" asked one southern colonizationist. "I am willing to pay $100 [toward a bondman's freedom], if you can succeed in raising the [$700] balance in the North," offered another. The transport of freedpersons to Liberia was "a case for northern charity," according to a third.[2] Many things had to occur for an ACS manumission to be effected; procuring financial contributions from northerners was often one of them.[3]

When it came to seeking funds for ACS liberations, few groups worked harder than the Pennsylvania Colonization Society (PCS), a state auxiliary of the ACS that was founded in 1826. Of course, many PCS partisans were indifferent to the group's emancipatory agenda: they had joined the PCS with the hope that black people would be removed from the Keystone State. Such members were destined for decades of disappointment. Between 1820 and 1860, the number of African-Americans in Pennsylvania grew from thirty thousand to fifty-seven thousand. During the same period, fewer than three hundred of the state's blacks went to Africa. PCS leaders continued to call for the expatriation of Pennsylvania blacks, but most of the colonizationists' time was spent raising money to facilitate the liberation and emigration of southern slaves. Pointing to their emancipatory endeavors, PCS officers claimed that they were fostering a national campaign in which northerners and southerners cooperated in a peaceful effort to dissolve black bondage.

If eroding slavery was the PCS's goal, the organization was an abysmal failure. Between the mid-1820s and 1860, the group facilitated the liberation of just a few hundred slaves. During the same years, the U.S. slave population increased from less than two million to nearly four million. Undeterred, PCS supporters continued to promote their program. The question, then, is why did so many realistic people cling to an emancipatory scheme that was so inadequate?[4]

Part of the answer is that they could not conceive of any other alternative. Their antislavery beliefs were sincere—proslavery ideologues were wrongheaded, they contended. Yet abolitionists who sought emancipation without expatriation were equally misguided, they added. The only solution to the "problem" posed by the presence of African-Americans and slavery in the United States, they pled, was colonization. Their certitude on the matter was absolute.

PCS supporters' tenacity also stemmed from their understanding of recent history and contemporary politics. Gradual emancipation laws had ended bondage in Pennsylvania, they reasoned. Along the way, many of the state's slaves had been sold southward. PCS devotees assumed that the same processes could work in the Border South. Indeed, many Border South statesmen were championing such policies. PCS members' historical and political sensibilities suggested that colonization was feasible, just as their racial ideology convinced them that their program was imperative.

The colonizationists' mindset left them impervious to evidence that conflicted with their preconceived views. As social psychologist Leon Festinger has noted, the greater one's commitment to a belief system, the more extensive one's efforts to reconcile incompatible information—that is, to reduce cognitive dissonance.[5] In this case, PCS leaders calibrated their opinion that colonization could do away with both slavery and black people with the program's patent failings. Given the gulf between their convictions and reality, PCS officials' mental labors were necessarily extraordinary. When abolitionists exposed colonization's shortcomings, when black northerners protested the scheme, when appalling reports from Liberia appeared, when census figures indicated that the slave population was growing by tens of thousands each year, PCS officers ignored, disbelieved, or reinterpreted these embarrassments.

Reducing cognitive dissonance involves more than disregarding or filtering disagreeable information; it also entails aggrandizing the presumed attributes of one's decisions—thus the importance of PCS-aided emancipations. The liberations were showcased as proof that colonization *was* working, that PCS partisans championed a worthwhile cause.

PCS officials adhered to this line of thought for decades. During the 1850s, however, the rapidly escalating conflict over slavery finally forced them to reevaluate their program. The slender reeds of manumission, those weak props upon which the colonizationists' world had been built, buckled under the weight of an impending civil war. Faced with the imminent bloodbath of battle, PCS leaders admitted that colonization was not the answer to the "slavery question" and consequently forsook their emancipationist aims. By 1861, the PCS was no longer a facilitator of manumission.

The Early Years: 1816–1839

Following the establishment of the ACS in 1816, white Pennsylvanians rallied to the colonization cause. The scheme's appeal transcended class lines. Disgruntled laborers caught in the nexus of urbanization, industrialization, and European immigration embraced colonization, venting their frustrations by calling for the expatriation of African-Americans. The state's elite was equally enthusiastic about the project. The well-known Quaker merchant and philanthropist Elliot Cresson worked on behalf of colonization, and he was joined for a short time by fellow Friends Sarah Grimké and Robert Vaux. Esteemed Protestant ministers such as John Breckinridge, George M. Bethune, and J. B. Pinney also lent their support. So did political and business leaders like the lawyer Joseph R. Ingersoll, Congressman Joseph Hemphill, pamphleteer and biographer Calvin Colton, diplomat William Short, physician John Bell, and the young activist Thomas Buchanan. Colonization sentiment was strongest in Philadelphia, but as the movement matured, supporters established auxiliary societies throughout Pennsylvania.[6]

Initially, Pennsylvania colonizationists anticipated black support for the ACS. Several of the state's African-American leaders, worried about the hard times that had befallen their followers, had intimated interest in the project. It soon became apparent, however, that the black masses reviled the scheme. Shortly after the founding of the ACS, nearly three thousand African-Americans gathered in Philadelphia to discuss the new organization. Despite interest in colonization among James Forten, Richard Allen, Absalom Jones, and John Gloucester, the attendees voted unanimously to oppose the ACS. Another large meeting, held eight months later in August 1817, protested the formation of a Philadelphia chapter of the ACS. Acknowledging that colonizationists had benevolent motives, the assembly nevertheless insisted that the program would ultimately harm both free blacks and slaves, and those present declared their "determination not to participate in any part of it."[7]

In the early 1820s, few African-Americans in Pennsylvania reneged on their vows of resistance. The state's black population numbered thirty thousand, but between 1820 and 1823 just sixty black Pennsylvanians moved to Africa. The tribulations endured by the few who emigrated confirmed the convictions of those who stayed. By 1825, one-third of the sixty colonists had died; among the survivors, nearly half had fled Liberia. Facing unremitting opposition, PCS leaders focused on other aspects of the movement, including the emancipation and emigration of southern slaves.[8]

Unlike ACS officials, Pennsylvania colonizationists freely acknowledged the movement's antislavery aspects. The PCS's constitution actually listed the emancipation of slaves as one of the group's goals. The inclusion of such objectives partly stemmed from colonizationists' early failures among black

Pennsylvanians. But the PCS officers also incorporated antislavery ideas into the organization's constitution because they longed for the gradual and peaceful demise of slavery. Indeed, PCS administrators even projected their desires on to the more cautious parent society, insisting that the ACS's founders had envisioned "the total extirpation of slavery throughout the Nation." The first step in the process, PCS officials reasoned, was to help individual slaveholders liberate their bondpersons.[9]

The PCS abetted manumissions in four ways. First, it contributed money to the ACS treasury—when the national organization transported freedpersons to Liberia, it did so with the financial support of Pennsylvanians. Second, the PCS periodically assumed responsibility for ACS expeditions, the parties of which consisted mostly of former bondpersons. Third, the group financed the transport of ex-slaves whose owners had liberated them, yet had not provided the means for carrying them to Africa. Finally, the PCS occasionally purchased slaves and then sent them to Liberia.

At first, the Pennsylvanians simply helped pay for ACS expeditions to Liberia. The PCS was less than a year old when it forwarded six hundred dollars to the parent society to help defray the costs of the ship *Doris,* which sailed to Liberia in 1827 with about one hundred emigrants, half of whom were freedpersons. Two years later, the Pennsylvanians resolved to send funds to the ACS, "on condition that they be applied exclusively to the outfit and transportation of slaves." In 1830, the PCS went even further by chartering its own vessels, the *Liberia* and *Montgomery,* which collectively transported ninety-one freedpersons to Africa. Pleased with their progress, the organization's leaders committed themselves to outfitting similar expeditions in the future.[10]

PCS leaders insisted that sending manumitted blacks to Liberia was the most cost-efficient way to end slavery. "By . . . [any] other mode," they explained in 1830, "a large expenditure is necessary to purchase the freedom of a single individual, whose situation is, but too frequently, rendered much worse by the change."[11] This statement was an avowal to parsimony; it was also a critique of the Pennsylvania Abolition Society, an older and more radical organization that occasionally purchased the freedom of slaves; and unbeknownst to the PCS, it was a portent of problems to come.

In the meantime, northern colonizationists' efforts in freeing slaves had done little to quell African-Americans' increasingly caustic opposition to the movement. Bostonian David Walker offered a searing condemnation of the ACS in his *Appeal* (1829), and black Pennsylvanians were soon expressing similar outrage. Whereas previous objectors had depicted colonizationists as misguided philanthropists, in 1831 African-Americans in Columbia, Pennsylvania, described the ACS as "a vicious, nefarious and peace-disturbing combination." Their counterparts in Lewistown thought colonizationists were "wolves in sheep's clothing" and warned that divine vengeance would soon visit them. In Pittsburgh, protesters denounced ACS supporters as "intriguers" who wanted to deport black leaders so that "the chain of slavery may be rivetted more tightly" and deemed any person "who allows himself to be colonized in Africa, or elsewhere, a traitor to our cause."[12] Few African-Americans in Pennsylvania endured such approbation. In the late 1820s and early 1830s, when the PCS was helping send scores of manumittees to Liberia, just a few black Pennsylvanians emigrated to the African settlement. Despite worsening conditions—economic hardship, relative population decline, ghettoization, race riots, and the specter of disenfranchisement—the state's black residents refused to leave America.[13]

By the early 1830s, white abolitionists like William Lloyd Garrison were also crusading against the ACS. Garrison preferred to focus his attacks on colonization ideology, a philosophy of race relations that he believed contravened the principles of American liberty and Christian love. Yet Garrison also took up the issue of ACS emancipations. He did so with some reluctance, however. In the preface to his *Thoughts on African Colonization* (1832), Garrison contended that moral questions were the only ones that mattered. Debates over whether colonization was practical, or whether Liberia was viable, or "whether any slaves have been emancipated on condition of their banishment" were immaterial. Even so, Garrison wanted to squash the notion that ACS manumissions were harbingers of slavery's demise. Colonizationists had to see that they were in a state of denial; they had to understand that, if anything, ACS emancipations aided slavery. The colonization program obstructed the progress of black freedom, argued Garrison, because "it dissuades . . . [slaveholders] from emancipating their slaves faster than they can be transported to Africa." Moreover, the liberation and removal of some slaves increased the value of those who remained in bondage. Also, calculating slaveholders would send only aged, infirm, and rebellious bondpersons overseas. Finally, freedpersons who landed in Liberia would encounter nothing but misery, poverty, and disease. "It is impossible to imagine a more cruel, heaven-daring, and God-dishonoring scheme," concluded the Boston abolitionist. Garrison's contentions concerning ACS ideology and manumissions irrevocably tarnished colonization's luster. Within a few years, Amos Phelps, James G. Birney, Arthur Tappan, Gerrit Smith, and several other well-known figures quit the ACS and joined Garrison's American Anti-Slavery Society.[14]

Garrison's: Amer. Anti-Slavery Society

Reeling from the abolitionist onslaught, colonizationists futilely sought help overseas. In 1831, Philadelphian Elliot Cresson traveled to Great Britain on behalf of the ACS. Hoping to gain the favor of the British public, Cresson claimed that thousands of American slaveholders were ready to send their bondpersons to Liberia. All that was needed to secure the slaves' emancipation and emigration, he declared, were generous contributions from philanthropists. Cresson even claimed that colonization would ultimately procure "the final and entire abolition of slavery." The mission appeared destined for success. The citizens of Edinburgh were especially receptive to Cresson's message, and he promised to name a settlement in Liberia "Edina" in their honor. After one year, Cresson had collected four thousand dollars, and he was making plans to establish a British Colonization Society.[15]

Then the venture suffered a series of setbacks. Abolitionist forces rallied against Cresson, with Charles Stuart of the British Anti-Slavery Society leading the campaign. Stuart insisted that colonization was logistically impossible, and, like American abolitionists, he bewailed the movement's ideological foundation. The ACS, he argued, "corroborates against the people of color, whether enslaved or free, one of the most base, groundless, and cruel prejudices, that has ever disgraced the powerful, or afflicted the weak." Stuart's invectives so incensed Cresson that the latter referred to him as "a 2nd Garrison."[16]

To Cresson's dismay, in May 1833 the real Garrison arrived in England. Cresson refused to debate this adversary. The Bostonian's talents as a public speaker were intimidating enough, but the fact that Garrison had with him the latest ACS publications—and Cresson did not—was equally troubling. Cresson assumed that Garrison would attempt to discredit colonization by misrepresenting statements that had been made in the ACS's *African Repository* and *Annual Reports*. Yet without these materials, Cresson was helpless to counter the abolitionist's charges. Cresson blamed ACS officials for the dilemma, thereby exacerbating tensions between the parent society and the Pennsylvania auxiliary. Frustrated and worn, Cresson finally left England in late summer 1833.[17]

Upon his return to America, Cresson discovered that abolitionists were still lambasting the PCS. In the mid-1830s, Garrison's followers founded the Pennsylvania Anti-Slavery Society (PASS). Committed to immediate emancipation and racial equality, PASS crusaders denounced colonization and challenged PCS leaders to public debates. The PCS declined, but the Garrisonians kept up the pressure. Colonization was founded on unchristian prejudice, they declared. Moreover, it curtailed manumissions: "Before the Colonization Society was organized, it was very common for slaveholders on their dying beds to emancipate their slaves," they proclaimed. "But since the scheme of expatriation has been got up, few have been willing in a dying hour, to incur the dreadful responsibility of banishing those whom they have already too deeply injured, from the land of their birth."[18] According to the PASS, even the most guilt-ridden slaveholders would not send their bondpersons to the wilds of Africa.

The abolitionists had a point. Liberia was a wretched place. Yet the emigrants' misfortune did not sap PCS leaders' confidence in colonization. Instead, they rationalized unfavorable reports from Africa, reinterpreting them in such a way that made the dreadful situation seem tolerable and colonization appear destined for success. They blamed the deceased, ascribing their deaths to "thoughtless exposure to the chilly nights." They insisted that better preparation would obviate any difficulties. They assured their followers that physicians would soon learn how to treat tropical diseases. And they placed these deaths in the best possible context: "There was as much sickness and loss, perhaps, as at Plymouth in the earlier days," contended the Pennsylvanians. All things considered, they averred, Liberia was in fine shape.[19]

The PCS's deteriorating relationship with the ACS was another issue altogether. The discord mostly concerned the insolvency of the parent society. The Pennsylvanians had voiced their displeasure over the matter as early as 1830, and the passage of time, in their opinion, had only provided further evidence of fiscal incompetence. ACS officials, they asserted, sent more emigrants to Liberia than the available means could justify, underestimated the cost of colonial administration, assumed large debts that could not be repaid on time, and harbored unrealistic expectations about the amount of money that could be raised by private donations. Indeed, by 1834 the ACS was forty-five thousand dollars in debt, and the group appeared ready to collapse.[20]

ACS officials consequently faced a dilemma when Dr. Aylett Hawes of Virginia died and willed that the ACS convey his 110 slaves to Liberia. Knowing that the national organization could not oblige Hawes's testamentary request, the Pennsylvanians took the opportunity to resolve their long-festering grievances. In April 1834, they created a new body, the Young Men's Colonization Society of Pennsylvania (YMCSP), which had only nominal ties to the ACS. The YMCSP then offered to send the Hawes freedpersons to Africa. ACS leaders lamented the splintering of the movement: "If the state societies take colonization into their hands," wrote one official, "we are a nullity."[21] Nevertheless, the ACS had little choice but to accept the Pennsylvanians' invitation. Later that year, the YMCSP banded with colonizationists in New York, and by October 1834 the Hawes company was headed to Africa. Wishing to start afresh, the colonizationists decided that the freedpersons would establish a new settlement to be called Bassa Cove, which would be located sixty miles south of Monrovia.[22]

The Pennsylvanians and New Yorkers had grand designs for their enterprise. For starters, they expected Bassa Cove's residents to Christianize Africans and, as religious role models, to practice temperance and pacifism. But with its inhabitants committed to nonviolence, Bassa Cove was an easy target for displeased Africans. In June 1835, King Joe Harris, a native chieftain who correctly perceived that the new community would threaten his slave trade interests, orchestrated an attack that resulted in the death of nearly twenty colonists. Settlers from Monrovia led a successful retaliatory raid, exacted concessions from Harris, and began rebuilding Bassa Cove.[23] Within a year, eighty-nine new emigrants arrived in the settlement. Almost all of them were former bondpersons. Just four were from Pennsylvania. The manumission and resettlement of slaves thus continued to be a central component of the colonization movement in Pennsylvania.[24]

In early 1837, the YMCSP united with the largely defunct PCS, adopting the latter's name. Whatever the organizational nomenclature, the goals stayed the same. "Let us foster the growing desire of masters to emancipate," beseeched the Pennsylvanians. They promised to advance the cause of black freedom by encouraging "citizens of every calling in the north to provide for the new freed-men a refuge in the land of their fathers."[25]

PCS leaders understood that without compliant slaveholders, there could be no manumissions, and they consequently glorified the sacrifices of their southern partners. "These gifts of emancipation," asserted Pennsylvanian Calvin Colton in his *Colonization and Abolition Contrasted* (1839), "are, in fact the most substantial supports of the cause, though the donors receive little credit for it." Colton calculated the value of bondpersons who had been sent to Liberia at $2.5 million. In 1838 alone, he argued, the PCS had been asked to transport 130 slaves, worth $78,000. "Many [slaveholders] have given their all and impoverished themselves and their heirs—a sacrifice, we imagine, which is rarely to be found in northern charities."[26] Manumissions thus provided a way for northern colonizationists to fancy southerners as noble allies in the fight to end slavery.

The same emancipatory endeavors allowed PCS leaders to distance themselves from abolitionists. In less than twenty years, they announced, colonizationists had helped hundreds of slaveholders liberate thousands of bond-

persons. "How many have the abolitionists emancipated during the same period?" they asked. The PCS alleged that their opponents, having refused to
work with slaveholders, resorted to harassing colonization agents and spreading misinformation. "The importance of the colonization plan," PCS leaders
rationalized, "is made the more evident by these efforts of the abolitionists to
paralize its operations."[27]

Embattled Pennsylvania colonizationists also continued squabbling with
ACS officials. In 1838, PCS leaders, along with colonizationists from other
parts of the North, finally seized control of the ACS by rewriting the organization's constitution. Previously, a yearly vote by ACS members determined
who would serve on the powerful board of managers. Under the new system,
the managers were replaced by a board of directors, and these positions were
divvied up according to the amount of money each state remitted to the parent
society, with additional weight given to those state societies that maintained
their own settlement in Liberia. With these rules in place, northerners began to
dominate the ACS.[28]

During the 1820s and 1830s, colonization officials in Pennsylvania championed both the expatriation of free blacks and the effecting of ACS manumissions. They were sorely disappointed with the results of their first objective and
generally pleased concerning the second. The satisfaction they derived from
the liberation and emigration of southern bondpersons buoyed their belief
that colonization would eventually destroy slavery and remove black people
from America. In the two decades before the Civil War, however, PCS leaders
found it increasingly difficult to keep their faith afloat.

The Antebellum Years: 1840–1861

The 1840s and 1850s were decades of growth, conflict, and change for the PCS.
For much of the period, Pennsylvania colonizationists continued to pursue
emancipationist goals. Indeed, in some respects, the group stepped up its efforts in this realm, an expansion of activities that ultimately created new problems for the movement. Those difficulties, when coupled with a glint of pro-
emigration sentiment among northern blacks and the looming threat of civil
war, prompted PCS officials to rethink their stance on manumission. By the
late 1850s, the PCS no longer concerned itself with slave liberations. Instead,
the organization was almost entirely devoted to the expatriation of black
Pennsylvanians.

With the reorganization of the ACS in 1838, the colonization movement started to revive. It was a slow process—in the ten years following the Society's restructuring, the group, in an effort to conserve money, sent a yearly average of just 130 emigrants to Liberia. Then, in 1847, Liberia became an independent nation. Financially stable and relieved of the burden of colonial administration, the ACS began transporting more emigrants to Africa. In 1848, 439 blacks departed for Liberia; the next year, 420 left; by 1850, the figure topped 500.

The PCS abetted the movement's revitalization. "Our duty as Colonizationists remains the same as ever," explained the editor of the PCS's journal, the *Colonization Herald*. Their first responsibility was to discredit proslavery theories by demonstrating blacks' capacity for self-government in Liberia. Having done that, colonizationists were then obliged to help slaveholders send their bondpersons to Liberia.[29] In fulfilling their second duty, the PCS board of managers resolved in 1848 to raise money for the 143 freedpersons who were to emigrate aboard the *Amazon* and *Nehemiah Rich*.[30] The next year, the *Colonization Herald* solicited donations to transport African-Americans who had been freed in Louisiana, Kentucky, North Carolina, and Virginia.[31] The emancipation and emigration of a few hundred bondpersons hardly crippled slavery, but PCS leaders remained steadfast. "Who refuses food to a hungry man because he cannot feed all the starving?" they queried. "We can send *some*; and those we send cease to be chattels or inferiors."[32]

The ACS's resurgence worried many African-Americans in Pennsylvania. "After all the professedly disinterested regard for us by the American Colonization Society," remarked a convention of black Philadelphians in 1845, "they have thrown off the mask of deception by their public acts." Forgetting that several African-American leaders had originally endorsed colonization, the conventioneers proclaimed that the ACS now openly admitted "what every philanthropist apprehended in the beginning of the Colonization scheme, viz., the premeditated, forcible ejectment of the free colored Americans from the land of their birth." Colonizationists' primary concern, they alleged, was the deportation of free blacks, especially northern free blacks. "It is we who are to be put down, if possible," the convention warned.[33]

Interestingly, colonization's renaissance helped mitigate divisions among abolitionists. In the late 1830s, the antislavery movement had been beset by disputes over Garrison's advocacy of women's rights, hostility toward ecclesiastical bodies, eschewal of electoral politics, and insistence on nonviolence. Those debates had climaxed in 1840, when Arthur and Lewis Tappan and their followers broke from the Garrisonian ranks and established their own abolitionist organization, the American and Foreign Anti-Slavery Society. Although northern opponents of black bondage continued to argue about policies and tactics, they were united in their opposition to colonization's revivification. The Garrisonian Pennsylvania Anti-Slavery Society relentlessly condemned the rejuvenated movement. The Pennsylvania Abolition Society gave no quarter either. Signs of progress, it argued, were seen "not so much in isolated instances of the emancipation of slaves as in the awakening of public attention to the enormity of the system."[34] Based on this criterion, both Garrisonian and non-Garrisonian abolitionists could assert that colonization actually sustained slavery, for the occasional PCS-aided manumission merely salved the consciences of slaveholders, absolved white northerners' complicity in black bondage, and tantalized bondpersons with token gestures of freedom.

Soon the abolitionists would add another charge against colonizationists: the latter engaged in the morally questionable business of buying bondpersons. As previously noted, the PCS's involvement with slave emancipations usually entailed financing the transport of freedpersons to Liberia. Sometimes it assumed entire responsibility for an expedition; at other times, it covered just part of the expenses. In either case, the organization did little beyond defraying the cost of settling former slaves in Liberia. But manumissions were not always tidy affairs. Situations arose wherein owners were not willing to simply free their slaves but instead insisted on being compensated. Carrying freedpersons to Africa was one thing; purchasing slaves and then sending them to Africa was another.

Consider the case of the Corpsen family of Virginia. In 1851, Elizabeth Herbert of Portsmouth freed Mary Corpsen and her sons, John and Hezekiah, on the condition that they emigrate to Liberia. Another slaveholder, David Griffith, then manumitted Mary Corpsen's husband, Kiah. The enterprise was far from finished, though, for the Corpsen family included three other enslaved children. David Griffith bought two of them, but obtaining the freedom of the family's last child, fifteen-year-old Jerry, was a more complicated matter. The young man was the slave of Edward Herbert, who figured that Jerry was worth six hundred dollars. Kiah pleaded with his son's owner, and the latter agreed to sell Jerry for four hundred dollars. Determined to liberate his son, Kiah began soliciting contributions from local townspeople, but after several months of toil, he had managed to accumulate only one hundred dollars. A three-hundred-dollar chasm still separated Jerry from freedom.[35]

"Feeling that we have already drawn too largely upon the liberality of a large portion of our readers," began an article in the PCS's Colonization Herald, "we have several times determined in our own minds, that we would make no more appeals ... at least for some time to come, in behalf of emancipated cases." But the Corpsen's plight was too compelling to ignore. New York colonizationists had already taken steps to help free Jerry Corpsen; now the Pennsylvanians joined the campaign. When PCS officials learned of this slave family's travails, they responded, and they expected their supporters to respond, too.

The *Colonization Herald* reminded its readers that, while northerners had been asked for financial contributions, it was southerners who made the real sacrifices. David Griffith and Elizabeth Herbert, the two Virginians who had done so much to secure the freedom of the Corpsen family, were presented as admirable examples of southern liberality. "A little of the same self-denial, on the part of a few of our citizens, will send Jerry along with them," cajoled the editor.

The solicitations proved successful. The *Colonization Herald* reported that $325 had been raised to free Jerry Corpsen. The donations came in small increments. The average contribution was about nine dollars; nobody sent more than twenty-five. All but one of the respondents were northerners.

Once Jerry Corpsen had been emancipated, colonizationists used the affair to curry public approval. As was the custom, the PCS celebrated southern generosity. The *Colonization Herald* printed a letter from George Bain, a Norfolk preacher who had helped orchestrate the purchase of Jerry Corpsen. According to Bain's missive, Edward Herbert had lost money on the transaction, but he had sold the bondman "cheerfully and freely." From the PCS's perspective, the lessons of the Corpsen story were manifest: southerners wanted to send slaves to Liberia, and it was northerners' responsibility to effect these laudable desires.

To hammer home the point, PCS leaders juxtaposed their efforts in freeing Jerry Corpsen against allegedly counterproductive tactics of antislavery radicals. "So far as we are aware," commented the *Colonization Herald*, "not a dollar of this money has come from an Abolitionist." While Garrison and other crusaders alienated southerners, the PCS claimed, colonizationists were mollifying sectional tensions. "True, the effort is a small one," the paper admitted, "but it evinces a disposition and a spirit, which will be ready for greater things, whenever any feasible plan for meliorating the condition of the slave can be devised."

The problem for the PCS was that no "feasible plan" could entail purchasing slaves' freedom. Paying for bondpersons raised three unwieldy problems. First, the financial obstacles were almost insuperable, especially if colonization remained a privately funded movement. From the start, the ACS's opponents

had claimed that sending millions of blacks to Africa was an impossible undertaking. Adding the expense of *buying* slaves only worsened the problem. Indeed, PCS leaders themselves had once argued that purchasing bondpersons
was an extraordinarily costly way to extinguish slavery. The $325 that they
raised to buy Jerry Corpsen, for example, if earmarked just for transporting
freedpersons to Liberia, would have sent approximately six individuals across
the Atlantic.

Second, purchasing slaves exposed colonizationists' ideological liabilities.
Abolitionists could charge that PCS advocates were comfortable regarding
African-Americans as chattel, as things that could be bought and sold. In this
sense, colonizationists' plan for weakening slavery also legitimized the institution. Of course, not all abolitionists asserted that buying a slave's freedom was
ethically reprehensible. Mainstream white northerners were presumably even
less sympathetic to such arguments. Still, the accusations had the potential to
damage colonizationists' image, for they came at a time when many northern
whites began questioning the morality of black bondage.[36]

Third, buying bondpersons undermined the idea that southerners were
eager partners in the colonization program. The PCS had long insisted that
slaveholders would free their bondpersons if given the opportunity to do so,
but the Corpsen episode suggested otherwise. David Griffith and Elizabeth
Herbert manumitted some of the Corpsen family, but Edward Herbert had
demanded compensation, as had the owners of Kiah Corpsen's other two children. Financially and ideologically, Pennsylvania colonizationists could not
afford to reimburse southern slaveholders.

As the PCS was helping liberate Jerry Corpsen and hundreds of other bondpersons during the late 1840s and early 1850s, the organization's leaders sensed
that black Pennsylvanians were ready to embrace colonization. After decades
of almost unmitigated opposition, prolonged economic and political deprivation, along with the enactment of the federal Fugitive Slave Law in 1850, convinced some African-Americans to leave the United States. Most free black
people still rejected Liberia as a refuge, but a few hazarded the transatlantic
voyage. Wearied and worried, thirteen black Pennsylvanians departed for Liberia in 1850; the following year, another seventeen emigrated to the African
nation; in 1852, thirteen more went. The PCS delighted in African-Americans'
apparent change of heart. "We want them to go *for their own good*," declared
the *Colonization Herald.* "We see no possible chance for them ever to acquire
in this country, social equality. We do see in Africa not a chance but a certainty of their elevation to the great brotherhood of man."[37] PCS officials eagerly awaited the seemingly imminent exodus.

Indeed, in the early 1850s, the PCS radiated optimism. The organization was helping emancipate slaves; it was transporting black Pennsylvanians to Liberia; its coffers were being replenished. In short, it was the ideal time to ask the state government for money.

In April 1852, two PCS officials, William V. Pettit and John P. Durbin, addressed the Pennsylvania legislature. Pettit spoke first. He opened with a short history of the movement and then explained how colonization created commercial opportunities, undermined the slave trade, and spread civilization and Christianity in Africa. Since the PCS was soliciting state monies, Pettit made sure to note that colonization would benefit Pennsylvania by removing its black population. Yet Pettit also directly addressed the enterprise's antislavery aspects. He twice acknowledged that the majority of emigrants to Liberia had been freedpersons, a fact, he believed, that showed "a strong disposition to emancipate, on the part of the owners." Pettit concluded by disparaging abolitionists, whom he claimed had lied about the colonizationists' motives, fabricated stories about Liberia, and deceived black Americans who contemplated going to Africa.[38]

The PCS's second speaker, John P. Durbin, was even more forthright about freeing bondpersons. Most of his speech concerned the threat that slavery posed to the nation, and how colonization could avert the impending disaster. But it could only do so with public aid. "In order to succeed, so as finally to remove the disturbing element of slavery from our country and separate the two antagonistic races," he explained, "the States, and finally the General Government, must espouse the cause of colonization." A native of the South, Durbin believed that slaveholders would embrace the program. "They see the danger in the distance, and would as gladly as we accept any safe and honorable remedy. Let them see that our measures are peaceful, are practicable, are effectual, and they will join us heartily."[39]

The PCS's appeal had mixed results. In 1852, Pennsylvania allocated $2,000 to the PCS. That sum was considerably less than what Virginia ($150,000), Maryland ($60,000), and Missouri ($30,000) had recently contributed to colonization, but it was on par with the amounts dispensed by northern states like Indiana ($2,000) and New Jersey ($2,000). The public funds also came with a catch—they only could be used to transport black Pennsylvanians to Liberia.[40]

The state subsidy sparked some controversy. Abolitionists predictably decried the measure, remarking that they viewed it with the "deepest abhorrence." Pennsylvania's colonizationists, of course, were happy to receive the aid and eager to spend it.[41]

The PCS used the funds to transport thirty-five black Pennsylvanians to Liberia aboard the *Isle de Cuba*. The *Colonization Herald* began touting the venture months before the vessel embarked. The paper ostensibly aimed its message at black northerners, encouraging that group to consider the advantages of moving to Liberia. Yet there is nothing to indicate that the *Colonization Herald* circulated widely among African-Americans. PCS officials were really targeting other white people and, in a way, themselves. In the parlance of social psychology, the expedition functioned as a dissonance-reducing cognition. Just as periodic manumissions helped them believe that colonization could end slavery, the *Isle de Cuba*'s voyage served as proof that the program appealed to northern African-Americans. This tiny undertaking of thirty-five souls, in other words, emboldened colonizationists who clung to the hope that America would one day be free of black people.[42]

The emigrants' journey began amid a torrent of protest. One of the party's leaders, Charles Deputie, feared that he would be unable to summon his sons for the voyage because it was "un Safe for me to do any thing the Excitement was so great among the Colord People."[43] The harassment prompted one colonizationist to conclude that "this event, with others, shows that to keep . . . emigrants from the influence of the false and designing, it would be wise to have them seek the sea-board by a more southern route."[44]

More frustration and disappointment awaited on the other side of the Atlantic. William Nesbit, for one, was appalled by what he saw. Claiming to have been induced to emigrate by "stool-pigeons (colored men) who decoyed me," Nesbit departed Africa after a short stay. According to his *Four Months in Liberia* (1855), Liberia was a horrid land, and persons who encouraged African-Americans to go there deserved derision:

> On stepping ashore, I found that we had been completely gulled and done for. The statements generally circulated in this country by Colonization agents, respecting the thrift and prosperity of that country, are most egregious falsehoods. Everything is exaggerated. The whole country presents the most woe begone and hopeless aspect which it is possible for a man to conceive of.[45]

Nesbit's denunciations, along with similar ones authored by other members of the *Isle de Cuba* party, naturally undermined colonizationists' efforts among African-Americans in the North.[46]

PCS leaders dealt with the setback in characteristic fashion. Unable to align the mission's failure with their belief that colonization was the only solution to America's racial problems, they concluded that the venture had not miscarried after all. PCS officials swore that those who brought negative news were mistaken. Emigrants who defamed Liberia, they argued, had not remained long enough to know that country's true bounty. Or, if their residency had been extended, the individual lacked gumption, intelligence, and energy. Liberia and the program that spawned it were almost never to blame.[47]

Having dispensed with the critical accounts, PCS officers focused on positive reports. This process led them to draw peculiar, even paradoxical, conclusions about their enterprise. They boasted, for example, that the colonization movement was prospering. "The intention to emigrate to Liberia is becoming popular among the people of color," began a January 1854 article in the *Colonization Herald*, "and applications for passage are pouring in." The number of emigrants, the paper predicted later that year, would soon be on the rise. Yet the truth was that black Pennsylvanians were not going to Africa: in the five years following the embarkation of the *Isle de Cuba,* just fifteen moved to Liberia.[48]

PCS officials were consequently obliged to reverse themselves and explain why African-Americans shunned Liberia. Since colonization was sagacious and Liberia was praiseworthy, they reasoned, the fault must lie with black people themselves. Thus the *Colonization Herald* complained in 1854 that despite "the receipt of favorable intelligence as a general thing, doubt, stupefied, heavy fearful doubt, hangs over a majority of our colored people in regard to facts which to all others are as clear as the noon-day sun." PCS officials' irate faultfinding, like their unwarranted optimism, reflected attempts to refashion reality to fit their colonizationist convictions.[49]

Southern freedpersons were still emigrating to Liberia, though, and the PCS continued to help send them overseas. In 1853, the *Colonization Herald* asked its readers to abet the transport of Betsy Gordon's thirty-one bondpersons abroad.[50] The following year, the PCS collected emigration funds for sixty-three former slaves liberated by Virginians George Love and Thaddeus Herndon.[51] Shortly thereafter, the organization successfully solicited donations to purchase the wife and seven children of the Rev. Hardy Mobley, a free black Alabamian who wanted to move to Liberia. The *Colonization Herald* also served notice of similar fund-raising activities in other northern states.[52] The success of these endeavors, insisted PCS leaders, demonstrated their program's popularity, especially among society's philanthropists. Colonization's constituency, they claimed, was "a noble band of men and women, unknown to each other, and separated by many a league or clashing interest, but united in considering this a cause of strict and pure benevolence."[53]

Some PCS contributors saw the cause as one of "strict and pure benevolence," and they voiced this belief when discussing southerners' willingness to cooperate on the slavery question. For example, Catherine Yeates of Lancaster, Pennsylvania, cheered northern African-Americans' burgeoning interest in Liberia, but she was equally excited about colonization's emancipatory aspects. In 1854, Yeates gave ten dollars to help convey new freedpersons to Liberia, commenting, "we rejoice to see this disposition manifesting itself amongst our southern brethren."[54] Thus Yeates, like PCS leaders, viewed colonization as a means of mollifying interregional discord over slavery.

Pennsylvanians also may have funded the PCS because the organization could show its supporters the concrete consequences of their contributions. When soliciting money, the Garrisonians offered hopeful pictures of abolition and racial equality—an image that few white northerners could fathom, and even fewer relish. Colonizationists, conversely, could review the characteristics of freedpersons, discuss their journey to Africa, publish their letters from Liberia, and so on. The "experiential" aspects of the PCS's antislavery activities, in other words, were critical to its fund-raising efforts.[55]

Pennsylvanians answered the PCS's solicitations for one more reason: they delighted in the idea that an ordinary person could help free a slave. No doubt many Pennsylvanians concurred with the sentiments of Luther Paul of Newton Centre, Massachusetts, who wrote, "[I] was somewhat surprised though not displeased that so humble an individual as myself should be invited to aid in the good work of giving freedom to any who are held in bondage." "My means are limited," Paul continued, "but I send you ten dollars to be used in sending them to Liberia."[56] That common folk could further the cause of freedom, and that their pecuniary contributions would help reconcile the North and the South and bring happiness to black people made the PCS's emancipatory endeavors seem, in the estimation of some white northerners, like projects worth supporting.

The exact number of manumissions abetted by the PCS is unknown. According to one report, by 1854 the organization had financed the emigration of nearly five hundred non-Pennsylvanian African-Americans to Liberia, most of whom were freedpersons. Obviously, this figure paled in comparison to the growth of the slave population during the antebellum era. Yet PCS officials maintained that the raw numbers were only part of the story. For them, the

group's antislavery endeavors, no matter how small, were symbolically important, rhetorically valuable, and psychologically comforting.[57]

Well into the 1850s, Pennsylvania colonizationists continued to hail the
emancipationist aspects of their program. In doing so, they regularly offered
positive portrayals of southerners in general and of slaveholders in particular.
When the Pennsylvania Anti-Slavery Society repeatedly rallied behind the slo-
gan "No Union with Slaveholders," when some abolitionists advocated the use
of violence to overthrow slavery, when even moderate white northerners fretted over a "slave power conspiracy," the PCS insisted that a latent antislavery
sentiment flowed beneath the southern soil and that only colonization could
tap that emancipatory well-spring.[58]

That idea, however, would not survive the 1850s. Two incidents in November 1854 indicated that PCS officials were having doubts about the wisdom of
their long-standing policy. First, they decided to investigate conditions in
Liberia. They acknowledged that they had received complaints for some time
and decided to send the editor of the *Colonization Herald* abroad to assess the
situation. "The safety and health of the new emigrants, and therefore the real
progress of the cause, may be promoted by such a visit," they explained.[59] The
second event involved Alfred Cuthbert Jr. of Eatonton, Georgia, who wanted
to transport his seventy slaves to Liberia. William Coppinger of the PCS expressed reservations about moving scores of destitute bondpersons to a country whose resources were already overextended. William McLain, corresponding secretary of the ACS, upbraided Coppinger, writing, "I am sorry to find
that you entertain so poor an opinion [of] 'newly emancipated negroes' as
companions for your gentlemen negroes!!"[60] Despite the rebuke, Coppinger
and his PCS associates became increasingly convinced that they needed to reevaluate their philosophy on emigration.

In January 1857, a PCS committee submitted a remarkable report that advocated significant changes for the organization. Specifically, it recommended
that the PCS stop financing the emigration of freedpersons and instead concentrate on persuading black Pennsylvanians to go to Liberia. The ACS's original purpose, the committee explained, was to send free black people to Africa.
The men who founded the Society had envisioned manumissions as only "an
incidental or consequential result" of colonization. Yet the group had become
chiefly a transporter of unskilled and impoverished freedpersons, a practice
that had had disastrous results for Liberia. This course of action had also been
harmful to the colonization movement in America. Auxiliary societies de-
volved into "anxious collecting agencies" that did little to encourage free Afri-

can-Americans to emigrate to Liberia. "It is not easy to see how . . . we are to acquit ourselves as a pennsylvanian society," the committee remarked, "while we make no effort to correct erroneous opinions, remove prejudices, soften the asperities of hostile feeling, and diffuse information about the true nature of our enterprise." The report concluded by stating that the ACS should circumscribe emigration, permit its auxiliary societies to focus on free African-Americans, and make Liberia more attractive to potential emigrants.[61]

Just two months after approving the committee's report, the PCS board of managers decided to employ two individuals, Henry Cole and Isaac Kendall, to cultivate support for colonization among the state's black population. Kendall himself planned on emigrating to Liberia, and the PCS consequently expected him to be an especially persuasive agent. Yet just one month later, the board dejectedly reported that the two men had accomplished little. Kendall had become consumed with his own business affairs; Cole "had withdrawn from the work, the way being closed up against him."[62]

Unbowed, the PCS pushed on. The organization hoped to convert more white men and women to the cause by publishing additional issues of the *Colonization Herald*. Previously, it had printed 2,500–3,000 copies. Now the paper's circulation topped 4,750. The PCS board of managers also resolved that any person who procured new subscribers to the *Colonization Herald* would retain one half of the first year's fees. It is not clear whether these endeavors affected white Pennsylvanians' attitudes toward colonization; it is certain, though, that emigration patterns changed markedly during this period.[63]

Between 1858 and 1860, 110 black Pennsylvanians moved to Liberia—about as many as had gone in the previous twenty years combined. Instead of devising ways to send freedpersons to Africa, the PCS board of managers now spent much of its time discussing which Pennsylvania applicants to convey to Liberia. To encourage further emigration, the organization hired a Liberian emigrant, Thomas W. Chester, to work among Pennsylvania's African-American population.[64] The PCS's decision to concentrate on removing the state's black residents—a choice that was bolstered by the 1857 *Dred Scott* verdict—proved successful beyond the organization's means. In a reversal of their previous financial roles, the PCS began asking the ACS for pecuniary help to transport black Pennsylvanians to Liberia. When ACS leaders responded favorably, the PCS determined it would "continue to send emigrants at their expense until directed to cease."[65]

The PCS's 1861 annual report reflected these new developments. It noted that thirty-three black Pennsylvanians had recently left for Liberia and that twenty more would soon depart. The African republic, the report continued, had ennobled its indigenous population and promised equal, if not greater, blessings to the free black men and women who might emigrate there. It even indicated that four thousand "recaptured" African slaves had been sent to the country, and that these persons were adopting the Liberians' ways. But the report contained no mention of manumission, no cheering of southern liberality, no solicitations for freedpersons. Simply put, the report lacked the interregional antislavery vision that had characterized the PCS since its founding in 1826.[66]

According to historian Kenneth Stampp, "1857 was probably the year when the North and South reached the political point of no return—when it became well nigh impossible to head off a violent resolution of the differences between them."[67] If Stampp's argument is correct, Pennsylvania colonizationists persisted in their emancipatory activities as long as one might expect.[68] For decades, they showcased manumissions, for such liberations comforted PCS leaders who chafed between colonization's failings and the conviction that the program would solve the country's problems concerning race and slavery. The emancipations, in other words, eased the officials' internal tensions. Yet those dissonance-reducing endeavors proved insufficient in the tumultuous late 1850s. Psychological stress intensified as colonization proved incapable of averting a civil war. "*The pressure to reduce the dissonance,*" posits social psychologist Leon Festinger, "*is a function of the magnitude of the dissonance.*"[69] For PCS officers, something had to change. They accordingly eschewed the antislavery aspects of their enterprise, and thereby stilled the tempest within.

5

—⚬◡⚬—

White Southerners' Responses
to ACS Manumissions

"In regard to objections argued against us from the south," wrote ACS corresponding secretary Ralph Gurley in 1832, "I am not aware, that in any instance has the Society been the occasion of discontent or disturbance among slaves, or that a single slave has left his master in consequence of the existence of the Society."[1] As Gurley's comments indicate, one criterion upon which southern whites evaluated the ACS was whether the organization's activities encouraged slave resistance. ACS-sponsored manumissions, in particular, brought the issue of slave recalcitrance to the forefront. Some white southerners decried these emancipatory episodes and rebuked the slaveholders who effected them; others ignored the affairs and left the emancipators undisturbed. How does one account for such a wide range of reactions? Why did some commentators believe that ACS manumissions threatened slavery while others held contrary views? The diversity of opinion stems from the fact that southern whites' thoughts on the subject were influenced by three different variables: the location of the manumission, the magnitude of the emancipatory operation, and the observer's proximity to the enterprise.[2]

Location of the Manumission

Local manumission rates shaped southern whites' responses to ACS emancipations. In urban locales and in the Border States, where economic forces and the potential for slave flight made slave liberations a *comparatively* common phenomenon, neighborhood whites usually did not protest the emancipation and emigration of bondpersons. Conversely, in the plantation districts and in the Lower South, where slaves rarely obtained freedom, nearby whites were more likely to take exception to ACS liberations. All other things being equal, a community's forbearance toward manumission varied directly with the frequency of such transactions.

The best data concerning popular reactions to ACS manumissions comes from Virginia, where more than one-third of all such liberations occurred. Let us first consider public responses in the state's eastern urban centers—to wit, Norfolk, Portsmouth, Fredericksburg, Richmond, and Petersburg. Compared to the Tidewater's and Piedmont's rural sectors, manumission rates in these towns were relatively high, largely because the cities' economic and demographic conditions compelled slaveholders to offer delayed emancipation to bondpersons who otherwise might have sought immediate liberty by blending into the free black population, slipping on board a vessel, or fleeing northward. In such locales, whites had been exposed to manumission, and as a result, local slaveholders who effected ACS liberations usually escaped reproach. Between 1820 and 1860, the five aforementioned Virginia cities were home to thirty different ACS manumitters. Only two of these individuals—Fredericksburg's outspoken mother-daughter tandem of Lucy and Mary Blackford—reported that they had been ostracized by whites for their emancipatory endeavors.[3]

Pockets of toleration could also be found in Virginia's rural areas. Loudoun County, located along the Maryland border in North Central Virginia, is a case in point. The western section of the county was populated by Quaker and German migrants from Pennsylvania and Maryland, and these settlers showed no ill will toward ACS manumitters. For example, in 1829 the brothers Albert and Townsend Heaton liberated a family on the condition that they move to Liberia, and neither the siblings nor the people they freed encountered trouble from local whites. Yet the Heatons' situation was unusual. The strong presence of the Friends, along with the comparatively small number of slaves in the county, made Loudoun different from many rural areas in eastern Virginia. In places where the bonded population was large, the opportunities for escape few, and emancipationist sentiment weak, neighborhood whites did not take kindly to ACS liberations.[4]

Several ACS manumitters in Central Virginia discovered just how strong the backlash could be. For example, when the Rev. John Paxton of Cumberland County sent a dozen slaves to Liberia, local whites quickly denounced the minister as an imprudent extremist. Forced to resign his ministry, Paxton moved to

Danville, Kentucky, where he believed his colonizationist affinities would be given a better reception. In a similar fashion, John Hartwell Cocke of Fluvanna County suffered a "frightful beating" after effecting an ACS manumission. Anne Rice of Prince Edward County, cringing under her community's glare, cloaked her antislavery views so thoroughly she could barely reveal them to friends who shared her beliefs. The residences of these beleaguered emancipators—Cumberland, Fluvanna, and Prince Edward Counties—were all in Virginia's Piedmont region. They were places where slaves made up between 46 and 62 percent of the population and where manumissions occurred infrequently. In this demographic and social milieu, ACS liberators like Paxton, Cocke, and Rice encountered more malevolence than did their peers in the cities.[5]

The pattern that was manifest in Virginia appears to have been replicated in other parts of the South. The surviving evidence on the subject is less than abundant, but the extant documents indicate that in areas where manumission rates were comparatively high, ACS emancipators operated without fear of rebuke. Urban centers, in particular, were relatively amenable to the transport of bondpersons to Liberia. Thirteen different ACS manumitters hailed from New Orleans; twenty-nine dwelled in Savannah; fourteen lived in Augusta; eleven came from Charleston; seven made their home in Baltimore. Most of these emancipators liberated just a few slaves. They were small-time manumitters residing in cities where the liberation of a slave or two was not an extraordinary event. Thus they did not endure the ire of their neighbors.[6]

Their rural counterparts faced a considerably different situation. In the countryside, planters worried that manumissions might arouse discontent among the enslaved masses. When Capt. Isaac Ross and Margaret Reed of Jefferson County, Mississippi, left wills that called for the emancipation and emigration of 350 bondpersons, a mob of several hundred armed men gathered to prevent the proposed manumission. In Orleans Parish, Louisiana, John McDonogh felt that area slaveholders would decry the allegedly deleterious effects that his emancipatory experiments would have on the vicinity's large slave population, and he consequently acted in a furtive fashion. Alfred Cuthbert Jr. of Putnam County, Georgia, also tried to remain socially liminal. "My neighbors will perish believing that there is some connection between Colonization & Abolitionism, notwithstanding all they may be told to the contrary," sighed Cuthbert.[7]

Some places discountenanced ACS manumissions more than others. As one Virginia colonizationist observed, individuals who treated their slaves above the neighborhood norm "had to do with a subject on which people quickly become violent, and on which too many Christians are soon angry." Yet local conditions were not the only factor shaping public opinion toward ACS manumissions; other variables figured into the equation, too. Among them was the magnitude of the emancipatory enterprise.[8]

Magnitude of the Operation

The scale of colonization operations influenced southern whites' attitudes toward them. The size of the affairs in turn depended on the method of manumission, the activities of emancipators, freedpersons, and ACS officials as the undertaking moved from plantation to port, and the Society's dockside endeavors. Generally speaking, the more expansive these ventures, the more caustic whites' responses.

The Method of Manumission

Most ACS manumitters used either deeds or wills to free their bondpersons. Many who utilized deeds avoided opprobrium because they liberated a very small number of slaves. Forty-four percent of nontestamentary ACS manumitters liberated just one bondperson, an act so inconspicuous that it was unlikely to attract notice, much less inspire maltreatment. But other emancipators who used deeds, and especially those who conducted "experimentalist" manumission programs, ran the risk of angering their neighbors.

"Experimentalist" manumission projects could test the tolerance of proslavery whites. Recall that many ACS liberators concocted emancipatory schemes that purportedly prepared slaves for life in Liberia. These "experimentalists" educated their bondpersons, or taught them special skills, or allowed them to purchase their freedom. Nearby slaveholders occasionally protested such practices. Moreover, as bondpersons pressed their own interests—as they tried to manipulate manumission agreements to their advantage—local opponents saw even more reason for complaint. Even as the terms of manumission were being negotiated, neighborhood whites sometimes detected causes for concern.

The tale of the Maryland slaveholder Margaret Mercer illustrates the point well. In the late 1820s, Mercer hoped to send the twenty bondpersons that she had inherited to Africa. Yet Mercer's manumission plans upset her neighbors in Anne Arundel County. Among other things, they denounced the manner in which Mercer was readying her slaves for Liberia. An educator herself, Mercer taught her slaves how to read. One bondman even received a medical education. These acts exasperated nearby slaveholders. Also, when the moment of emancipation arrived, some bondpersons refused to emigrate. Initially, Mercer insisted that these individuals remain slaves, but in time she allowed them to go free, with one family heading to Baltimore and one bondwoman moving to the North. This, too, rankled slaveholders in her community, and they pressured her to discontinue the venture. Mercer persevered, but under duress. She confessed that if her slaves had not been "human flesh and blood, souls belonging to the God that made them, I should have yielded. But I have determined to abide by the consequences." Those consequences, her memoirist contended with rhetorical flourish, were a life filled with "anxiety, toil, and poverty."[9]

ACS liberators could avoid such unpleasantness by using testamentary devices to free their slaves. Having passed away, the manumitters dodged face-to-face confrontations concerning their emancipatory deeds. But their postmortem directives exposed to censure colonization agents, executors, and others who were responsible for carrying out the testamentary instructions.

Part of the problem, in the opinion of those who opposed such enterprises, was the effect that postmortem manumissions had on bondpersons after their owner died. If the prospect of freedom supposedly sedated slaves while their master or mistress was alive, the interim between their owner's death and their actual liberation, according to the ACS's opponents, was a period fraught with dangerous anticipation and untoward excitement. When James McGill's will called for the emancipation of Robin McGill and his family, for example, one local resident complained that the bondman and his wife had become brazen as they neared freedom. "While they were under the protection of their master & mistress," wrote William Eagleton, "they maintained a very good character. Since their death Robin has at times been involved in difficulty." Testamentary liberations were worrisome in the minds of proslavery southerners because they could take months and even years to effect, and all the while would-be manumittees waited and waited, the infection of freedom growing among them and spreading to others.[10]

Postmortem manumissions often placed many bondpersons in that limbo between slavery and freedom. For testamentary emancipators, the median size of liberation was ten bondpersons (with a mean average of nineteen slaves). ACS opponents feared the consequences of having large numbers of bondpersons occupying the netherworld of semislavery. "Are such [prospective manumittees] likely to be good servants?" asked Justice Joseph Lumpkin of Georgia. "On the contrary, are they not likely to sow the seeds of insubordination, perhaps revolt, among the slaves in the neighborhood?" For Lumpkin, the answers were obvious, as was the solution: "[A]ll postmortem manumissions of slaves should be absolutely and entirely prohibited."[11]

The enhanced size of posthumous liberations also created additional pressure for conjunctive emancipations. The math was simple: the more slaves that had the opportunity to go to Liberia, the more requests there would be to secure the freedom of bonded kin. Even small testamentary liberations could expand geometrically. For example, in 1854 Sarah Inskeep's will provided for the emancipation and emigration of just two men, George Holt and Solomon Keys. One of Inskeep's relatives freed Keys's wife and daughter. Neighbor James Gibson then emancipated Holt's spouse and child. Thereafter, another slaveholder permitted three more bondpersons to join the group. A party of two had become a company of nine. If small postmortem emancipations multiplied in this manner, larger ones could proliferate all the more.

ACS emancipators insisted that they were moderates at heart, that they abhorred antislavery radicalism as much as other white southerners. And many manumitters never heard an unkind word, partly because they disavowed abolitionism and partly because their emancipatory projects were minute affairs. Yet the methods by which colonizationists freed slaves—that is, experimentalist manumissions and testamentary liberations—could also make for socially conspicuous ventures. When ACS emancipations became high-visibility events, proslavery southerners were apt to protest.

From Plantation to Port

ACS manumissions required colonizationists to attend to many matters, and each activity could increase the magnitude of the Society's operations. Contacting the ACS, acquiring information about Liberia, orchestrating conjunctive emancipations, securing transportation funds for emigrants, and moving manumittees to port often attracted the attention of local slaves. Once bondpersons stirred, proslavery whites declared that the colonizationists' transactions were discord-inducing enterprises.

Emancipators had to correspond with ACS leaders, and even this seemingly benign endeavor entailed risks. This was especially true in the Lower South. "Do not give me any publicity to this as I deem it private & confidential," enjoined a Mississippian. "[I]f you think it worthwhile, show this letter to . . . [ACS officials] Mr. Latrobe & Mr. Gurley . . . but to no one else," suggested a Georgian. "Confidential," scribbled one Arkansan, "My situation requires it." Although hundreds of southern colonizationists wrote to the Society without fear, others penned letters with trepidation.[12]

Many epistlers wanted to learn more about the colonization movement, and ACS leaders often responded by sending them copies of the *African Repository*. Over time, however, the Society's periodical was branded as an incendiary publication in some parts of the South. In South Carolina, for example, those who read the journal did so at their own peril. According to one individual who asked the ACS to stop sending the paper to his home, abolitionist agitation had produced in slaveholders "a deep aversion to everything which *may appear adapted* to excite a spirit of insubordination among the colored population." The Society's periodical, which discussed emancipation and emigration at length, evidently fell under that category. During the 1840s and 1850s, the ACS received numerous letters from anxious South Carolinians requesting that the organization discontinue their subscriptions to the *African Repository*.[13]

Yet if the colonization program was to succeed, information about the enterprise had to be distributed. ACS publications had to circulate; colonization agents had to promote the project; and former emigrants had to return to America and champion the cause. This last necessity continually placed the colonization movement on thin ice in the South. Indeed, the more effective the recruiter—the more excitement he or she generated about Liberia—the thinner the ice. ACS agents therefore searched for boosters who could tackle the Sisyphean task of interesting blacks in Liberia without alarming whites.

The case of Thomas Fuller, a Virginia free black who had emigrated in 1852, demonstrates the dilemma well. ACS officials were quite hopeful about Fuller, printing articles about him in the *African Repository* and conferring among themselves about his potential recruiting abilities. "Thos. Fuller would be a special advantage to the cause of colonization," wrote ACS agent William Starr from Norfolk, Virginia. "But I fear he would not be comfortable here, nor acceptable to the white population," he continued. "There is such a foolish sensitiveness, especially of late, on every subject relating to free negroes or slaves—and such antipathy against every darky, free darky, coming from other states."[14]

If Thomas Fuller would have attracted too much attention, other Liberian spokespersons would have garnered too little. Consider a situation that arose in Clarke County, Virginia. In 1851, J. W. Ware of that county wrote to the ACS, informing the organization about a recent testamentary manumission. According to Ware, the testator's slaves had reservations about Liberia and the heirs-at-law were fueling the bondpersons' fears. Ware suggested that a previous emigrant be sent to allay the slaves' concerns, but he repeatedly counseled that this should be done in secrecy. There is no evidence that the ACS took Ware's advice. Such an emissary's range of operations would have been too limited to be helpful to the organization, and such clandestineness would have lent credibility to the proslavery charge that colonizationists were undercover abolitionists.[15]

ACS supporters desperately sought former colonists who could walk the recruiter's tightrope. Some thought that John Morris might have been able to perform the requisite balancing act. ACS agent William Starr believed that the fifty-one-year-old farmer and hack-driver would be influential among blacks and acceptable to whites. Another colonizationist, William Kennedy, agreed. Stationed in Morris's former hometown of Elizabeth City, North Carolina, Kennedy asserted that many neighborhood blacks were interested in emigrating, but "they seem unwilling to make any move until John Morris returns." "I have no doubt he will induce many to return with him," predicted Kennedy. Morris was the ideal spokesperson for the ACS: a man trusted by blacks and tolerated by whites, a person who could warm up interest in colonization without overheating passions about the program. Still, such a remarkable talent did not come cheaply. Morris did not work for free; he wanted the ACS to help him acquire a steamboat. When contemplating Morris's demands, agent Starr remarked that Morris could aid the ACS, and then added, "And he is aware of it."[16]

If contacting the Society, reading the *African Repository*, and escorting former emigrants around the South could place colonizationists in ill stead among proslavery whites, so too could going to court. Much to the Society's detriment, trials sometimes became public spectacles. ACS officials consequently grew weary and leery of suits involving slaves. "I have frequently said We ought to keep clear of such extraneous encumbrances," commented ACS officer William McLain after becoming entangled in litigation.[17] The hoopla surrounding the emancipation of Dorthea Bratton's slaves elucidates why McLain and his colleagues came to this conclusion. The episode piqued many whites in Christiansburg, Virginia. "Such a day of trial I never before spent," remarked colonization agent William Ruffner:

A large number of people were in town, [and] all had heard of Mrs. Bratton's intention to send her negroes to Liberia & all had their disapproving remarks & looks to throw around. Some thought that Mrs. B. was in her dotage, others thought that [Bratton's son-in-law] Dr. Kent ought to put his veto upon the whole transaction; some thought almost all the emigrants died directly after they reached Liberia, some that it was an abolitionist scheme—all very knowing upon the whole subject (*facts* only excepted) & all very ready to express an opinion, & were not very particular who heard them.[18]

Such scenes contrasted sharply with the colonizationists' claim that ACS man-umissions would entail little or no commotion. As Ruffner noted, even though it was understood that Bratton's slaves were to be sent to Liberia, some onlook-ers insisted that the affair was an abolitionist plot.

Like public trials, conjunctive emancipations could irritate slaveholders who valued social stability and wanted to limit their slaves' thoughts of free-dom. The saga of Edmund Brown of Fairfield, Virginia, a small town located just west of the Blue Ridge Mountains in Rockbridge County, exemplifies the disorder that could attend conjunctive emancipations. In 1854, the heirs of Robert Stuart freed Brown, who set out to liberate various family members so that they could accompany him to Africa. Capt. Hugh Adams manumitted Brown's wife and three of his children. Brown himself purchased four other kin and was trying to buy two more when some slaveholders began protesting his conduct. "This reflex influence is against Ed. and I do sincerely regret it," the Rev. James Paine informed the ACS. "There is no occasion for it. Ed. has acted wisely, prudently; he has 'put no mischief in anybody's head.'" Intentional or not, Brown's efforts were deemed disruptive, for local slaves had started asking for the same opportunities. "Some think the thing must be checked," Paine explained. Indeed, the objectors succeeded in stymieing Brown's efforts, and on 6 November 1854, the freedman left for Liberia without his son and daugh-ter-in-law.[19]

Hoping to steer clear of such controversies, some ACS emancipators hired out their slaves, figuring that the bondpersons could use their wages to pur-chase their own freedom and that of their loved ones. In cities like Baltimore, Norfolk, and New Orleans, such arrangements were commonplace and un-worthy of comment. But when the transactions occurred in rural areas, local slaveholders occasionally voiced their opposition. In Warren County in Cen-tral Tennessee, William White learned this the hard way. White hired out his bondpersons with the expectation that they would be able to finance their journey to Liberia. White's neighbors labeled him a subversive. "Some . . . are speaking hard of me on account of my course towards my slaves," he lamented. They say "I am ruin[in]g thare slaves by laying the examples before theirs[,] making them believe that it is right that thare masters should do as I have done." The outcry finally overwhelmed White, and he abandoned his manu-mission plans.[20]

For those individuals who did not forsake their emancipatory schemes, more social hazards awaited. Conveying freedpersons to port, for example, often necessitated prudence on the colonizationists' part. Here the number of emigrants in the party proved important. Rarely did a single manumittee leave his or her county alone, unaccompanied by other Liberia-bound blacks. More often than not, a handful of manumittees would travel together, and it was not uncommon for them to be joined by a group of free blacks. For parties that included at least one manumittee, the mean number of emigrants departing a county was fifteen, with the median average being seven. Some contingents were noticeably large. One in five had twenty or more members. A few had over one hundred in tow.[21]

The departure of a sizable emigrant party from a southern community rarely went unnoticed. When Nathaniel Hooe's 104 slaves began their journey from King George County, Virginia, to Liberia in 1845, a crowd of over two hundred persons, including many blacks, gathered to witness the affair. Such an assemblage, it seems safe to suppose, did not sit well with local slave-holders.[22] As one anticolonizationist remarked of such episodes:

> [I]t is spreading a dangerous influence among the negroes of this coun-
> try, for slaves of whole plantations to acquire their freedom, take leave of
> the country, and make their departure with great pomp and parade, pro-
> claiming liberty for themselves and their posterity; . . . it renders those
> who are left behind, dissatisfied, refractory, and rebellious; and . . . it may,
> probably will, if not checked in time, lead to insubordination and insur-
> rection."[23]

Apprehensive about encountering opposition on the way to port, some emancipators asked the ACS to send a representative who could handle any troubles that might arise during the trek. The Society obliged these individuals when possible, yet even the most skilled, upstanding, and conciliatory agents struggled to appease disgruntled southerners. The simple fact was that freed-persons who trooped through a neighborhood were anathema to proslavery whites.[24]

In some places, such processions appeared surprisingly often. ACS records clearly reveal what demographers call "chain migration"—that is, successive companies exiting from the same locale over time. The data from Virginia are striking. Between 1820 and 1860, ACS emigrants left from sixty-four different Virginia counties. Most of the counties (thirty-seven) experienced such epi-sodes more than once. Certain areas nearly qualified as regulars: Dinwiddie County saw the departure of Liberia-bound blacks on sixteen different occa-sions; Albemarle County, ten times; Southampton, nine times; Campbell and Jefferson Counties, eight times each; and Augusta, Frederick, Hanover, Rockbridge, and Spotsylvania Counties, seven times apiece. These periodic events hardly made the ACS a fixed feature in the aforementioned places. But emigrant departures occurred with enough frequency to suggest that, in such districts, colonization was never wholly out of view, and perhaps then, never entirely out of mind.[25]

The "chain migration" pattern resulted from blacks' pre- and postemigration activities and from emancipators' philosophy on manumission. For most ACS liberators, manumission was a long-term mechanism of slave management, a system of control that might require more than one act of emancipation. Ultimately, fifty ACS manumitters (about 9 percent of all known manumitters) sent multiple companies of freedpersons to Liberia. To an extent, the colonization movement was dependent on these "multiple manumitters": those 9 percent effected one-fifth of all ACS emancipations, and they liberated, collectively, over one-fourth of all freedpersons.[26]

"Repeat emancipators" could miff their proslavery neighbors. Consider the case of Ann R. Page. In the early- to mid-1830s, Page sent three separate companies (totaling twenty-four freedpersons) to Liberia. Although she lived in Frederick County, Virginia, a place where bondpersons constituted "just" 28 percent of the population, Page felt ostracized for her emancipationist sympathies. "The fear of God," she explained, "enabled me to overcome the fear of man." Page was probably guilty of a little hyperbole—the horror of divine retribution was not so alarming as to prompt Page to liberate her slaves in toto, and the dread of public castigation was not so intense as to dissuade her from effecting multiple manumissions. Still, her story reminds us that popular reactions to ACS manumissions were the product of many forces, and the size and nature of the emancipatory endeavor were among the most important.[27]

ACS manumissions were complicated affairs. Colonizationists had to acquire information about Liberia, secure funding and supplies, win court cases, coordinate conjunctive emancipations, convince skeptical blacks to emigrate, and shepherd the willing to port. As the scope of these enterprises grew, so did the possibility of harassment at the hands of proslavery individuals. Moreover, colonizationists' problems did not end once the emigrant party reached the port of embarkation. If anything, their predicaments became even more complex.

The ACS in Port

Prior to the Civil War, the Society sent 143 expeditions to Liberia. Initially, most ACS vessels left from Norfolk. Then, as ACS manumissions slowly shifted south- and westward, colonization officials began using other ports. For example, between 1841 and 1852, more ACS emigrants set out from New Orleans than from any other city. Savannah, Georgia, also became a point of departure for ACS ships, at least until town authorities clamped down on colonizationists in the mid-1850s. By the end of the antebellum period, ACS embarkations were once again largely confined to the Chesapeake region, with Norfolk and, to an even greater extent, Baltimore reigning as the locations from which most emigrants left for Liberia.[28]

The expansiveness of ACS operations in Norfolk, Baltimore, New Orleans, Savannah and other ports influenced local whites' attitudes toward them. The scale of the Society's endeavors in these seaside locales was determined by a variety of variables. Some the colonizationists could control, such as the size of the emigrant parties and the amount of publicity that the ACS purposely generated. Others factors, such as free black protests, emigrant indocility, and logistical difficulties, were beyond the colonizationists' realm of power.

There was a direct relationship between the number of ACS emigrants entering a port and the amount of proslavery opposition plaguing colonizationists. During the early- to mid-1820s, for example, the Society sent out from Norfolk one or two ships a year, with each carrying just a couple score of colonists. These modest enterprises did not worry local leaders. In the aftermath of Nat Turner's Rebellion, however, many more ACS emigrants began arriving in Norfolk. In a span of four years, over one thousand African-Africans came to Norfolk with the expectation of leaving for Liberia. The city itself had only 928 free blacks at the time, and the onrush of free and soon-to-be-free African-Americans alarmed proslavery whites. The backlash became so intense that colonizationists hid emigrants throughout the borough. Ultimately, city officials demanded that each ACS emigrant post a five-dollar bond for good behavior.[29]

A similar but more drastic turn of events occurred in Savannah, Georgia, in the 1850s. The ACS had sporadically used this port during the 1820s and 1830s, but as the number of Lower South manumissions grew, the Society employed Savannah more frequently. Over nine hundred ACS emigrants sojourned through Savannah in the late 1840s and early 1850s, and local authorities were not pleased. In 1856, the city placed a two-hundred-dollar tax on every emigrant leaving Savannah. The mayor, James P. Screven, stated unequivocally that the measure was designed "to prevent any further shipment of Negroes from this port to Liberia." The instrument had the desired effect: only one other ACS vessel came to Savannah, and in this quixotic episode, colonizationists skirted the municipal ordinance by ferrying emigrants to the ship as it floated in the harbor.[30]

Like large emigrant parties, excessive self-promotion could jeopardize ACS operations. Society supporters consequently had to manage their public relations carefully. They needed to generate enthusiasm and support for their enterprise yet do so in way that would not upset slaveholders. In the end, colonizationists scaled their publicity according to local social conditions.

In some instances, the Society utilized the press aggressively. This was the case in Norfolk during the 1820s and 1830s. The city's colonizationists advertised their meetings, solicited aid for needy emigrants, trumpeted the embarkation of ACS vessels, and candidly championed the emancipatory aspects of their program. Yet even in Norfolk, ACS members had to temper their public proclamations. They disavowed "enthusiasts"; they counseled "moderation"; they extolled "prudence." As the years passed, ACS editorials in the Norfolk papers grew more conservative. In 1839, when the *Saluda* embarked with thirty-nine emigrants, the *Herald* exercised restraint, focusing its story not on the manumittee majority on board but rather on the ship's free black passengers.[31]

The cautiousness that seized Norfolk colonizationists had held their New Orleans peers for years. Even in the early 1830s, ACS agent James G. Birney had encountered opposition from whites who feared that merely discussing colonization would incite unrest among slaves. In light of these circumstances, newspaper editorials about ACS activities in New Orleans tended to be discreet. Between 1841 and 1852, twelve ACS ships departed from the Crescent City. The *Daily Picayune* covered many of these events, but the paper's accounts were always understated and usually published *after* the vessel set sail.[32] Another New Orleans daily, the *Commercial Bulletin*, paid less attention to ACS embarkations, and the stories that it did run had a proslavery tint. For example, when the *Renown* left in 1843, the *Commercial Bulletin* claimed that periodic departures of "industrious, honest, and intelligent manumitted negroes" demonstrated the virtues of "their subjection to the whites."[33] So ACS partisans publicized their doings in New Orleans, but they did so warily, knowing, as agent Birney once remarked, that there was "no popularity to be gained by openly espousing the cause of Colonization."[34]

If ACS advertising was relatively bold in 1820s Norfolk and more circumspect in 1840s New Orleans, there were towns in which colonizationists could not engage in any self-promotion. Charleston, South Carolina, was such a place. When over one hundred Charleston free blacks expressed their intention to go to Liberia in 1848, an ACS representative in the city begged Society officials to refrain from publishing any statements on the matter. "[T]he whites are yet much opposed to colonization," wrote the agent, "I shall be able to do more by keeping silence."[35] Like Charleston, Savannah, Georgia, became a town where colonizationists operated covertly. In the late 1840s, an ACS field worker there encountered "great difficulties & strong opposition" when running newspaper advertisements and holding public meetings. By the 1850s, such pre-embarkation activities had been abandoned altogether. When the *General Pierce* was scheduled to sail from Savannah in December 1854, ACS officer William McLain decided that secrecy was necessary for success. "I desire to say to you very quietly," he wrote one local sympathizer, "that we shall start a vessel from Savannah the 30th Dec. . . . We shall not publish any notice. We do not want the authorities of your city to know anything about it."[36]

If the ACS's conspicuousness in port partly depended on things the organization could regulate like the size of emigrant parties and the vociferousness of its agents, the Society's dockside visibility was also determined by factors that colonizationists could not control. Foremost among the latter forces were free blacks. In Baltimore, free blacks repeatedly disrupted the embarkation of ACS ships, causing in at least one instance "great confusion" on the wharves. In Norfolk, too, free blacks engaged in "artful temptations" to dissuade emigrants from sailing. Large crowds of African-Americans also gathered in New Orleans and Savannah upon the departure of ACS ships, and although the extant evidence does not describe the assemblages' moods and dispositions, it is reasonable to suppose that some of individuals present were opposed to the proceedings.[37]

Nor could Society supporters restrain local bondpersons, who sometimes saw ACS activities as opportunities to strike for freedom. When the *Colonel Howard* docked in Savannah in 1849, one resident reported, "letters are coming in from various places saying that slaves have run away & will get on board this vessel." Baltimore also witnessed controversies over whether emigrants were "legitimate" freedpersons or fugitive slaves. Indeed, ACS officials literally had to run a tight ship, for while runaway slaves tried to sneak onto Liberia-bound vessels, manumittees attempted to abscond off them. Colonization leaders took precautionary measures—they appointed agents to oversee emigrants, guarded against "suspicious" activity, and withheld manumittees' freedom papers. Even so, there were limits to how effectively they could enervate African-American agency.[38]

Logistical matters also vexed ACS organizers in Norfolk, New Orleans, Savannah, and other ports. Coordinating the arrival and departure of Society ships proved especially problematic. During the early years of the movement, ACS vessels embarked at random times. This chaotic mode of operation resulted in confusion and delays—in one instance, a group of emigrants wandered about Norfolk for three months while awaiting the Society's ship. By the late 1840s, however, the ACS had packets departing at fixed, biannual intervals. Regularizing embarkation dates solved some of the ACS's logistical problems, but not all of them. For one thing, there was no telling when emigrants would arrive in port—some showed up too early; others, too late. Moreover, even if the parties gathered at the agreed-upon time, colonizationists could not guarantee that the ship would be ready to carry them overseas. Transportation was notoriously unreliable during the antebellum period. Postponements were inevitable, and the sight of freedpersons lingering about—sometimes for weeks, sometimes for months—displeased proslavery whites.[39]

The Society's dockside detractors, like white anticolonizationists across the South, feared that ACS operations would inspire restlessness among slaves, that the affairs would weaken whites' control over bondpersons. To them, the visibility of the Society's enterprises was a vital matter. The more conspicuous the episode, opined proslavery southerners, the greater the likelihood for servile insubordination. So, in regard to white southerners' reactions to ACS manumissions, the magnitude of the episode was as salient as the locale in which it occurred. As shall be seen, the proximity of the observer was equally important.

Proximity to the Enterprise

Neighborhood critics' complaints against colonization differed from those brought by faraway proslavery ideologues. The locals bemoaned the movement's tendency to invite slave resistance. The theorists claimed that enterprise was logistically untenable and that black people were unfit for freedom.

Initially, proslavery writers' arguments paralleled the condemnations voiced by local opponents of colonization (that is, that ACS operations promoted restiveness among bondpersons). In 1825, South Carolinian Whitemarsh B. Seabrook penned *Concise View of the Critical Situation*, which attacked the emancipationist drift of the ACS. Two years later, Robert J. Turnbull of the same state published a series of articles in the *Charleston Mercury*, wherein he asserted that colonizationists sought to "disturb the peace in the Southern

States."[40] Virginian "Caius Gracchus" railed against colonization in the *Richmond Enquirer,* calling the program visionary and subversive. The Georgia legislature leaped into the fray in 1827, denouncing ACS activists for making slaves "discontented with their present situation."[41] In deeming colonization dangerous, these writers implied that it was feasible. After all, that which is impossible cannot be very threatening. Vigilance was necessary, they warned, because ACS advocates were no daydreamers.

Thomas R. Dew's *Review of the Debates of the Virginia Legislature of 1831 and 1832* (1832) challenged that assumption and thereby transformed the southern debate on colonization.[42] Dew tellingly entitled one section of his work "The impossibility of colonizing the blacks." After analyzing the enterprise's costs and logistical difficulties, Dew declared, "the whole plan is utterly impractical."[43] Having exposed the venture's inoperability, Dew then questioned the morality of sending ill-prepared freedpersons to Liberia. Mockingly, he wrote:

> We are to send out thousands of . . . [bondpersons], taken from a state of slavery and ignorance, unaccustomed to guide and direct themselves, void of all the attributes of free agents, with dangerous notions of liberty and idleness, to elevate them at once to the condition of freedmen, and invest them with the power of governing an empire, which will require more wisdom, more prudence, and at the same time more firmness than ever government required before.[44]

Dew had heard enough nonsense. Colonization, he proclaimed, was a "*stupendous piece of folly.*"[45]

In highlighting the impracticality of colonization and the immorality of sending blacks to Africa, Dew leveled charges against the ACS that were different from those made by individuals who denounced actual emancipators. The brand of opposition experienced by John Paxton, Margaret Mercer, Ann R. Page, and other liberators—all of whom had been cast as troublemakers in their communities—emphasized the public dangers of colonization, not the irrationality of the scheme or the moral wisdom of its adherents.

Why did Dew fail to discuss the tumult that sometimes attended ACS manumissions? He had plenty of opportunities to learn about the emancipatory affairs. At the time, ACS liberations were on the rise. Moreover, many well-known Virginians were sending slaves to Liberia. In addition, the enterprises were discussed in the ACS's *African Repository* and *Annual Reports.* Dew nevertheless focused on logistical questions. He had good reasons for doing so.

Dew wanted white Virginians to understand that colonization was no solution for slavery. Dew himself thought that the state's bondpersons might be diffused southward and that state-funded internal improvements and an influx of white migrants would abet the process. In Dew's mind, Virginia lawmakers would never move on such matters if they remained bedazzled by colonization. Thus he labored to prove the program unfeasible.[46]

Dew's treatise proved a boon to proslavery partisans. Ignoring Dew's ideas about sending Virginia bondpersons to the Lower South, they assumed that Dew's anticolonization tract had obliterated the middle ground in the debates over slavery. Dew had shown that black people would remain in America, they grinned, and that fact would force white southerners to join either the abolitionist or proslavery camp. Bondage's defenders were certain that southern whites would choose the latter, but just to make sure, they began churning out proslavery propaganda.

The works of William Harper and James Henry Hammond illustrate how southern intellectuals used Dew's piece as a proslavery springboard. "After President Dew," wrote Harper in *Memoir on Slavery* (1838), "it is unnecessary to say a single word on the practicability of colonizing our slaves." Harper then took the next logical step, contending that African-Americans were unfit for freedom, "that nothing but the coercion of slavery can overcome their propensity to indolence."[47] Seven years later, Hammond presented similar arguments in his *Two Letters on Slavery* (1845). Hammond did not even mention colonization, instead framing the debate as a choice between the virtues of slavery and the recklessness of abolitionism. Hammond's and Harper's arguments were natural extensions of Dew's position on colonization: since African-Americans were here to stay, they were best off in slavery.[48]

Both Harper and Hammond contended that morally squeamish slaveholders were courting disaster. Hammond noted that "excessive indulgence" on the part of masters inspired resistance among bondpersons. Harper likewise opined that "weak" and "timid" slaveholders sometimes fell prey to abolitionist sophistry. Over time, he continued, these tormented dupes grew more desperate. They sold their slaves, an act that only injured the bondpersons, and left the South, foolishly relocating to alien and uncongenial areas. According to Harper, everyone lost. "Society is kept in an unquiet and restless state," he argued, "and every sort of improvement is retarded."[49]

Harper's and Hammond's brief accounts of ethically anxious slaveholders illuminate why proslavery ideologues concentrated on colonization's imprac-

ticality and black people's presumed slavishness and ignored the social discord that sometimes accompanied ACS operations. In associating antislavery sentiment with servile resistance, for example, each author implicitly
suggested that African-Americans, far from being contented and loyal dependents, in fact, were displeased with thralldom. Moreover, in acknowledging that "unquiet and restless" conditions existed, proslavery authors would
eventually need to explain how government authorities could squash these
threats to (white) society's safety. In other words, they would have been required to opine on the ways in which the state could circumscribe slaveholders' personal and property rights. For intellectuals who wanted to confirm
whites' right to own blacks, digressions concerning governmental impositions
on those prerogatives were unpalatable. So proslavery theorists, if they discussed colonization at all, rarely strayed from safer criticisms of the scheme
—namely, the enterprise's alleged impracticality and blacks' supposed ser-
vility.[50]

During the late 1840s and 1850s, many proslavery writers disregarded colonization altogether, as if it no longer merited debate. Several authors who appeared in E. N. Elliott's proslavery anthology *Cotton Is King* (1860), including
Albert Taylor Bledsoe, Thornton Stringfellow, Samuel A. Cartwright, and
Charles Hodge, overlooked the subject.[51] A number of the apologists who were
not cited in Elliott's compendium, such as Henry Hughes, Nehemiah Adams,
Edward A. Pollard, and George Fitzhugh, were equally indifferent.[52] When
proslavery intellectuals did take notice, they offered perspectives that were distinct from those expressed by local foes of colonization.

There were some exceptions. In 1851, the *Southern Quarterly Review* objected to a proposed congressional appropriation for a line of steamers that
would convey free blacks to Africa. "The whole scheme looks like gross imper-
tinence," snarled the journal's editor, E. H. Britton. "To send off free negroes
will very soon conduct to the manufacture of free negroes." Britton continued with his attack, insisting that ACS advocates had disturbed communities
across the South. "The Colonization Society, without designing it, has exercised almost as mischievous an influence upon the peace of our people, and
the safety of our slave institutions, as the direct assaults of the abolitionists,"
he complained. This editorial was unusual. Few critics of colonization analyzed the social ramifications of ACS activities that, as we have seen, were the
very things that could place ACS emancipators and their white neighbors at
odds.[53]

De Bow's Review published numerous articles that zealously disparaged the ACS. But repetition and ardor were no substitutes for ingenuity. Most of the essays simply echoed Dew's 1832 argument that colonization was logistically impossible and subsequent writers' contention that black Americans were unsuited for freedom. "Besides the expense of such a system, which renders it impractical," intoned the author of an October 1849 piece, "it is attended with the death of from one-fourth to one-half of the emigrants by the coast fever."[54] In an 1851 article, Josiah Nott, the famed proslavery physician, commented, "it is utterly inconceivable to my mind, how so many men of intelligence could be led to favor a scheme so impractical."[55] Having convinced themselves that colonization was utterly unworkable, the ideologues then repeated the standard incantations about black dependency and submissiveness. "His experiments in self-government have been hideous failures. . . . Sierra Leone and Liberia are experiments in the face of all experience," argued one writer.[56] "My purpose is not to depreciate that noble scheme . . . but only to show the repugnance of the free colored race among us to perform the indispensable labors of cultivated and civilized life," announced another.[57] "Were a tithe of the increase of the slaves of the United States . . . discharged on Liberia, a speedy return to barbarism would be the inevitable result," declared a third.[58] In short, proslavery writers' anticolonization arguments were still quite different from the indictments that ordinary southern whites made against ACS emancipators.

De Bow himself sounded off against colonization. When introducing an August 1853 article in which the author praised the ACS, De Bow inserted the editorial remark, "We have less faith than he has in the practical value of colonization."[59] In 1856, De Bow again took aim at colonization, claiming that the movement's failings had proven "that slavery is morally, socially, industrially, politically, *right*—the best for the master and the slave, *and necessarily to be maintained at any and all hazards.*"[60] Over the next few years, De Bow intermittently denounced the ACS.[61] The most devastating critique to appear in *De Bow's Review,* though, came from the pen of the celebrated agricultural reformer Edmund Ruffin.

In 1859, *De Bow's Review* published several lengthy essays by Ruffin.[62] Like previous proslavery writers, Ruffin noted the logistical difficulties of colonization and the supposed immorality of transporting blacks to a woebegone place like Liberia. Only "blind fanatics" could endorse such a scheme, he insisted. Up to this point, Ruffin's commentary, though more elaborate than his predecessors, had not broken new ground.[63]

Then Ruffin's ire fell upon ACS emancipators. Looking back on the early days of the movement, Ruffin argued that some southern whites had believed that the Society was a benevolent institution. At the time, kindly slaveholders conjectured that bondpersons could be inculcated with proper values and steady work habits and that these characteristics would help blacks become self-supporting members of an independent African community. In providing a repository for freedpersons, slaveholders had thought that the ACS offered a valuable service to southern society.[64]

Yet ACS leaders were not satisfied with such mundane activities, charged Ruffin. They intended to destroy slavery. Operating in secrecy, they deceived impressionable and confused slaveholders, cajoling them into sending their bondpersons to Liberia. Southern women, in particular, were easy prey for the fast-talking colonizationists.[65] Deluded by ACS agents, the emancipators, fe-male and male alike, assumed that they had performed meritorious and pious acts. The ACS would then publicize the manumissions, adding to the libera-tors' fame and cultivating "vanity, ostentation, self-righteousness, and self-worship." Meanwhile, the freedpersons suffered in Liberia, victims whose wel-fare and happiness had been "greatly impaired, if not totally sacrificed on this shrine of false benevolence and humanity."[66]

Ruffin was not finished. The trouble with ACS manumissions went be-yond arrogant emancipators and downtrodden freedpersons. Ruffin noted, for example, that the liberations deprived the South of valuable workers, and labor was the greatest need in the agricultural region. "But there is still a much worse effect," he warned. ACS emancipations—especially prospective, testamentary manumissions that took years to effect—encouraged discon-tent among slaves. Colonizationists had to persuade bondpersons to accept freedom in Liberia, and in the process of doing so, they needed to convince would-be manumittees that they were unhappy with their condition as slaves. And planting these notions in the head of a single bondperson was just the beginning of the problem. "Such lessons, when designed to operate on one individual, and even without having direct effect on that one, may reach hundreds of others, to the injury of their contentment, and their worth as laborers and slaves."[67] Here, in 1859, Ruffin had finally explained what local opponents of colonization had known all along: that ACS manumissions could be socially disruptive.

As Ruffin pointed out, the issue of slave unrest largely determined south-ern whites' attitudes toward ACS liberations. After contemplating the sub-ject, some onlookers denounced the emancipatory enterprises; others, conversely, were untroubled by the episodes. The differences of opinion should not be surprising. ACS liberations were not uniform events. They varied in site and size. Consequently, a manumission's location and magnitude, along with the proximity of the observer, shaped white southerners' responses to the affairs.

6

ACS Manumissions and the Law

ACS manumissions raised two interrelated legal questions. The first involved the extent to which the state could circumscribe a slaveholder's property rights (in this case, an individual's right to disown bondpersons). The second question concerned whether the state would sanction slave agency in ACS operations. Both issues were vitally important to southern colonizationists, who discovered that the answers to these questions varied by time, place, and circumstance. In general, the more southern the state, the later the date, and the greater the slave agency, the harsher the governmental response to ACS emancipations.[1]

Public Policy and Statutory Law

Manumission law pitted emancipators' rights against their white neighbors' interests and "the public good." One's right to free bondpersons was not absolute. It was curbed, on one side, by another individual's right to the "quiet enjoyment" of their slave property, and, on the other side, by (white) society's welfare. But where did those boundaries lie, and what were the criteria for making such determinations?

Southern states' answers to these questions changed over time. During the early nineteenth century, southern states usually resolved these matters by outlawing "domestic manumissions" (that is, liberations wherein the freedpersons remained in the state) but permitting "foreign emancipations" (that is, liberations wherein the freedpersons left the state). Manumission guidelines, in other words, were initially designed to prevent increases in a state's free black population, a group whose very existence seemed to undermine the South's racially based slave system. However, by 1840, proslavery advocates in the Lower South began campaigning for more rigorous manumission policies. Over time, this movement spread northward, with its paladins importuning states to declare themselves opposed not just to free blacks but to manumission itself. Antimanumission crusaders defended their cause by arguing that slave emancipations—even out-of-state ones—were inherently threatening to slavery; that restrictive emancipation laws implied an aversion to manumission in general and not just the presence of freedpersons; that the anti–free black principle itself authorized a ban on slave liberations; and that interregional tensions between the North and South as well as intrastate disputes between nonslaveholders and slaveholders necessitated stronger safeguards for slavery, including a complete prohibition on manumission. By 1861, slave liberations had been outlawed in several states and were nearly impossible in many others.

The Revolutionary Era through 1840

During the Revolutionary era, many southern states, emboldened by Enlightenment ideology and Christian egalitarianism and alarmed by slaves' own assertiveness in securing freedom, liberalized their manumission laws. In 1782, for example, Virginia empowered slaveholders with the right to liberate bondpersons by deed or will, and for the first time in ninety years, allowed new manumittees to lawfully remain in the state. Following Virginia's lead, Delaware, Maryland, Kentucky, and Tennessee revised their emancipation statutes. The drive for flexible manumission codes was stonewalled in some places, however. South Carolina and Georgia refused to revamp their restrictive emancipation laws, while North Carolina, after a few ill-fated attempts to secure more moderate statutes, began passing increasingly stringent measures in the late 1780s. Nevertheless, in the aftermath of the Revolution the trend in the South was toward more liberal manumission laws. Most slaveholders did not take advantage of these permissive statutes, but hundreds, perhaps thousands, did emancipate bondpersons.[2]

The increase in slave liberations swelled the size of the southern free black population. So, too, did the inflow of Saint-Domingue refugees, greater numbers of runaway slaves, and natural population growth. Between 1790 and 1810, the number of free blacks in the South rose from 32,000 to 108,000, an increase of 238 percent. Most of the growth occurred in the Upper South, but the upward trend was evident in the Lower South too. Simply put, free blacks had become the fastest-growing segment of the southern population.[3]

This demographic development worried many white southerners who claimed that free blacks refused to work without compulsion, engaged in criminal activities, harbored fugitive slaves, and organized insurrectionary plots. These objectors not only encountered resistance from free blacks, but they also faced opposition from fellow whites who relied on free black labor. Even so, state lawmakers usually sided with the detractors and passed statutes that were designed to diminish the size of the free black populace. To achieve this goal, the legislators employed a three-pronged strategy: first, they attempted to prevent bondpersons from joining the ranks of the free by toughening manumission laws; second, they prohibited free African-Americans from entering their states; and third, they encouraged the already-free to emigrate by circumscribing their rights and sponsoring relocation programs.

Southern legislators tried to dam up one of the primary sources of free blacks by rewriting state manumission codes. In 1800 and 1801, respectively, South Carolina and Georgia prohibited domestic emancipations. Prior to the ban, both states had witnessed sizable increases in their small free black populations, a development that was due in part to the arrival of Saint-Domingue exiles. A proliferating free black population and a brush with rebellion also precipitated a prohibition on in-state manumissions in Virginia in 1806. There, the number of free blacks had increased tenfold between 1782 and 1800, and Gabriel's plot had alarmed anxious whites. In explaining the need for restrictions on manumission, one Virginia lawmaker asserted that, under the permissive 1782 law, slave emancipations had been "destructive to the happiness of the state."[4]

Other states did not outlaw domestic emancipations in the early 1800s, but they did revise their manumission codes with the hope of fixing the alleged "free black problem." Some lawmakers reserved for themselves the final say on prospective liberations. This was the case in the Mississippi and Alabama territories, where would-be emancipators were required to secure legislative permission before freeing their slaves. Southern officials also delimited the sorts of bondpersons who could be liberated: Delaware, Maryland, Missouri, Arkansas, Louisiana, and several other states prohibited the freeing of young and old slaves—persons presumed most likely to become public charges. Finally, legislators in Kentucky, Maryland, North Carolina, and Tennessee guarded against the supposed depredations of free blacks by requiring emancipators to post security bonds for freedpersons. Although most states had stopped short of banning domestic manumissions, they had done much to discourage liberations of this type.[5]

A second method for arresting the growth of the free black population involved preventing the caste's members from entering the state. Virginia outlawed free black immigration in 1793; South Carolina did likewise in 1800. After Virginia declared domestic manumissions illegal in 1806, Maryland, Kentucky, and Delaware, worried that Virginia manumittees would take up residence in their environs, denied free blacks admission into their states. North Carolina and Georgia still allowed free blacks to settle in their territories, but they required such persons to post hefty bonds or pay special taxes.[6]

In addition to enacting new manumission and immigration statutes, southern lawmakers' legislative assault on free blacks also entailed revoking the group's civil liberties, limiting their economic opportunities, and championing their deracination. Virginia, Georgia, Maryland, and Tennessee all endorsed colonization in the mid- to late 1810s. As noted in chapter 1, during this period, colonization enjoyed the support of both proslavery and antislavery partisans in the South. For a short while, the campaign to remove free blacks was entangled with the crusade to expatriate all blacks. In time, proslavery advocates extricated themselves from the colonization coalition.[7]

By the mid- to late 1820s, all of the Lower South states had registered their opposition to a national emancipationist program of colonization. In Georgia, for example, lawmakers recanted on their previous support for colonization, arguing that they had been misinformed about the nature of the enterprise. The legislators now believed that ACS leaders intended to remove all African-Americans, not just free blacks, and, worse still, colonizationists wanted the U.S. government to "effect this object, so wild, fanatical, and destructive." The lawmakers' counterparts in South Carolina voiced the same sentiments, warning that they would not allow slavery "to be meddled with, or tampered with, or in any manner regulated, or controlled by any other power, foreign or domestic, than this legislature." Over the next few years, Lower South politicians, true to their word, railed against every attempt to establish a national colonization project.[8]

The 1820s controversies over the ACS, when coupled with the rise of Garrisonian abolitionism, the bloodshed attending Nat Turner's Rebellion, the Virginia Slavery Debates, and the continued growth of the southern free black population, prompted southern legislators to revise their manumission laws once again. Previously, only three states had insisted on the removal of new manumittees. Now the majority of the southern states required their departure. Florida outlawed domestic manumissions in 1829, as did Louisiana and North Carolina in 1830, Tennessee in 1831, Maryland in 1832, Alabama in 1833, and the Republic of Texas in 1836. The new codes were not the harbingers of a novel policy on manumission and slavery; they did not represent a giant stride toward the "positive good" view of black bondage. Rather, they were the last step in a long-developing, older policy of limiting the size of the free black population.[9]

This was certainly how southern judges understood the manumission laws. In the Upper South, jurists repeatedly argued that their states disfavored free blacks, not slave emancipations. In *Elder v. Elder* (Va., 1833), Judge Henry St. George Tucker wrote in a concurring opinion that neither the law nor "the policy" of Virginia forbade "an emancipation by transportation to a free colony." Tennessee judge John Catron likewise contended in *Fisher's Negroes v. Dabbs* (Tn., 1834) that the goal of the state's manumission policy was to minimize the number of free blacks in the state and, if possible, in the entire country. Similar ideas were expressed in North Carolina, where Judge Thomas Ruffin opined in *Cox v. Williams* (N.C., 1845) that "the policy is avowed of encouraging emancipation, upon the sole condition, that the people freed . . . keep out of our borders."[10]

Lower South jurists also contended that public policy permitted foreign manumissions. In *Frazier v. Frazier* (S.C., 1835), Judge John Belton O'Neall held that a testamentary, out-of-state emancipation was "legal and valid, and must be obeyed." Similar rulings were handed down in Mississippi. In *Ross v. Vertner* (Miss., 1840), for example, the plaintiffs claimed that such liberations fostered "insubordination and . . . insurrection," but the Mississippi Supreme Court dismissed these arguments. According to the justices, out-of-state emancipations were not so disruptive as to justify a ban on them. Georgia's justices likewise ruled in favor of foreign manumissions in *Jordan v. Bradley* (Ga., 1830), *Roser v. Marlow* (Ga., 1837), and *Vance v. Crawford* (Ga., 1848), for as Judge Joseph Henry Lumpkin explained in the latter case, "neither humanity, nor religion, nor common justice, requires of us to sanction . . . domestic emancipation," but "*foreign* emancipation . . . is in accordance with our declared policy."[11]

Out-of-state manumissions were thus perfectly legal in Georgia and other southern states during the early nineteenth century. Yet this position did not go unchallenged. Indeed, Judge Lumpkin himself, after conceding that a testamentary foreign liberation was within Georgia's "declared policy," remonstrated that "such wills cannot be regarded with particular tenderness and favoritism by the Courts of Justice." As Lumpkin's comments imply, by the 1840s there was mounting pressure to change manumission policy in the South.[12]

The Antebellum Era

During the antebellum years, proslavery southerners believed they had reason to fret about the security and future of black bondage. Northern abolitionism and free-soil ideology represented dangers from abroad, while slave escapes, insurrection scares, nonslaveholder disgruntlement, and a revived colonization movement all constituted threats from within.[13] In this period of acute tension, southern legislators and jurists debated whether their states should adopt new manumission policies, ones in which slave emancipations would be proscribed altogether. The antimanumission movement began in the Lower South around 1840 and slowly spread northward. On the eve of the Civil War, slave liberations had been banned in several states and were subject to strict regulations in many others.

In the Lower South, the push for a new manumission policy commenced at a relatively early date. In the late 1830s, some proslavery partisans argued that slave emancipations, by their very nature, threatened black bondage and should be outlawed in the name of "the public good." In *Trotter v. Blocker* (Ala., 1838), for example, the Alabama Supreme Court began with the usual premise that the state's welfare required "suitable guards around the institution of slavery." The justices then contended that slave emancipations disturbed "the quiet of the country." Such dangers must be minimized, the jurists reasoned. Therefore, only manumissions that were explicitly sanctioned by state laws were permissible. The court consequently ruled that a testamentary foreign manumission was illegal because postmortem liberations were not authorized by Alabama's manumission code. The *Trotter* decision was later overruled, but the notion that slave liberations were intrinsically detrimental to societal interests could not be quashed.[14]

Some judges responded to this brand of logic by insisting that, whatever the dangers of manumission, outlawing them would only worsen the problem. Bondpersons would become so disgruntled and desperate, the argument went, that whites' safety would be placed in even greater peril. As Virginia judge William Brockenbrough remarked, "[I]s there no danger that oppression and tyranny . . . may drive them [slaves] to despair?" Ebenezer Starnes of Georgia likewise reminded his colleagues that "it would not be for the best interests of the slave holding community" to eliminate all forms of manumission. For justices of this ilk, the prospect of freedom anesthetized slaves.[15]

The drive for more restrictive manumission policies continued nonetheless. South Carolina and Mississippi proscribed testamentary liberations in 1841 and 1842, respectively, and jurists in the two states were soon debating whether the bans reflected a change in manumission policy (that is, whether their states were now opposed to slave emancipations in principle). South Carolina judge John Belton O'Neall lamented that such a transformation had occurred, protesting, "the state has nothing to fear from emancipation, regulated as that law [the law of 1800] directs it to be." In Mississippi, jurists seemed unsure whether their state had revised its philosophy on manumission, ruling in an 1846 case that "it is the policy of this state . . . to prevent the increase of free persons of color therein" and then opining, two years later, that the state could "discountenance" foreign emancipations. The Mississippi justices continued to vacillate in the 1850s. After reviewing the pertinent litigation in an 1859 suit, Judge William L. Harris observed that in some decisions the court had held that "our policy is against emancipation," while in others it had maintained that "our State policy is only opposed *to the increase in free negroes in this State.*" An exasperated Harris tried to resolve the issue and rewrite history, proclaiming, "[I]t *now is and ever has been,* the policy of Mississippi to . . . prevent emancipation generally of Mississippi slaves."[16]

If the outlawing of postmortem liberations gradually weakened the ACS's legal standing in Mississippi and South Carolina, the passing of stringent manumission laws elsewhere had a more ambiguous impact on the colonization movement. In 1852, for example, Louisiana state legislator Francis DuBose Richardson introduced a bill that would have required manumittees to emigrate specifically to Liberia. During the ensuing debate, it became clear that some lawmakers construed the measure as an explicit endorsement of foreign emancipation, while others perceived it as the forerunner of a comprehensive antimanumission policy. The bill's opponents contended that the proposed legislation represented a complete reworking of the manumission system, that it constituted, according to one legislator, an "entire prohibition of all emancipations." Richardson pushed aside these arguments, insisting that the measure would simply better enforce the old principle of reducing the size of the state's free black population. After the bill became law, the man charged with its implementation, Governor Paul Octave Hébert, adopted Richardson's line of thought, remarking, "It is the settled conviction of the people of the southern States generally, that it is impolitic and dangerous to permit the increase, by emancipation or introduction from abroad, of the free colored population." Thus interpreted, Louisiana's manumission code placed the ACS in an exceptional legal position: if the state's slaveholders wanted to free their bondpersons, they had to send them to Liberia. Many observers nevertheless worried that this law merely presaged less colonization-friendly statutes.[17]

In the meantime, the new regulation contributed to a small upswing in ACS emancipations in Louisiana. During the period in which the 1852 removal-to-Liberia statute was in force, the number of ACS manumissions in Louisiana rose from .5 per year to 3 per year. Interestingly, Tennessee passed a comparable law in 1854 and witnessed a similar increase in ACS liberations (from 1.7 per year to 3.4 per year). In both Tennessee and Louisiana, a rewriting of the manumission code was followed by an upturn in ACS emancipations.[18]

The campaign against manumission even made headway in Kentucky. Unlike most southern states, Kentucky had refrained from proscribing domestic emancipations. In 1850, however, lawmakers there finally joined the southern majority by banning in-state manumissions. Proslavery advocates rejoiced at their long-awaited victory, but Kentucky's jurists reminded them that the state had merely adopted an anti–free black policy, not an antimanumission one. As Judge Stites explained in *Smith v. Adam* (Ky., 1858), it was whites' concern over the burgeoning free black population that had inspired the restrictions on slave emancipations. Kentucky, in other words, would not leapfrog its sister states in a rush to outlaw manumissions of every sort.[19]

In Mississippi, South Carolina, Louisiana, Tennessee, and Kentucky, antimanumission advocates defended their crusade by pointing to new legislative checks on slave liberations. In Georgia, the proponents for change needed other rationales for lawmakers there had not revised the state's emancipation code since 1818. Bereft of a statutory springboard, individuals intent on overhauling the state's manumission policy turned to the old anti–free black principle, arguing that it authorized the prohibition of foreign liberations. For instance, Judge Henry L. Benning wrote scathing dissents in *Adams v. Bass* (Ga., 1855) and *Sanders v. Ward* (Ga., 1858), contending that banished freedpersons would ignore the penalties for reentering the state and would come back to Georgia. The free black population, Benning predicted, would increase by these means. He complained, "Already one or more of the negroes manumitted by the *Waters Will* . . . have returned from Liberia—a feat far more difficult, than the return of such negroes from any one of the free States."[20]

Benning's colleague, Joseph Henry Lumpkin, personally detested foreign emancipations. As a judge, however, he felt obligated to uphold the laws as they were written and public policy as he perceived it. He therefore thought Benning's arguments rather specious. According to Lumpkin, the occasional returnee from Liberia did not justify banning out-of-state emancipations. Would it be reasonable, he asked, "to cut off the right so highly prized by a large portion, *if not a majority* of our people, to guard against the return of a few straggling negroes?" Thus Lumpkin reluctantly opined in favor of foreign liberations. Even so, he virtually begged the legislature to change the state's manumission statutes. "Let that body speak, and no one will take more pleasure than myself in obeying their behest," he wrote in *Sanders*.[21]

By the end of the antebellum era, some jurists were calling for an anti-manumission policy, not because their states had passed severe emancipation laws or because they had come to a new understanding of the anti–free black principle but rather because they believed that turbulent societal conditions necessitated the outlawing of all slave liberations. Consider the case of *Bailey v. Poindexter* (Va., 1858), in which the justices appeared to have broken precedent and voided a foreign emancipation. Judge William Daniel, writing for the majority, insisted that *Bailey* was different in small but significant ways from previously adjudicated cases, and therefore the court had not adopted a new philosophy on manumission. In his dissenting opinion, Judge Richard Moncure argued that there was no distinction between *Bailey* and other out-of-state emancipation cases and that his colleagues were using the tumultuous times as an excuse to overhaul the state's stance on manumission. Moncure admonished the majority, reminding them that justices were obliged "to expound the law as it is written and settled, and not as it ought to be, or as it may be supposed that public opinion would have it be."[22]

By the late 1850s, the campaign for an antimanumission policy, having started in the Lower South twenty years earlier, had reached the Upper South. Those who wished to circumscribe slaveholders' "emancipation rights" presented several interrelated arguments. Slave liberations disquieted the bonded population, they insisted. Stringent manumission laws implied a general antipathy toward black freedom, they pled. A correct understanding of the anti–free black principle justified a ban on manumission, they declared. The impending showdown over slavery necessitated protections against antislavery enemies at home and abroad, they averred. By the 1850s, such arguments were being proffered throughout the South. They were not universally accepted, though. Even during the "decade of crisis" manumission policy was still contested terrain.

The indeterminate outcome of these policy debates was evident in two monographs on slave law. William Goodell's abolitionist tract *The American Slave Code* (1853) explained the southern rationale for restrictions on manumission by quoting from Jacob D. Wheeler's *A Practical Treatise on the Law of Slavery* (1837), wherein the author contended that the regulations were justified because the public had a right to protect itself from "stupid, ignorant, and vicious [freed]persons." Thus Goodell, taking his cue from Wheeler, intimated that anti–free black objectives still dictated manumission policy in the South. Yet Goodell also enumerated the many legislative and judicial obstacles to emancipation, implicitly suggesting that southern states had gone beyond their customary concern over size of the free black population.[23]

Similar uncertainties showed up in Thomas R. Cobb's proslavery work, *An Inquiry into the Law of Negro Slavery in the United States of America* (1858). According to Cobb, southern states had not yet embraced new manumission policies; the anti–free black principle continued to rule in this realm, he contended. Yet Cobb acknowledged that this principle was subject to different interpretations. Cobb himself advocated "the middle way, in which is safety." Cobb nevertheless evinced more conservatism than many when he argued that slaves who were liberated via a foreign manumission had to leave "immediately" because states needed to minimize the number of *statu liberi*—that is, bondpersons who had a vested right to freedom. In the end, Cobb admitted that the current method of adjudicating manumission cases, because it depended on each state's interpretation of the anti–free black idea, had produced a "contrariety of decisions."[24]

The antimanumission campaign, though foiled in some states, had impaired the colonization movement in the South, or so ACS spokespersons claimed. "We are often called upon to record instances where Wills are set aside, the intentions of testators defeated, and funds designed for benevolent societies appropriated by distant heirs," lamented an 1854 article in the *African Repository*. ACS managers had become so accustomed to such disappointments, the piece continued, "that we dare say it is quite refreshing to them to meet with a case of an opposite character." Entering the courthouse had become an uncertain, frustrating, and often disheartening experience for southern colonizationists. Manumissions had become, as one ACS official wrote, "a case of Conscience or Law."[25]

The ACS's legal prospects only worsened in the late 1850s. Georgia declared postmortem liberations illegal in 1859, as did North Carolina in 1861. Mississippi and Louisiana proscribed emancipations entirely in 1857; Arkansas went the same route in 1859; Alabama and Maryland followed suit in 1860. By the end of the antebellum era, slaveholders' manumission rights had been largely if not totally extinguished.[26]

Slave Agency in Colonization Cases

Although most southern states tolerated foreign manumissions until the late 1850s, adjudicating colonization cases was no easy endeavor. The difficulties inherent in viewing humans as property proved especially troublesome. Southern jurists acknowledged slaves' humanity in many ways. Bondpersons were liable for criminal acts, and masters could not murder slaves with impunity, for example. Yet these were necessary and beneficial concessions that improved the South's control over bondpersons and its image in an antislavery world. The matters raised in colonization cases were not as manifestly advantageous to the slave regime. Could slaves accept a bequest of freedom from their owners? Could bondpersons choose between slavery in America and freedom in Liberia? Could they be hired out to extinguish estate debts and fund their own transport to Africa? For most of the antebellum era, jurists answered these questions in ways that gratified colonizationists. Then, as antimanumission forces gathered strength in the 1840s and 1850s, southern justices began narrowing the legal confines of slave agency.

Giving and Receiving Freedom

Emancipation entailed more than discontinuing property rights in a slave. This made bondpersons distinct from other forms of property. If an individual relinquished their claim to, say, a chair, another person could rightfully take possession of the object. Liberated blacks, conversely, required protection from being owned. Manumission had to be seen as more than merely disposing of one's goods.[27]

Many jurists utilized property law ideas when deciding manumission cases, essentially arguing that emancipation gave bondpersons property rights in themselves. In this formulation, freedom was regarded as a commodity or title that passed from slaveholders to bondpersons. Judge Ephraim M. Ewing adopted this rationale in *Nancy v. Snell* (Ky., 1838), as did Judge Ara Spence in *State v. Dorsey* (Md., 1848). According to Spence, manumission conferred upon slaves "the identical rights, interests and benefits, which would pass, if the testator had bequeathed the same slave to another person."[28]

Viewing freedom as an entity—as an item that slaveholders willed to bondpersons—raised several unwieldy problems. First, it was unclear whether slaves had the capacity to receive that special gift. Judge O'Neall of South Carolina was certain that they did not. As O'Neall contended in *Lenoir v. Sylvester* (S.C., 1830), "a legacy cannot be given to a slave; for he can have no right, whatever, which does not, the instant it is transferred to him, pass to his master." Eight years later, Chief Justice Henry W. Collier of Alabama made the same point in *Trotter v. Blocker* (Ala., 1838). From this view, bondpersons, as individuals without civil status, were not legitimate parties to testamentary action.[29]

Most jurists refused to follow O'Neall and Collier and instead concluded that bondpersons could take a beneficial interest in a will. Perhaps the most forceful expression of this view came from Judge William Gaston of Tennessee in *Ford v. Ford* (Tenn., 1846):

> A slave is not in the condition of a horse or an ox. . . . He has mental capacities, and an immortal principle in his nature. . . . the accidental position in which fortune has placed him . . . cannot extinguish his highborn nature nor deprive him of many rights which are inherent in man. Thus while he is a slave, he can make a contract for his freedom, which our laws recognize, and he can take a bequest of his freedom, and by the same will he can take personal or real estate.[30]

Other southern jurists echoed Gaston. In *Leech v. Cooley* (Miss., 1846), Judge Alexander M. Clayton plainly asserted that "the bequest to the slaves is not void for want of capacity in the legatees to take." In North Carolina, the court ruled in *Cox v. Williams* (N.C., 1845) and *Thompson v. Newlin* (N.C., 1851) that slaves' right to accept or decline freedom existed in nature. The Maryland Supreme Court also admitted slaves' agency in these matters. On the whole, jurists who viewed freedom as a transferable entity tended to concede bondpersons' ability to receive it.[31]

Conceptualizing freedom as a commodity brought up a second problem: if one could take freedom, one could sell it, too. Yet slavery was an involuntary condition, and the ability to sell oneself into bondage seemed to defy the essence of the institution. Despite such arguments, property law analysis was simply too tempting to pass up. Most jurists employed it; justices who foreswore it inadvertently slipped property law ideas into their reasoning and rhetoric; and southern legislators implicitly endorsed it by enacting voluntary enslavement laws in the 1850s. This was all well and good for the colonization movement, for jurists' and lawmakers' utilization of property law concepts allowed slaves to "take" the freedom that their owners had willed to them.[32]

ACS supporters nevertheless understood that potential hazards lurked in every courtroom. Some judges refused to think of freedom as a title that passed from slaveholders to bondpersons; others doubted whether slaves had the legal capacity to accept freedom; and there was no guarantee that these perspectives would remain minority views. Faced with this uncertainty, southern colonizationists sought to bolster their legal position. Their options in this pursuit included contending that manumissions were charities, encouraging jurists to employ the doctrine of cy pres, and having slaveholders will their bondpersons to the ACS.

Some litigants averred that manumissions fell under the legal category of charities, and a handful of southern justices agreed with them. The Virginia court embraced this argument in *Charles et al. v. Hunnicutt* (Va., 1804), ruling that "devises in favour of charities, and particularly those in favour of liberty, ought to be liberally expounded." The North Carolina bench followed a similar course in *Cameron v. Commissioners* (N.C., 1841), declaring that a will that devised slaves their freedom as well as funds for their settlement in Liberia was valid because manumission, if consistent with public policy, was a charitable bequest. At the time, foreign manumission was within the bounds of public policy in North Carolina, and thus the freedpersons were permitted to emigrate to Africa.[33]

ACS advocates occasionally entreated jurists to use the doctrine of cy pres, which allowed courts to overlook a will's technical problems and to order executors to carry out "as near as possible" the testator's intentions. Sometimes justices complied. Take the case of *Young v. Vass* (Va., 1855), for example. Philip E. Vass willed that several of his slaves be emancipated and resettled in North Carolina. He also bequeathed them two thousand dollars. The lower court held that since North Carolina prohibited the immigration of free blacks, the will was void. The Court of Appeals reversed the decision. The slaves should decide between moving to the North or Liberia, opined the justices, and the legacy should be "applied in the manner most beneficial to them." An even more remarkable verdict was handed down in *Prater's Administrator v. Darby* (Ala., 1854). In this instance, the Alabama court actually validated an emancipator's will that omitted provisions for removing freedpersons. According to the justices, there was nothing in the will that required the executors to liberate the slaves in Alabama. If the bondpersons received their freedom beyond Alabama's borders, the jurists explained, the state had no reason for complaint.[34]

Such liberal applications of cy pres irritated many observers. Indeed, the *Prater* decision in Alabama was overturned five years later, when the court ruled in *Evans v. Kittrell* (Ala., 1859) that judges could not "engraft . . . a term, not inserted by the parties . . . to carry the slave out of this State." Jurists elsewhere in the South likewise balked that the principle of cy pres granted tribunals too much discretionary power. Judge Lumpkin of Georgia deemed it "odious." His associate Benning thought it "monstrous" and ruled accordingly. When Benning and others on the Georgia bench examined a will that directed slaves to be liberated and sent to a state that prohibited the immigration of free blacks, they refused to employ the principle of cy pres and send the would-be freedpersons elsewhere. "It cannot be said, with any degree of confidence," wrote Benning in the 1855 decision, "that he wished them to be free in Ohio or Massachusetts, Canada or Congo, Liberia or wherever else his executor or some Court might say."[35]

In addition to arguing that manumissions were charities and urging jurists to utilize the doctrine of cy pres, southern colonizationists sought to enhance their legal prospects by having the ACS inherit slaves. The organization could take an interest in wills because Maryland had granted the ACS a charter of incorporation, specifying its purpose as "colonizing with their own consent upon the coast of Africa, the free people of color residing in the United States." Free black emigration was emphasized to assuage proslavery southerners' fears that colonizationists were stealthy abolitionists. But the charter's wording created legal problems for the ACS: the Society's detractors contended that an organization established to remove "free people of color" was incapable of inheriting slaves.

Southern jurists rejected these arguments and almost always confirmed the ACS's legal capacity to take and transport bondpersons to Liberia. In *Maund v. M'Phail* (Va., 1839), the Virginia court held that even when a testator misnamed the organization "the new colonization society in Africa," the ACS could receive bequeathed slaves. Seven years later, the Mississippi bench likewise ruled that the ACS could inherit bondpersons. "It is true the charter confers no right to transport *slaves* to Africa," Judge Clayton opined in *Wade v. The American Colonization Society* (Miss., 1846), "But the slaves . . . have an inchoate right to freedom. As soon as they are taken beyond the limits of this state, that right is so far consummated, that by the terms of the charter they may be transported and colonized." Even Judge Lumpkin and his associates on the Georgia court upheld a devise of bondpersons to the Society in *Vance v. Crawford* (Ga., 1848). Yet Lumpkin disliked ACS manumissions, and his simmering antipathy toward colonization eventually led him to rethink the legality of willing slaves to the ACS.[36]

Late in the antebellum era, Lumpkin and a few other judges repudiated precedents and insisted that the ACS could not inherit bondpersons. In *American Colonization Society v. Gartrell* (Ga., 1857), the Georgia court ruled that, since the ACS's charter specified the colonization of free people of color, the organization was not qualified to receive slaves. Like the Georgia bench, Mississippi's high court overturned previous decisions and ruled against the ACS. "The holding of slaves, not for emancipation," Judge Handy opined in *Lewis v. Lusk* (Miss., 1858), "is irreconcilable with the policy and true spirit of the society, and hence . . . this bequest was not valid." The courts of Mississippi and Georgia were the only tribunals that invalidated testamentary bequests of slaves to the ACS. In the rest of the South, such provisions were, as Judge Clayton wrote in *Wade,* "repeatedly carried into effect . . . without objection."[37]

Even when jurists conceded the ACS's capacity to receive slaves, or even when they admitted bondpersons' ability to accept liberty, the justices had to resolve one last matter: when exactly did bondpersons become free? Was it before or after they left for Liberia? Answering these questions proved difficult, especially when justices examined wills that ordered slaves to be freed and removed (instead of removed and freed). In Mississippi, North Carolina, and Alabama, the juxtaposition of terms was deemed irrelevant. As Judge Clayton wrote in *Leech v. Cooley* (Miss., 1846), "The mere collocation of words, if their meaning be the same, cannot vary their construction." Late in the antebellum era, however, the Georgia bench ruled in *Drane v. Beall* (Ga., 1857) that such directives were illegal. "The emancipation . . . was to take effect in Georgia," Lumpkin wrote for the court, though it "was intended to be *enjoyed* in Liberia, California, or some other free State or Territory."[38]

Conundrums concerning the giving and receiving of freedom challenged jurists. A slaveholder's right of emancipation did not automatically admit a bondperson's capacity to accept liberty. Nor was it clear whether the ACS could inherit slaves. Southern judges usually adjudicated these matters to the benefit of colonizationists, at least they did so until the late 1850s. For most of the antebellum period, ACS advocates could expect to fare well in court if their manumissions were consistent with public policy—that is, if the slaves agreed to leave the state. But this raised the question of whether slaves could legally make such decisions.

Election Cases

ACS emancipators knew that their bondpersons dreaded privation in Liberia and separation from kin. Consequently, most allowed their slaves to select between liberty in Africa and bondage in America. Southern jurists usually conceded slaves' capacity to *accept* freedom, but permitting them to *choose* between liberty and slavery ostensibly constituted a greater concession to bondpersons' agency. Given the prevalence of these emancipatory provisos, judicial sanction proved critical to the colonization cause.

In the Upper South, judges consistently upheld slaves' right to choose freedom. In *Elder v. Elder* (Va., 1833), the Virginia court validated a will that gave slaves the option of bondage in America or freedom in Liberia. "Every instrument conferring freedom," Judge William Cabell wrote in a concurring opinion, "should be construed liberally, in favor of freedom." Jurists throughout the Upper South followed the ruling in *Elder*. Kentucky's high court concluded in *John v. Moreman* (Ky., 1847) that a bondman "had an inchoate right to freedom as soon as he made his election to go to Liberia." Similarly, in *Hayden v. Burch* (Md., 1850), the Maryland court upheld a will that gave bondpersons the option of freedom in Africa or slavery in America. Judge Ruffin defended this principle in *Cox v. Williams* (N.C., 1845) and adhered to it throughout the antebellum period. "It is not true in point of fact or law," Ruffin opined in *Redding v. Long* (N.C., 1858), "that slaves have not a mental or a moral capacity to make the election to be free." "They are responsible human beings," he continued, "having intelligence to know right from wrong, and perceptions of pleasure and pain, and of the difference between bondage and freedom, and thus, by nature, they are competent to give or withhold their assent to things that concern their state."[39]

The Tennessee high court was even more accommodating. When James McGill died in 1833, he left a will that stated that his wife could hold his slaves during her lifetime, whereupon the bondpersons could then choose between being free in Africa or remaining bonded in America. When McGill's widow passed away in 1840, several slaves expressed reservations about emigrating to Liberia. McGill's heirs then claimed the bondpersons for themselves. The Tennessee bench would hear nothing of it. "There were only casual conversations . . . in which some [slaves] . . . expressed their unwillingness to go to Africa," wrote Judge Nathan Green in *Isaac v. McGill* (Tenn., 1848). "To hold that such conversations . . . should be their solemn decision to remain slaves, rather than be free, would outrage every principle of justice."[40]

Judges in the Lower South also initially sided with colonizationists in election cases. In 1837, the Georgia court held in *Roser v. Marlow* (Ga., 1837) that bondpersons, when given the option by their owners, could choose between slavery in America and freedom elsewhere. In the early 1840s, the Mississippi court also dismissed arguments that permitting slaves to select freedom was contrary to the rights of heirs and the logic of slavery. Louisiana judges likewise held in *Executors of Henderson v. Heirs* (La., 1856) that would-be manumittees could decide to move to Liberia.[41] Yet the ACS's good fortune in election cases eventually expired. Ultimately, four southern states repudiated the idea that bondpersons could make legally binding decisions concerning their own fate and status.

Alabama was the first to do so. In what legal historian Helen T. Catterall called "a blunder," the Alabama Supreme Court misinterpreted a previous verdict and held in *Carroll v. Brumby* (Ala., 1848) that slaves could not choose between bondage and freedom. Thirteen years later, Alabama judges reasserted this principle in *Creswell's Executor v. Walker* (Ala., 1861). The justices acknowledged that blacks were "rational *human beings*," and therefore considered persons in criminal trials, but "because they are *slaves*, they are . . . incapable of performing civil acts," including opting to be free.[42]

Virginia jurists also reversed themselves. Since 1833, the state's high court had consistently ruled in favor of slave elections. In *Forward's Adm'r v. Thamer* (Va., 1853) and *Osborne v. Taylor* (Va., 1855), the justices stuck to the precedents but avoided explaining why slaves could choose liberty. Colonizationists soon discovered that the court's silence masked the judges' intensifying aversion to slave elections. In *Bailey v. Poindexter* (Va., 1858) and *Williamson v. Coalter* (Va., 1858), the Virginia court finally declared that slaves lacked the legal capacity to select between bondage and freedom. "The operation of this will as an instrument of emancipation . . . is made to depend on the choice of the slaves," complained Judge William Daniel in *Bailey*. A bondperson who chose liberty had seized, in his estimation, "*the uncontrollable and irrevocable power*" of self-emancipation. In both cases, the court's slim majority failed to persuade Judges Richard Moncure and Samuel B. Green. "A slave can become free only by the act of his master," Moncure posited in his dissent in *Bailey*. Slaveholders could attach any lawful contingency to the liberation, including obtaining the consent of the bondpersons to be free. "[I]t is the act of the master, and not the happening or performance of the condition which confers the right to freedom," he argued. Moncure had deftly shifted the debate from slaves' capacity to select freedom to the erosion of whites' rights. It was shrewd, though unsuccessful, judicial politics.[43]

In Georgia, too, the court came to rule against slave elections. In *Cleland v. Waters* (Ga., 1855), the justices decided that slaves could choose between bondage in Georgia and freedom elsewhere. To rule otherwise, Judge Lumpkin explained, would impugn "the whole train of decisions in this and our sister States, as well as of every other civilized country." In 1860, however, Georgia's judges decided in *Curry v. Curry* (Ga., 1860) that slave elections were illegal. In fact, the court went so far as to void a will in which the testator permitted bondpersons to name their next master. Such postmortem provisos, argued Judge Lyon, encouraged slaves to wander about the state "until such person should be found who would give them the largest liberty for the least consideration." "I cannot imagine a condition . . . more hurtful to a proper and necessary regulation of the slave population," he asserted. In actuality, there were many situations that represented greater threats to black bondage. Permitting slaves to choose freedom in Liberia, as Georgia and many other states had done for decades, was arguably one of them.[44]

Since most of the ACS's testamentary emancipators granted slaves the option of freedom in Liberia or bondage in America, favorable rulings in election cases were vital to Society operations in the South. This was especially true in the 1840s and early 1850s, when postmortem emancipations became an increasingly important feature of the colonization movement. The ACS's successes, in other words, were partly due to a tradition of judicial openness toward slave elections, while its failures were partially the result of a late-developing judicial hostility toward this brand of slave agency.

Inheritances and Hiring Out

Freedpersons' fate in Liberia was often determined by their financial condition upon embarkation. Their owners knew that poverty plagued the African colony, and many bequeathed their bondpersons outfits for emigration. But could property inherit property? Granting slaves a legacy of freedom was one thing. Yet since bondpersons could not technically own anything, allowing them to take tangible possessions was a more complex matter. For southern jurists and Liberian emigrants alike, determining whether slaves could receive property was a substantial concern.

The same principles that allowed bondpersons to accept bequests of freedom, southern jurists reasoned, permitted them to take other devises. In *Cameron v. Commissioners* (N.C., 1841), North Carolina's judges upheld a legacy to slaves because it was for a charitable purpose. Mississippi's court ruled in *Leech v. Cooley* (Miss., 1846) that slaves could take a bequest if they complied with stipulations established in the will. In *Alvany v. Powell* (N.C., 1853), Judge Richmond Pearson opined that the law that required the removal of freedpersons did not imply they lacked "a capacity to take property until after they have left the State." For the most part, jurists contended that would-be freedpersons could be legatees.[45]

Yet for many ACS liberators, the question was not whether bondpersons could receive a testamentary gift but rather whether there would be anything to take. Many emancipators accumulated debts that jeopardized their own manumissions schemes. When their wills were probated, creditors swooped in, contesting those wills in court. The law was usually on the creditors' side: most southern legislatures passed statutes that safeguarded lenders from manumissions. Judicial interpretations of these laws, however, varied greatly. Jurists sometimes construed these statutes in ways that gratified ACS supporters and prospective manumittees.

Judges in the Upper South were especially adept at balancing claims of freedom against the rights of creditors. In *Nicholas v. Burruss* (Va., 1833), Virginia jurists ignored ordinary laws of equity and held that both real and personal property had to be exhausted before creditors could claim slaves whom a testator wished freed. Kentucky judges ruled in *Nancy v. Snell* (Ky., 1838) that slaves who were to be liberated by will constituted "the most favored class of legatees" and that freedom could be withheld only when the testator's debts made its denial "inevitable." Two years later, the same court decided in *Snead v. David* (Ky., 1840) that creditors claiming an individual who had been manumitted possessed "no right to his person or services, but only to his value." The freedman could retain his liberty, the jurists explained, by paying the creditors his former market price. Kentucky's court was exceptionally liberal, but other tribunals sought just solutions, too. Although Maryland judges wavered on the issue, they amazingly ruled in *Thomas v. Wood* (Md., 1848) that manumitted persons were "not assets for the payment of debts." If creditors proved the estate to be in arrears, the justices vaguely promised that "proper relief would be accorded to them."[46]

One solution to the problem of indebtedness was to hire out slaves. The bondpersons' wages could be used to pay their former owners' bills and help fund their own conveyance to Africa. But was this kind of slave hiring permissible under the law? Did bondpersons under this arrangement come dangerously close to acting as free persons? The issue came before the Virginia court in one of the first and most important colonization cases, *Elder v. Elder* (Va., 1833). Herbert Elder willed his bondpersons the option of freedom in Liberia or enslavement in America. Elder's executor found the estate to be insolvent, and Elder's brother sued to break the will. Writing for the court, Judge Dabney Carr noted that the executor who encountered the debts "could not discharge

them without selling some of the negroes, or hiring them out. He very properly preferred the latter." Other states adopted the Virginia jurist's reasoning.
Across the South, justices ordered that slaves be hired out to finance their passage to Africa.[47]

Only Georgia's judges explicitly rejected this position, but the repudiation
came rather belatedly. In 1830, the court ruled in *Jordan v. Bradley* (Ga., 1830)
that if James Bradley's assets were insufficient to send his slaves to Liberia, the
bondpersons should be hired out. This precedent remained undisturbed for
over a quarter century. But in *Thornton v. Chisholm* (Ga., 1856), the Georgia
bench bewailed situations wherein slaves inched "nearer and nearer to the confines of freedom." The following year, in *Drane v. Beall* (Ga., 1857), Georgia's
judges decided that bondpersons laboring for emigration funds enjoyed an
illegal condition of quasi-slavery, remarking, "can it be denied, that . . . these
slaves are working for themselves?" The justices had laid bare the logical impli-
cations of this type of slave hiring, but their counterparts in other states continued to condone it.[48]

One of the canons of southern jurisprudence was that justice stood before
generosity. Jurists throughout the South recited this maxim, but many interpreted it creatively. The Georgia court notwithstanding, southern judges usually asserted that hiring out slaves satisfied the wishes of testators and bondpersons without injuring creditors. On this one issue, colonizationists usually
claimed victory, even as they suffered defeat on others.

The attitudes of southern legislators and judges toward manumissions
changed considerably over the years. During the early nineteenth century,
emancipation policy was largely designed to minimize the size of the free black
population, and by the early 1830s domestic liberations had been banned in
most parts of the South. Within this context, the ACS, when it went to court,
could expect favorable rulings on important issues. According to most jurists,
slaves could take freedom; they could also choose between slavery in America
and liberty in Liberia; and they could be hired out to pay for their transport
overseas. As time passed, though, antimanumission advocates began a successful campaign for more restrictive emancipation regulations. By the mid-1850s,
ACS supporters were openly fretting about their legal problems, as southern
legislators enacted tougher manumission codes and southern jurists reversed
themselves on issues like slave elections. By the end of the antebellum period,
the law was no longer on the colonizationists' side.

7

⸺ ᴏᴄᴏ ⸺

Liberia

Freedpersons' Experiences in Africa

When the ACS began transporting black Americans overseas, sixteen tribes occupied the region that would become Liberia. The Society made its first land acquisition in 1821, when U.S. naval officer Robert Stockton leveled a pistol at King Peter's head and thereby convinced the latter to sell some of his people's territory. Over the next few years, anxious natives witnessed the arrival of several hundred emigrants who founded settlements such as Monrovia, Caldwell, and Millsburg. Most of these pioneering "Americo-Liberians," as the colonists were known, were southern free blacks who emigrated with capital, connections, and entrepreneurial experience. By the mid-1830s, however, recent manumittees began to outnumber free blacks among the emigrant population. This trend continued throughout the antebellum period. Both groups suffered appalling mortality rates, thanks to African diseases, the hazards of settler life, and conflicts with native peoples. Those who survived sought to replicate American ways of life and to expand the colony's boundaries. By the middle of the nineteenth century, Liberian authorities claimed the rights to over 10,000 square miles of land. With the colony's population and territory growing, the settlers declared their national independence in 1847 and subsequently ratified the Liberian Constitution, a document modeled after the U.S. Constitution. For the rest of the nineteenth century, the African republic remained a three-tiered social order, with light-skinned, nepotistic free blacks dominating national affairs, a larger contingent of ex-slaves clinging to the middle rungs of society, and masses of marginalized natives searching for ways to stem the forces of disempowerment.[1]

Liberia was thus a place of both peril and prospects for freedpersons, and the ACS's fate rested heavily on their assessments of the country. In this sense, the colonization movement was a transatlantic phenomenon. Emancipators, ex-slaves, and ACS officials all understood that the events that transpired in Africa were just as important to the enterprise as those that occurred in America. Each party knew that the emigrants' reports shaped manumitters' thoughts about the program, informed black Americans' decisions concerning emigration, and provided both pro- and anticolonizationists with proof for their positions. Simply put, freedpersons' experiences in Liberia greatly affected the colonization movement in America.

During their first year in Liberia, freedpersons grappled with the consequences of familial emigration, the myriad emotions they felt upon disembarkation, dreadful mortality rates, and an insufficiency of American and ACS aid. Thereafter, they tried their hand at agricultural and commercial ventures but enjoyed little success. It was during these times that manumitted emigrants expressed their gravest concerns about Liberia. Even so, as individuals who had escaped slavery, freedpersons were not the type of people to despair in the face of adversity. Moreover, the difficulties they encountered were partially offset by the social, political, and cultural advantages that Liberia offered recently emancipated blacks. Indeed, as the years passed, the ex-slaves grew fonder of their adopted home. For longtime Liberians, high morality and economic deprivation steadily waned while opportunity and autonomy gradually increased. In short, freedpersons who survived a few years in Liberia usually ended up liking the country, and their sanguine attitudes proved a necessary (though hardly sufficient) cause for the continuation of ACS operations in the American South.

The First Year

Demography

The freedpersons who embarked for Africa were demographically similar to other American slaves. Although abolitionists insisted that ACS emancipators liberated only aged and infirm bondpersons, statistical evidence proves otherwise. Slaves' desire to emigrate with their families, when coupled with the in-adequacies of the emancipators' "training programs," meant that the bond-persons who went to Liberia were comparable to those who remained in America. Ordinary slaves, in other words, would face extraordinary circum-stances in Africa.[2]

ACS emancipators often claimed that their manumission programs readied bondpersons for the travails of colonization, but as far as vocations were con-cerned, emancipated emigrants were typical slaves. The vast majority of freed-persons were agricultural workers. Approximately 15 percent were artisans or semiskilled laborers. About 5 percent were domestics. Just a handful could be classified as professionals. These figures remained constant over time, a simi-litude that suggests that the manumitters of the 1820–40 era, who regarded colonization as a cautious emancipatory experiment, did not "prepare" their slaves any differently than the more broad-sweeping testamentary liberators of the 1841–60 period. When it came to occupations, manumitted emigrants were no more ready for life in Liberia than other slaves would have been.[3]

If freedpersons differed at all from their fellow bondpersons, it was in the area of education. This should not be surprising, since schooling was an essen-tial part of some slaveholders' manumission programs. Emancipators edu-cated slaves for many reasons. Among them was the expectation that the man-umittees, once in Liberia, would write back and provide information that would help their former owners assess the merits of emancipation and coloni-zation. As a result, between 1820 and 1840, 15 percent of liberated emigrants age sixteen or older could read or write, making their literacy rate three to five times higher than that of the general slave population. Not coincidentally, freed-person literacy rates declined to 9 percent during the 1840–60 period—an era when more indiscriminate testamentary manumissions became increasingly common.[4] As they sailed toward Liberia, freedpersons could not claim any vocational distinctiveness, but an unusual number of them would be able to write about their experiences in Africa.

Those experiences, more often than not, were going to involve their kin. The sex ratio and age distribution of the freedperson population demonstrate that the journey to Liberia was a family affair. Relatives provided ex-slaves with emotional and financial support, but there were also drawbacks to familial emigration. Most important, traveling with kin meant that there were many dependents among freedpersons. Forty percent of the manumitted emigrants were age twelve or younger. An additional 3.5 percent were sixty or older. All totaled, adults between the ages of twenty and fifty were a minority among the ex-slaves. ACS officials informed emigrants that they would have to be self-reliant in Liberia, but nearly half of the former slaves were either too young or too old to support themselves.[5]

Needless to say, adult freedpersons faced an enormous challenge once they reached Africa. Although they were an exceptionally literate group, most were ordinary farmers who were responsible for many dependents. Upon docking at Liberia, ex-slaves carried ashore the heavy burden of their own demography.

Freedpersons' Initial Attitudes toward Liberia

Freedpersons knew that Liberia was no Eden. Their preemigration intelligence had made it clear that they would encounter problems aplenty in Africa. The extent and resolvability of those problems were the real mysteries. Newly arrived emigrants breathed a sigh of relief upon landing in Liberia, for the country appeared to meet—and in some cases exceed—their expectations. But after this flush of enthusiasm came a chill of disappointment. Ex-slaves soon reported that they had greatly underestimated the country's shortcomings. The magnitude and complexity of those imperfections startled, depressed, frustrated, and occasionally inspired first-year freedpersons in Liberia.

Typically, emancipated emigrants would disembark and state that the settlements looked satisfactory. For example, Jacob Gibson arrived in Cape Palmas on 23 August 1833, and one week later notified two colonization officials, "I can say that I have realized all that I expected." Yet initial impressions were just the first step in the evaluation process. Most freedpersons wanted to investigate Liberia further. Their subsequent inquiries often revealed conditions that surpassed their direst fears.[6]

Jesse and Mars Lucas's attitudes toward Liberia exemplified this pattern of response. When these brothers arrived in Liberia with their respective families in January 1830, they initially indicated that their new home exceeded their expectations. Mars announced to his former owner that he was much pleased with the colony and would not have believed its splendor unless he had seen it for himself. Then the undertaking suddenly unraveled. Jesse's wife passed away; three of his children died shortly thereafter. The Lucases began reassessing their situation. The despairing siblings concluded that they had been misinformed about the colony. "The reports is all a lie, merely to encourage people to come to this country," complained Mars in June 1830.[7]

Many freedpersons were not content to waste away in such a dismal place. Hundreds quit Liberia. Not surprisingly, three-eighths of those departing left after less than twelve months in the colony. Those who remained often penned disconsolate letters to their acquaintances in America. Unfavorable first impressions of Liberia were so common that the ACS warned its members to be wary of missives sent by recent emigrants. "[D]uring this state of trial, many have wished themselves back in America, even in slavery," explained an article in the *African Repository.* "[B]ut invariably, as soon as they get entirely better, and able to act for themselves," the piece continued, "they are then ashamed of themselves, and will hardly acknowledge what they have said, or perhaps written, to their friends in the United States derogatory to their new country." The trauma associated with relocation and the "acclimating fever," insisted ACS officials, warped new colonists' perceptions of Liberia.[8]

One might expect that freedpersons' responses to Liberia would have changed over time. It would seem reasonable to suppose that, as the years passed and transatlantic communications regarding Liberia became more extensive and frequent, American slaves would have acquired better intelligence about the colony and thus would have been more knowledgeable about the conditions there. After all, by 1847, Liberia had been around for a quarter century. During those twenty-five years, dozens of ACS vessels had departed for Liberia; scores of blacks had returned to the United States with their assessments of the colony; and hundreds of emigrant letters had been received by American correspondents. It is somewhat surprising, then, that freedpersons' reactions to Liberia varied little over the years. Manumitted emigrants continued to go through the same sequence of initial satisfaction and subsequent disillusionment.

There were several reasons for this consistency. For starters, ex-slaves' attitudes toward Liberia tended to become more favorable the longer they lived there. By the 1840s and 1850s, Liberia's longtime residents, who usually liked the country, were more numerous than its new arrivals, who usually held contrary opinions. The detractors were simply outnumbered. They were outgunned as well. Liberia's most vocal advocates were often literate and skilled individuals, and as such they disseminated their views more widely and effectively than did its critics. Finally, the changing nature of ACS manumissions contributed to American bondpersons' misconceptions about Liberia. In the two decades before the Civil War, ACS manumissions were increasingly associated with the Lower South, rural districts, and testamentary decrees. The communication network among southern African-Americans was wide-ranging, but as far as Liberian news was concerned, Lower South ruralites who had been freed by will during the late antebellum era lived on the remotest informational tributaries. Simply put, many deliberating bondpersons had difficulty accessing intelligence about Liberia, and the reports that they did secure tended to reflect the views of the country's most enthusiastic partisans.

Thus the standard reaction to Liberia—wary optimism followed by alarmed disenchantment—persisted over time. The Ross freedpersons, for example, responded in this oft-replicated fashion. Emancipated by the wills of Capt. Isaac Ross and his daughter Margaret Reed, the Ross emigrants reached Liberia in March 1848. Just a few days after docking at Greenville, several settlers praised their new surroundings. In time, the same individuals became less enthused with Liberia. One member of the company, Sarah Woodson, accounted for the change in succinct fashion, stating simply, "I did not find the country as good as I hoped for or expected."[9]

Woodson then jotted down two addendums. First, she reported that, although Liberia had not lived up to her preembarkation expectations, she was starting to like the county. This was the case for many ex-slaves. Although the emphasis here has been on freedpersons' initial reactions to Liberia, the evaluation process was evolutionary and protracted. A final verdict, if it came at all, was years in the making.[10]

Woodson's second addendum concerned her health. She explained that her burgeoning affinity for Liberia was directly related to her physical well-being. "I am becoming quite satisfied," she stated, "especially since I have got my health as well as I have." As Woodson's comment suggests, avoiding sickness and death represented major triumphs for first-year freedpersons in Liberia.[11]

Immunity and Acclimatization

Liberia is located between four and eight degrees north latitude, in the region of Africa known as the Grain Coast. Lowland plains edge along the nation's seaboard, gentle hills undulate farther inland, plateaus sweep across the middle of the country, and mid-sized mountains rise above its eastern border. The entire area has a tropical climate, with rainfall sufficient to make the coastlands swampy and the interior thick with dense forests. This environment made Liberia home to diseases that freedpersons had never encountered. If the ex-slaves' imperfect access to information shaped their initial assessments of Liberia, their immunological defenses largely determined whether they would survive in their new country.

Almost all ACS emigrants were born in the United States. Having never set foot in West Africa, the settlers were susceptible to the region's diseases. Malaria, commonly called the "African fever," was especially deadly. There are four different species of malaria, and each has multiple strains. The most lethal species, *Plasmodium falciparum*, decimated the emigrant population in Liberia.[12]

In the nineteenth century, it was not known that mosquitoes were the vectors by which malaria spread. Rather, a "swamp theory" was usually offered as an explanation for the disease's propagation. According to this line of thought, heavy rains triggered the rapid growth of vegetation, which quickly died and decayed in stagnant ponds. Hot, humid tropical air then animated the principles of malaria, which wafted over human settlements on hazy, muggy mornings. New settlers were told to avoid the menacing miasmas, but the fever struck them down nonetheless.[13]

Freedpersons were especially hard hit. All other things being equal, exslaves' mortality rate was 15 percent higher than that of free black colonists. This differential stemmed from the fact that freedpersons had less access to medical care, inferior diets, and probably arrived in Liberia in worse physical condition than free blacks.[14]

One's first year in Liberia was the most precarious. An emigrant was four times more likely to die during that period than in subsequent years. Newcomers were felled by tuberculosis, pleurisy, anasarca, influenza, pneumonia, and other maladies, but malaria was the big killer. Some seasoned colonists opined that new arrivals' foolishness and carelessness hastened their demise. ACS officers adopted similar attitudes. "[S]ome die during their first few months of residence in Liberia," reported one colonization publication, "—not always in consequence of the violence of the fever, but frequently in consequence of not exercising the necessary precautions in the preservation of health." In effect, the ACS blamed the deceased for their own misfortune.[15]

White colonizationists nevertheless took steps to decrease the death rate among emigrants. For example, some emancipators sought to "season" would-be freedpersons by sending them to the Lower South or to Tidewater areas prior to their embarkation for Africa. ACS leaders also addressed the issue of emigrant mortality. Since they subscribed to the "swamp theory" of malaria, the officials assumed that Liberia's rainy season, which ran from May to October, was particularly insalubrious. They consequently tried to send vessels to Liberia between November and April, a period that was putatively more congenial to the new settlers' health. The ACS also attempted to establish upland communities. Colonization leaders theorized that interior settlements would be healthier than those located amid the coastal lowlands. From the ACS's perspective, the founding of inland towns would mean more robust colonists and further domination of the hinterland. This plan encountered two obstacles, however. First, colonization officials wanted to control as much of the seaboard as possible and accordingly acquired territory from Cape Mount to Cape Palmas, a distance of 350 miles, and founded cities such as Edina (1832), Bassa Cove (1834), and Greenville (1838). Second, the interior settlements proved no more salubrious for first-year emigrants than did the coastal ones. Colonists at Bexley, Caldwell, Millsburg, and other interior sites had the same mortality rates as did those along the shore. Although ACS leaders and long-time settlers boasted that they were winning the battle against malaria and other diseases, death continued to relentlessly stalk new emigrants.[16]

According to demographer Antonio McDaniel, Liberian colonists apparently suffered "the highest rate of mortality ever reliably recorded." Indeed, one astonished emigrant remarked that Liberian graveyards "always look[ed] fresh." For first-year freedpersons, illness and death were constant and unwelcome presences.[17]

The Limits of American and ACS Aid

The ACS promised to feed and shelter new emigrants for six months. After that, the colonists were on their own. "They will not have any friends there who will think and act and contrive and plan for them," Society leaders warned. "They must rely on themselves." Despite colonizationists' sanctimonious proclamations concerning self-reliance and hard work, many freedpersons complained that one simply could not establish a homestead in half a year's time. The ex-slaves were right. Once the ACS withdrew support, individuals who were still coping with disillusionment and sickness were further burdened by economic adversity.[18]

ACS officials evinced little sympathy for the struggling freedpersons. Considering how important emigrants' opinions were to the colonization movement, the organization's seeming indifference to the settlers' travails is remarkable. Nevertheless, Society agents remained unmoved, even when the provisions they provided were inadequate to the task at hand. In fact, Society leaders were known to reprimand desperate emigrants who sought to improve their lot. When one group of distraught settlers left Greenville for Monrovia in 1848, ACS officer William McLain reproved the whole party, dismissing them as "malcontents" who had forfeited any right to assistance:

> Those who went to Monrovia sent me a beautiful little piece of *personal abuse* which I trust they may live to become ashamed of. I entirely approve of the policy pursued by Mr. Murray of withholding their provi-

sions from them. If emigrants refuse to stay for six mos. after we place them, they must take the responsibility of their own support.[19]

Settlers who remained literally and figuratively "in their place" did not fare much better. When one of the Greenville residents, Joseph Corker, asked Mc-Lain for financial help, the Society's corresponding secretary answered with a polite but steely refusal. "I observed the list of goods that you desire me to send you," replied McLain. "I wish it was in my power to comply with your request," he continued, "But you are very much mistaken if you think *I am made out of money.*" Having denied Corker's request, McLain declared that he would be greatly disappointed if Corker failed to prosper in Liberia, a patronizing statement that no doubt exasperated the empty-handed emigrant.[20]

Henry B. Stewart, a freedman who had emigrated in 1849, commented extensively on the settlers' penury. Stewart noted that ACS provisions lasted three months, not six, and that that such shortfalls were a chronic problem. "[I]t has Bin the generl complant in most all the Emigrant privus [previous] to ous," he observed. ACS supplies were neither long-lasting nor lavish, he continued. Grown men were receiving just six pounds of food each week, and children were getting half that amount. "[A]nd from the Looks of things," he added, "it will have to be a greadill less."[21]

Besieged by destitution, illness, and familial obligations, some former bondpersons asked their previous owners for help. Such requests often went unheeded. Most ex-slaves did not obtain aid from overseas, and of those that did, the sums received were usually quite small.[22]

Many freedpersons were liberated by testamentary decree and consequently could not solicit assistance from their former masters and mistresses. Overall, 46 percent of the manumitted emigrants were freed by will, and this figure rose as time passed. By the 1850s, over half of the freedpersons arriving in Liberia had been emancipated upon their owners' demise. This fact alone suggests that most ex-slaves secured little, if any, relief from America.

Owners who were still alive might withhold aid from their former slaves. Some did so because they were financially unable to honor the freedpersons' requests. While few liberators went bankrupt sending their slaves to Africa, some simply lacked the resources to help when freedpersons asked for assistance.[23] Emancipators also had philosophical reasons for refusing ex-slaves' solicitations. Many insisted that only a strict adherence to self-reliance would prove blacks' fitness for freedom. "You are now your own masters," Albert Heaton explained to his former bondmen, "and it depends greatly on your own conduct whether you will do well and prosper . . . [or] whether you will abuse your liberty, do badly, and drag out your existence in want and misery." For individuals like Heaton, assisting freedpersons undermined the Liberian experiment in black self-governance.[24]

Even if their owners were still living, even if such persons were economically secure, and even if they were inclined to send aid, there was still no guarantee that the ex-slaves would receive provisions. Items could be lost in shipwrecks; they could be ruined in transport; or they could be stolen at any point in the journey. Some manumitted settlers speculated that the ACS itself was taking goods. When the former slaves of Capt. Isaac Ross failed to receive their promised inheritance, one member of the group, Horace Ross, pointed the finger at the ACS. "Somtime we thinks that Why we are treeted So [is] be couse we ware poore, mancipated & ignorent people," Ross wrote to a colonization official. "If so," he warned, "God will Judg beteen us & you who are members of that Society." From the ex-slaves' perspective, such remonstrations helped protect the aid that came their way. Ultimately, though, there was not much to defend, for testamentary manumissions, slaveholders' philosophical outlook and alleged indigence, and the difficulty shipping goods overseas all meant that freedpersons received scant assistance from America.[25]

Life was fairly bleak for many first-year freedpersons. The ex-slaves had arrived in Liberia, family in tow, with high hopes only to be waylaid by disappointment. Thereafter they grappled with malaria and other diseases. Then they faced economic uncertainty as aid from the ACS and America proved unsatisfactory. For some ex-slaves, the misery was overwhelming. As one young freedwoman remarked, "Sometimes I think I am thire [in Virginia] and when I awake I am here in Liberia & how that dos greave me."[26]

Agriculture and Commerce in Liberia

Agriculture in Liberia

ACS leaders expected emigrants to engage in agrarian pursuits. Colonists who raised crops for consumption, they promised, would enjoy contentment and autonomy. "[A]ny man in Liberia . . . who does not live comfortably and independently," they asserted, "may charge the deficiency to his own account." Yet farming was difficult in Liberia. Repeated setbacks in this realm, when combined with the lure of commerce, prompted many freedpersons to eschew agriculture. Moreover, emigrants who did work the land wanted to become planter-merchants, not self-sufficient yeomen.[27]

The ACS tried to abet agricultural production. On one hand, the organization dangled "positive incentives" before settlers. For example, Society officials gave new emigrants up to ten acres of land. On the other hand, the ACS also brandished "negative incentives," withholding rations and revoking the land titles of emigrants who failed to improve their holdings to the satisfaction of colonial authorities. ACS officers thus wielded both sticks and carrots in the hope of transforming Liberia into Africa's agricultural epicenter.

Many freedpersons wanted to oblige the organization—most had been field hands and were no strangers to the soil. Yet even settlers who were accustomed to such work had difficulty applying their talents in Liberia. There were many obstacles to farming there. Most obviously, individuals from the United States had little knowledge of the climate, land, crops, and pests of West Africa. Even after familiarizing themselves with the area, freedpersons had little hope for success. On the coast, the land was marshy and spotted with mangrove swamps. Farther inland, impassable undergrowth and imposing forests turned away dispirited colonists. "It is true we both drawd land," wrote one former bondperson, "but [we] was not ab[l]e to improve it and in consequence it went back to the publick again." Repossessed lots were often purchased by Liberia's free black elite, who owned the country's largest farms and who employed gangs of cheap African laborers to work them.[28]

Freedpersons who kept their holdings toiled without the aid of dray animals and proper tools.[29] Although horses, cattle, and oxen were occasionally brought into the country, such beasts of burden rarely survived. In a like manner, the flimsy hoes that the ACS provided had a short tenure in Liberia. Many manumitted colonists never acquired satisfactory equipment. Peter Ross, who emigrated aboard the *Nehemiah Rich* in 1848, urged prospective settlers to supply themselves with as many domestic, mechanical, and agricultural implements as possible. "[T]hey will need them," Ross wrote, "for they cannot be got here."[30] Ex-slaves thus had difficulty obtaining the basic instruments of agriculture, and securing the items necessary for large-scale enterprises was almost impossible for most freedpersons.

Many manumitted emigrants quit farming altogether. Between 1820 and 1843, almost 38 percent of the settlers who had been agricultural laborers in America abstained from such work in Liberia. A fair number became petty traders; even more ended up unskilled laborers. Some eschewed farming because it reminded them of slavery. Most left the land because it was unprofitable.[31]

For those who continued to till the earth, more difficulties arose. Part of the problem concerned what to grow, and here ecology conspired against the freedpersons' tastes. Born and raised in the South, ex-slaves longed for wheat flour, cornmeal, and other staples of their native land. Yet such items could not be produced in Liberia. Moreover, emigrants' affinity for American foodstuffs was matched by their aversion to indigenous produce. Many settlers complained that their diet consisted mostly of fruits and roots. Cassava was singled out for special scorn. Seaborn Evans, a freedperson who liked Liberia, opined that cassava was suitable only for farm animals' consumption. William Nesbit, one of the country's most severe critics, likewise described it as "a course, tough, clammy, tasteless root, which nothing but dire necessity would induce a man to eat." Ultimately, foodstuffs were not grown in abundance in Liberia. Cash crops took top priority.[32]

From the start, colonists tried to plant export commodities. Both sugarcane and tobacco were introduced in the mid-1820s. Tobacco failed utterly. Sugarcane showed more promise, but a lack of capital and concerns about intemperance inhibited its production. Later, settlers planted cotton, but it did not grow well along the coast, took years to turn a profit, and could not be sold in small quantities. During the last third of the nineteenth century, coffee finally emerged as Liberia's major export product. By then, however, the fate of most freedpersons had already been sealed. The ex-slave Titus Glover knew this all too well. "If they live at all," Glover said of his countrymen in 1869, "it under great restraint."[33]

Commerce in Liberia

At first, most ACS emigrants were southern free blacks. Financially secure and experienced in the world of entrepreneurship, these initial settlers quickly established themselves as the colony's merchant elite. Other emigrants were left with the "country trade," a local market where even the shrewdest peddlers realized only marginal profits. The free blacks then converted their economic influence into political power. They won every presidential election in the nineteenth century and controlled the Colonial Council as well. Not surprisingly, they enacted policies that favored traders, especially large ones, over African business people, foreign competitors, and even their fellow colonists.[34]

Among those other colonists were freedpersons who, unlike the early-emigrating free blacks, generally moved to Liberia in the 1840s and 1850s. Few of the new emigrants could compete with the entrenched ruling class. Many, in fact, believed that the Liberian elite were the source of their troubles. The freedpersons consequently accused them of myriad improprieties, from enslaving Africans to usury and thievery.

Even ex-slaves who emigrated at a relatively early date resented the elite's power. Peyton Skipwith arrived in Liberia in 1833 and spent the last fifteen years of his life struggling to support his family, always sensing that impoverished settlers faced unemployment because affluent colonists used African "apprentices" as slaves. Robert Leander Sterdivant emigrated in 1842 and quickly surmised that the wealthy acquired their fortunes through unscrupulous means. Items sent through Liberia's public store, Sterdivant informed an American correspondent, would never reach their intended recipient. Under such conditions, little wonder that Abraham Blackford, an ex-slave who moved to Liberia in 1844, merely wished to "do as well as those who . . . come to this country years before me."[35]

Things only got worse for freedpersons in the 1850s. Edward James Patterson emigrated in 1851, and despite years of unremitting labor, still lived in poverty. Patterson blamed creditors for his destitution. "As to undertake to make the money here you neve will Getit," he explained, "because when you . . . [work] Right hard, then you pay tuice before you can getit." Wilson Coalman came to Liberia in 1856 and, like others before him, suspected that aid from overseas was being pilfered by those in power. For latecomers like Patterson and Coalman—and most freedpersons were latecomers—achieving economic security, much less prosperity, was no easy feat.[36]

Most freedpersons arrived too late to unseat the Liberian elite, and they were too principled to deal in one of the country's most lucrative commodities: slaves. Although the Grain Coast never rivaled Sierra Leone and Senegambia (to the north) and the Gold Coast and the Bight of Benin (to the south) as a marketplace for slaves, the regional trade in bondpersons was prominent enough. Yet freedpersons would have nothing to do with the nefarious business. In fact, Liberia's Constitution prohibited residents from buying and selling slaves, and many freedpersons risked their lives attacking the baracoons that dotted the seaboard. "[W]e had to contend with the natives which fought us two days very hard," explained one former bondman after an 1839 raid, "but we got the victory."[37]

Constitutional proscriptions, military forays, and foreign naval patrols did little to slow the traffic in slaves in Liberia. The vicinity around Cape Mount alone exported fifteen thousand bondpersons each year between 1840 and 1850. Indeed, the *Regina Coeli* was anchored at Cape Mount in 1858, looking for more slaves, when those on board rebelled. "I sincerely hope that this may be the breaking up of this abominable slave traffic in human flesh," remarked the freedman William C. Burke after the event. Burke's wishes went unfulfilled.

Two years later, he witnessed the disembarkation of fifteen hundred "recaptured" Africans at Monrovia. "The horrors of the slave trade is more than I can find language to express," he sighed. If Burke could not describe the trade's ghastliness, it was not because he lacked opportunities for observing its terrors.[38]

Freedpersons, though, remained committed to "legitimate trade." In doing so, they forsook the valuable European and American merchandise that slaves fetched. From the settlers' perspective, foreign guns, alcohol, and cloths were a pittance compared to moral profits one reaped in shunning and even destroying the slave trade. As one freedman declared after a successful assault on a Spanish slaving operation, "It proved . . . that God is on our side & if he be for us who can be against us[?]"[39]

Economic development in Liberia quickly diverged from ACS leaders' original plan. If manumitted emigrants did not embrace agriculture as colonization officers had hoped, it was because conditions in Liberia offered little prospect for success in such fields. The former bondman John Page Jr. epitomized freedpersons' economic attitudes. Page owned a plot of land where he grew export commodities like coffee, ginger, arrowroot, and dried peppers. He also owned a store in Bassa Cove where he kept close track of commercial trends. Engaged in both agricultural and mercantile ventures, Page spent most of his time in the store and dropped by the farm "when I have no business to do."[40] Ultimately, Liberia failed to become the yeoman republic that ACS leaders had long envisioned.

Society and State

Though beleaguered by tribulations, ex-slaves were sanguine about their worldly affairs. Of course, cheerfulness was neither universal nor immutable. "Sum time I fild [feel] happy hear," explained one ex-slave, "and Sum time Cold and Dule and Sum time Cast Down in heart and mind." Nevertheless, many freedpersons predicted prosperity for themselves and their country. Perhaps their hopefulness should be expected. As Americans, former slaves knew the creed of inevitable progress. As freedpersons, they had the experience of manumission to justify optimism. Often disheartened during their first year in Liberia, most emancipated emigrants eventually embraced their new country.[41]

Some freedpersons vowed never to reside in the United States and ridiculed settlers who contemplated returning to America. According to the ex-slave

James W. Wilson, only blacks lacking moral fortitude would leave Liberia, "for Whare thire is a sine of a sole With in a man it Panc [pants] for fredom." The repatriation issue could engender personal conflicts, as in the case of John H. Faulcon, who flatly asserted that "he or She that hate Liberia don't like John H. Faulcon." Faulcon probably had his share of run-ins, for there were always some emigrants leaving Liberia. Even so, a large number of settlers shared Faulcon's sentiments and refused to quit their adopted land.[42]

Liberia's devotees boasted that their country was unsoiled by white supremacy. Abraham Blackford, a student of ACS physician J. W. Lugenbeel, juxtaposed the respect accorded to blacks in Liberia against epithets common in the United States. "I call him Dr. Luvenhal," he explained to his former owner, "and his . . . Repli [is] Mr. Blackford. It is much Bether than to be in the state [where the practice is] for them to call you Boy."[43]

Just as freedpersons cheered the absence of racism, they also trumpeted the freedoms that graced the pages of the Liberian Constitution. The former slaves enjoyed rights—free speech, trial by jury, bearing arms, among many others—that were routinely denied to black Americans. In a like fashion, Liberia's adult male citizens could sit on juries, hold office, serve in the military, and, if they owned real estate, vote. In comparing the political condition of United States blacks with that of Liberian freedpersons, one ex-slave remarked that the former slouched under the weight of oppression while the latter achieved "the full stature of men."[44]

Freedpersons were especially proud of Liberia as a land of religious liberty. Reflecting on their experiences in America, where whites had tried to interfere with blacks' religious practices, the Americo-Liberians reversed the relationship between churchgoers and the state. Not only did individuals have the right to worship freely, the government was responsible for protecting them. Indeed, the authors of the Constitution thought the matter of religious freedom so important they addressed it in the opening sections of that document's "Declaration of Rights," ahead of the provisions banning slavery, guaranteeing due process, and outlining suffrage.[45]

Indigenous peoples were not protected under the Liberian Constitution. Most emigrants recoiled at Africans' dress, manners, and beliefs, and saw little reason to afford them the blessing of citizenship. As the ex-slave Peyton Skipwith quipped, "[I]f we have any ancestors, they could not have been liked these hostile tribes in this part of africa." But the depth of the freedpersons' ethnocentrism reflected, in a way, their faith in human elevation. Although they excluded Africans from the body politic, former bondpersons maintained that, despite centuries of "savagery," natives could be brought within the pale of civilization and Christianity. Peyton Skipwith's own daughter, Diana Skipwith James, informed an illiterate African that God had endowed blacks and whites with the same abilities. By learning to read and write, she explained, Africans would escape superstition and barbarism. In the end, however, Americo-Liberians rarely attempted to integrate indigenous persons into their communities, and Africans usually resisted these periodic efforts.[46]

Emigrants who purportedly abused their freedom were accused of sullying the country's reputation. Idlers and idiots, claimed the nation's partisans, were fueling the myths about black baseness that other settlers were trying to extinguish. Just six months after obtaining his own liberty and passage to Liberia, Samson Ceasar lashed out against the slackers. According to Ceasar, white Americans should

> keep their slaves that they have raised as dum as horses at home and send those here who will be a help to improve the country ... as for virginia as far as my knowledg extends I think she has sent out the most stupid set of people in the place . . . they feal so free that they walk about from morning till evening without doing one stroke of work . . . by those means th[e]y becom to sufer ... people in the united states out [ought] to have more regard for Liberia than to send such people here.[47]

Yet most emancipated emigrants did not regard freedom as a plaything for their amusement. Rather, they deemed it a tool for building a better life—a life in which one could further their education, liberate their bonded kin, and, for some women, achieve a degree of independence.

Freedpersons arrived in Liberia with unusually high literacy rates, and education remained a central aspect of their lives thereafter. By 1843, there were sixteen schools in Liberia. Most of the attendees were youngsters, but adults also sought instruction and requested learning materials from their American correspondents. "I hop that you will send me some books," wrote one freedman to his former owner, "as you will see by this that I am trying to make some thin of myself." For freedpersons, liberty and education went hand-in-hand.[48]

Settlers also used their freedom to liberate their loved ones in the United States. Familial separations were excruciating, and ex-slaves averred that they suffered in ways that whites could not understand. Jacob Gibson spoke for many when he wrote to two colonization officials, "Neither of you, perhaps, know the pain which a father feels at being separated from his own offspring." Extant records do not indicate whether Gibson secured the liberation of his children. Some of his counterparts rescued their kin from bondage, though. How many emigrant tales ended with familial reunions is not known.[49]

If freedpersons of all sorts hoped to advance their education and emancipate their kin, female ex-slaves also sought individual empowerment. Several scholars have contended that Americo-Liberian women exalted Victorian values. Female emigrants' goals, according to this argument, were to teach natives "civilized" sensibilities, to ensure that settlers engaged in respectable activities, and to exude middle-class femininity themselves. Such attitudes were evident in Liberia, especially among the residents of Monrovia. But freedwomen's actions also suggest a different set of values, ones that stressed personal autonomy and financial security.[50]

Consider the case of Lucy and Mary Clay, two nineteen-year-olds who were emancipated by the will of Kentuckian Sidney B. Clay and who left for Liberia in 1851. Both women had children, but neither mentioned having husbands. Nor did they show any signs of wanting one. Although there were plenty of eligible men in Liberia; although the Clays were young, literate, and propertied; and although the two struggled in Liberia, Mary and Lucy never married. Equally interesting, both were happy in Africa. "Myself and Aunt [Mary] has been much afflicted since we have been here," wrote Lucy in 1853, "but notwithstanding I feel quite satisfied with the place, and like it very well. I have not as yet regretted that I left my native home, though I have often been unwelcomly circumstanced." The Clays' situation was unusual, of course—men normally accompanied women on the voyage to Africa. Yet women who emigrated with men could also find themselves single shortly after landing in Liberia.[51]

Widowhood was widespread in Liberia. Emigrants and ACS officials alike commented on the number of females who had lost their husbands. One former slave who asked the Society for aid justified his request by explaining that "We hav So meney old women and widows amoung us." The matter was so serious that the Liberian Constitution contained a section concerned exclusively with widows' rights. The question, then, is, why were widows so numerous in Liberia?[52]

Governmental policy did not dissuade widows from wedlock. Liberia's Constitution granted married women substantial property rights. Any possessions that a woman owned at the time of marriage, or any that she acquired thereafter, remained under her management and could not be seized for the payment of her husband's debts. Moreover, upon the demise of her spouse, a woman was entitled to one-third of his real and personal property, even if the estate was insolvent. From a strictly legal standpoint, matrimony did not impair a woman's control over her assets, and we must therefore seek other explanations for the prevalence of widowhood in Liberia.[53]

Demography was not at fault either. Although the sex ratio of the freedperson population was remarkably balanced, there were always more men than women in the country. There was no scarcity of marriageable men in Liberia, in other words. Nor does the high death rate explain the pervasiveness of widows. Mortality figures for men and women were nearly equal—Liberia was home to approximately the same number of widows and widowers. Why didn't they wed each other? The answer, it seems, is that some females simply chose not to remarry.[54]

Marriage was a dicey proposition for freedwomen. While wedlock might bring economic security, it might also result in economic hardship. With marriage usually came children—children who would financially burden a freedwoman should her husband die. Life was a fragile thing in Liberia; one could perish at any time. If a woman's husband were to pass away, she would be saddled with youngsters. Avoiding a second marriage, and thus additional offspring, could have represented a studied calculation on the part of freedwomen.

If some women decided to remain widows, others remarried under very specific conditions. Matilda Skipwith Lomax was twenty-seven years old when her husband drowned, leaving her with three small children. "[I]f I Ever in all my life needed Help," she wrote to her ex-owner, "it is now."[55] A washerwoman, Lomax relied on assiduity and charity to provide for her family. She did not remarry, though she liked to joke about matrimony with her former owner's daughter. Personally, Lomax regarded herself as a "poor widow" who took great pride in the progress of her children's education.[56] Finally, in 1854, Lomax, now age thirty-one, decided to give wedlock another whirl. Her choice was revealing. Lomax's second husband was James Richardson, a thirty-year-old freedman who had been in Liberia less than two years. Often described as a lazy, uneducated, ne'er-do-well, Richardson lacked the qualities that could make him a leading figure in Liberia. But he did not have any children either, a fact that probably made him an attractive partner to Lomax (and others like her). Indeed, when Richardson died six years later, in 1860, the couple had only one additional child. The following year, the twice-widowed freedwoman admitted that she had "seen a great deal of trouble," but, all in all, she was quite content.[57]

Liberia provided freedwomen with opportunities for autonomy and independence. The experiences of females who never wed, widows who forsook a second marriage, and individuals who remarried on their own terms all suggest that freedwomen may have seen colonization as a means of empowerment. Liberia hardly qualified as a paragon of gender equality, but its imperfections in this regard were no reflection on the women who tried to make it one.

If Liberia protected individual freedpersons from bigotry, religious persecution, and sexism, the country itself stood as a garrison against racism. According to its supporters, Liberia—an independent, Christian, prosperous member of the family of nations—was a bulwark against the forces of racial prejudice. "It is all idle talk and not true when it is Said that black people can not govern them selves," the ex-slave Seaborn Evans explained to his former owner, "and you would Say So if you could inspect liberia or visit this republic for a short time." As Evans's comments suggest, freedpersons were sure of their abilities, and they expected that whites everywhere would soon acknowledge them too.[58]

For most ex-slaves, the journey to freedom had been long and arduous. Yet the manumittees had completed the trek, and it would be remiss to forget how important that was to a people who had been enthralled in America for two hundred years and who, as individuals, had defied the odds in obtaining their liberty. Even destitute and forlorn settlers took solace in their freedom, and many wore it as a badge of pride while enduring what they called the "Hard Times."

Freedpersons knew all about Hard Times—they had been slaves, after all. They had vanquished this foe in America despite having had imperfect resources for battle, and they were undaunted by its reappearance in Liberia. Indeed, few freedpersons avoided its company altogether. Yet if Hard Times traveled widely, it stayed but briefly. As the years passed, one's prospects in farming or trading usually improved, as did one's chances for survival. Even when Hard Times hung around, refusing to leave, Respect, Opportunity, Education, and Autonomy came by as well. And Freedom was ever-present. When all was said and done, freedom bore bittersweet fruit in Liberia, but for most manumitted emigrants, it was sweet enough.

Conclusion

Colonization played a vital role in the Civil War. This was especially true during the first two years of the conflict, when African-American leaders harbored reservations about the future of race relations in the United States and President Lincoln repeatedly peddled emancipation and expatriation schemes to the loyal Border States. Ironically, the ACS faded to the background during this period. A privately funded organization that was wedded to Liberia, the Society neither could compete with government-sponsored emigration projects nor could diminish African-Americans' antipathy toward its program. During the Civil War, in other words, the colonization cause was largely in the hands of Congress and the president, who made it a central component of his geopolitical war strategy.

By the time of Lincoln's election, African-American interest in emigration was at an all-time high. Many black leaders eyed Haiti as a site for relocation, and several hundred black Americans moved there in the late 1850s and early 1860s. Africa also had its adherents, among them Henry Highland Garnet, who helped found the African Civilization Society and promoted settlement in Yoruba, and Alexander Crummell, who championed Liberia. By January 1861, even Frederick Douglass's opposition to emigration had waned. African-American abolitionist James McCune Smith, who still opposed all expatriation projects, was gravely concerned about the popularity of these schemes and implored Garnet to "shake yourself free of these migrating phantasms."

"We have lost Crummell, and we have lost Ward, and Frederick Douglass's eyes appear dazzled with . . . [Haiti]," Smith continued. "Do not, I beseech you, follow their example, and leave an earnest and devoted people without a leader."[1]

Lincoln gave African-Americans little reason to believe that their condition would improve. After the fall of Fort Sumter in April 1861, Lincoln had many constituencies on his mind, and black northerners were not among his foremost concerns. Instead, he thought about the disparate opinions of northern Democrats, Radical Republicans, Union soldiers, the British and the French, Border South whites, and southern secessionists. After sizing up these countervailing groups, Lincoln, along with General Winfield Scott, designed a war strategy that would broaden the president's appeal at home and abroad, while exacerbating divisions among southerners. The first military objective of their Anaconda Plan was to hem in the Confederacy by securing the Border South and establishing a blockade around the rebel states. Thereafter, a three-pronged attack would occur, with northern troops invading Virginia, a western army penetrating down the Mississippi River, and naval forces capturing New Orleans and then heading upriver. With the Confederacy divided in two, federal armies would head for the mountains of Tennessee to "liberate" that area's Unionists. This approach to war, predicted Lincoln, would prevent Border South whites from seceding, mobilize southern loyalists, and sap rebel morale. With the Union's prodding, the Confederacy would collapse upon itself.[2]

Along with rallying northern support for the war, retaining the Border South's allegiance was one of Lincoln's most critical goals. To appease the region's proslavery forces, Lincoln pledged to enforce the Fugitive Slave Law, rejected black Americans who signed up for military service, and promised that the conflict would not become a "remorseless revolutionary struggle." When some hard-core secessionists continued to preach disunion, Lincoln adopted harsher tactics, deploying military units, suspending the writ of habeas corpus, and incarcerating dissidents. In the end, Lincoln's use of positive and negative incentives kept the Border States in the Union. His triumph deprived the Confederacy of considerable resources, with manpower being among the most important. Some 200,000 white citizens of Delaware, Missouri, Kentucky, and Maryland fought for the Union—one-fifth the total number of soldiers mustered by the Confederacy. "To deprive" the enemy of the Border South, remarked Lincoln, "substantially ends the rebellion."[3]

Lincoln also sought to take advantage of slave restlessness without alarming his Border South and northern constituencies. The conflict was less than a month old when bondpersons fled into Fort Monroe in Virginia, leaving the Union general Benjamin Butler unsure as to what to do with the fugitives. Reluctant to send the bondpersons back to their owners, yet not authorized to liberate them, Butler decreed the runaways "contrabands of war" and put them to work. Lincoln approved of the general's decision, and Butler's contraband rule was incorporated into the Confiscation Act, which the president signed into law in August 1861. The contraband policy served several of the administration's needs at once, for it deprived secessionists of black workers, added to the Union's labor pool, mollified white northerners who feared that southern African-Americans would migrate northward, and assured Border South slaveholders that this was not a war for abolition.[4]

By December 1861, Lincoln was offering compensated emancipation and colonization to the Border States. If such a program were adopted, thought Lincoln, a slave-free Border South would have no reason to join the rebellion. Lincoln identified Delaware, with its mere two thousand bondpersons, for a pilot project. To the president's dismay, Delaware's legislators rebuffed his overture. Unshaken, Lincoln took his case to Congress. In March 1862, he urged lawmakers to set aside federal money for emancipation. Congress soon obliged, passing a joint resolution supporting the president's proposal and establishing a Select Committee on Emancipation and Colonization (which was staffed almost entirely by Border South men). The following month, federal legislators passed the District of Columbia Emancipation Act, a law that paid Washington slaveholders for their bondpersons and earmarked $100,000 for colonization. With compensated emancipation and black expatriation projects gaining momentum, in May 1862 Lincoln urged several Border State congressmen to take advantage of these programs, promising that their implementation "would come gently as the dews of heaven, not rending or wrecking anything." His audience ignored the proposition, much to Lincoln's displeasure.[5]

Disappointed but not defeated, Lincoln turned his thoughts to where freedpersons might be sent. As early as December 1861, he had urged Congress to recognize Haitian and Liberian independence and to establish official relations with the two republics. For years, southern congressmen had stonewalled such initiatives, declaring that black envoys must not be allowed to mingle among white dignitaries. Lincoln dismissed such notions, arguing that he could not discern a single "good reason" for withholding recognition from Haiti and Liberia. Lincoln contended that such a course might procure "important com-

1862

Recognize Haiti Liberia

mercial advantages" and increase black emigration. The three issues of black diplomats, economic interests, and future emigration dominated the subsequent congressional debates. In the end, the measure passed both houses, and Lincoln signed the bill into law on 5 June 1862.[6]

By the time Lincoln put his signature on the Haiti and Liberia bill, there was mounting pressure on the president to issue a broad-sweeping antislavery proclamation. Lincoln understood that political considerations, diplomatic concerns, and military needs might compel him to make a dramatic move, regardless of what Border South slaveholders and northern conservatives thought. Thus in early June, the president began drafting an emancipation proclamation. For weeks, he kept the matter mostly to himself, but the perspicacious might have detected that something was afoot. "What I *cannot* do, of course I *will* not do," wrote Lincoln, "but . . . I shall not surrender this game leaving any available card unplayed."[7]

1862 vs slavery

The tide of freedom rose quickly during the summer of 1862. In mid-June, Congress abolished slavery in the western territories. One month later, national lawmakers passed the Second Confiscation Act, which liberated the bondpersons of disloyal slaveholders, and the Militia Act, which authorized the employment of black people in "any military or naval service for which they may be found competent" and granted freedom to slaves so employed. Shortly thereafter, Lincoln told his cabinet that he intended to issue a proclamation that would free slaves in rebel-controlled areas. Still fearful that the emancipatory actions would alienate northerners and Border South slaveholders, Lincoln and his congressional allies pitched colonization proposals more fervently than ever.[8]

Black removal

Many of the antislavery measures of mid-1862 came accompanied with recommendations for black removal. In mid-July alone, Lincoln warned several Border South congressmen that the war had made all slave property insecure and that they would be wise to take compensated emancipation and colonization while it was on the table; the Select Committee on Emancipation and Colonization strongly urged the adoption of a black expatriation program; and Congress passed the Second Confiscation Act, which included $500,000 for colonization. With abolition's ascension, colonization became a vital feature of the administration's geopolitical war strategy. The prospect of deporting freedpersons, Lincoln hoped, would keep white northerners in the war and the Border South out of the Confederacy.[9]

The symbiotic rise of emancipation and colonization continued in late 1862. From August through December, Lincoln investigated numerous black

symbiotic rise of emancipation and colonization

emigration projects. In early August, after meeting Joseph Jenkins Roberts, the former president of Liberia, Lincoln reiterated his belief that an African venture would be financially difficult and unpopular with black Americans. On 14 August 1862, he informed a delegation of black men that African-Americans ought to emigrate. In September 1862, Lincoln issued the Preliminary Emancipation Proclamation, which included a meditation on black expatriation. He also pursued a colonization scheme in the Chiriqui region of New Granada. After that ill-fated enterprise, the president asked several European nations whether they would open their Latin American possessions to African-American settlers. Thereafter, Lincoln took an interest in Haitian emigration. In December 1862, the president devoted nearly two-fifths of his address to Congress to the subject of compensated emancipation and colonization. As Navy Secretary Gideon Welles noted, Lincoln's aggressiveness on abolition partly stemmed from the president's confidence in colonization. "I have sometimes doubted," wrote Welles, "whether he would not have hesitated longer in issuing the decree of emancipation had he been aware that colonization would not be accepted as an accompaniment."[10]

The Emancipation Proclamation of 1 January 1863 reflected the president's increasingly futile efforts to counterbalance bold measures with conciliatory gestures. On the one hand, the decree itself was more radical than Lincoln had originally envisioned. Unlike the preliminary proclamation (issued in September 1862), the January 1863 version did not mention colonization. Equally important, the final draft authorized the use of black soldiers, a decision that the African-American abolitionist H. Ford Douglas predicted would "educate Mr. Lincoln out of his idea of the deportation of the Negro." On the other hand, the president still hoped to appease his white critics in the North and Border South. Lincoln continued investigating black expatriation schemes, for example. On 31 December 1862, just hours before the Emancipation Proclamation went into effect, Lincoln signed a contract pledging federal money to transport 5,000 black Americans to Haiti. Moreover, the president sought to stave off his conservative detractors by defending the Emancipation Proclamation on military grounds, a justification that made his edict, in the opinion of the *Weekly Anglo-African,* "no more humanitarian than a hundred pounder rifled cannon." In addition, Lincoln's proclamation did not pertain to areas under Union control, including the Border South. Slaveholders there, wrote Lincoln, "can have their rights in the Union as of old."[11]

Lincoln was stretching the truth. Slavery was tottering in the Border South.

From the start, the region's bondpersons had taken advantage of wartime disruptions by running away and committing other acts of resistance. With Border South bondage reeling, antislavery crusaders went for the kill. In West Virginia, legislators enacted a gradual emancipation statute. In Maryland, an emancipationist movement blossomed. In Missouri, antislavery forces rallied against their proslavery foes. Whether freed by congressional act, military decree, presidential proclamation, state law, or their own actions, hundreds of thousands of slaves obtained liberty in 1863.[12]

Colonizationists hoped that the new freedpersons would leave America, but several developments suggested that their wishes would go unfulfilled. First, many observers conceded that blacks' battlefield sacrifices entitled African-Americans to citizenship. Second, northern reformers were moving to the Sea Islands of South Carolina, and their efforts to establish schools and homesteads for ex-slaves did not bespeak a zeitgeist that countenanced the deportation of black southerners. Third, Radical Republicans in Congress called for the establishment of a Freedman's Bureau that would assist former bondpersons. Fourth, African-Americans were being put to work on plantations in the Union-controlled areas of the Mississippi River valley, suggesting to observers that a mass exodus of freedpersons was not forthcoming. Finally, a federally funded expedition of black Americans to Haiti ended in disaster. By the end of 1863, black expatriation was at a standstill. In the span of one year, colonization had gone from a critical geopolitical force to a peripheral project.[13]

In 1864, Lincoln, black Americans, and Congress all drifted still farther from colonization. The president stopped pitching the program in public, and while some doubt remains as to his personal thoughts, his private secretary, John Hay, believed that Lincoln had "sloughed off" the notion of black removal the previous year. African-Americans in the North likewise recovered from the "emigration fever" of the early 1860s, and, as Secretary of the Interior J. P. Usher observed, freedpersons manifested "little disposition . . . to leave the land of their nativity." Congress, too, turned against colonization. Several bills that would have set aside western territory for black settlement were defeated in 1864, and in July of that year, Congress froze its previous allocations for colonization. In the end, only $38,000 of the $600,000 appropriation was spent, a discrepancy that was due to Border South obstinacy during the early stages of the war, black protests and ill-conceived emigration enterprises during its middle phases, and the ferment of freedom throughout the conflict.[14]

The advance of emancipation neared its apogee in January 1865, when the House debated a constitutional amendment to abolish slavery. The body had rejected the measure the previous June, and Lincoln knew that the upcoming vote would be close. He consequently summoned Congressman James A. Rollins of Missouri to the White House. The president was delighted to learn that his "Old Whig friend" was going to support the proposed amendment. Rollins cast a critical ballot; the measure passed by just two votes. The Lower South's planters' nightmare had become reality: Border South men were helping nail slavery's coffin shut.[15]

Slavery's demise did not change ACS leaders' ideological outlook one bit. Insisting that African-Americans were unfit for citizenship in the United States and that white people would inevitably crush black aspirations, Society officials eagerly anticipated a postwar upsurge in emigration. The organization was in a position to make good on its claims, for it had conserved its financial resources during the war and had continued receiving large bequests from departed members. When the war ended, the Society made arrangements for new settlements in Liberia, purchased the 1,000-ton *Golconda*, and blitzed black Americans with entreaties to emigrate. The abolition of slavery, proclaimed ACS spokespersons, was merely the "beginning of the negro question."[16]

Black Americans understood this all too well. During the immediate postwar years, most freedpersons, flushed with hope, spurned the ACS's offers. Even so, over two thousand African-Americans went to Liberia between 1866 and 1871. Black interest in expatriation grew thereafter as Democrats regained control of the South. Unfortunately for colonizationists, the postbellum upswing in emigration left the ACS virtually broke by the mid-1870s. As a result, even though applications for emigration continued to increase, the financially exhausted Society sent ever-dwindling numbers of black Americans to Africa during the 1880s and 1890s. The last person to depart under the ACS's aegis left in 1904. The Society finally admitted defeat, conceding, "it is now regarded as chimerical to attempt to send the entire mass of Negroes back to their native land."[17]

The ACS functioned as a Liberian aid society thereafter. The organization donated most of its records to the Library of Congress in 1913, with the remainder being deposited in the early 1960s. Around the time that the last of the Society's documents were being turned over, Martin Luther King Jr. gave his "I Have a Dream" speech in Washington. In envisioning a racially harmonious

America, King implicitly rejected the racial pessimism that had undergirded colonizationist thought for generations. With the ACS entombed at the Library of Congress, King's famous oration was, in a way, a eulogy for a movement that had profoundly shaped the debates on slavery, race, and freedom in America.

Tables

Table 1. ACS emigration, 1820–1860

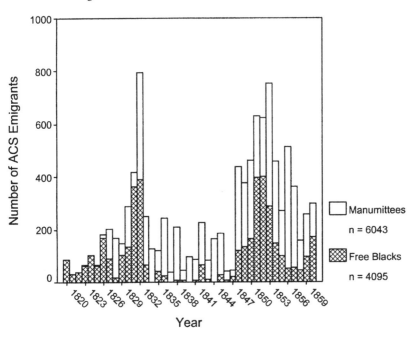

Source: ACS Database.

Note: This graph does not include information on "recaptured" Africans, "purchased" emigrants, and emigrants whose status is not known.

Table 2. ACS emigration by period, 1820–1860

	1820–1833	1834–1847	1848–1860	Total	Percentage
Africans	236	44	5	285	2.6
Free Blacks	1,710	218	2,167	4,095	37.4
Manumittees	1,124	1,483	3,436	6,043	55.2
Purchased	32	55	236	323	3.0
Unknown	58	91	44	193	1.8
Total	3,160	1,891	5,888	10,939	100.0

Source: ACS Database.

Table 3. ACS emancipators by state

	Number of emancipators	Percentage
Upper South		
D.C.	5	0.9
Kentucky	107	19.0
Maryland	43	7.7
Missouri	9	1.6
North Carolina	36	6.4
Tennessee	51	9.1
Virginia	186	33.1
Upper South Total	437	77.8
Lower South		
Alabama	9	1.6
Georgia	64	11.4
Louisiana	18	3.2
Mississippi	12	2.1
South Carolina	15	2.7
Texas	1	0.2
Lower South Total	119	21.2
Other		
Choctaw	1	0.2
Indiana	2	0.4
New Jersey	1	0.2
Ohio	1	0.2
Unknown	1	0.2
Other Total	6	1.1
Total	562	100.0

Source: ACS Database.

Note: The sum of percentages may not equal 100 due to rounding.

Table 4. ACS manumittees by state

	Number of manumittees	Percentage
Upper South		
D.C.	37	0.6
Kentucky	589	9.7
Maryland	243	4.0
Missouri	71	1.2
North Carolina	691	11.4
Tennessee	506	8.4
Virginia	2,214	36.6
Upper South Total	4,351	72.0
Lower South		
Alabama	44	0.7
Georgia	762	12.6
Louisiana	251	4.2
Mississippi	486	8.0
South Carolina	113	1.9
Texas	21	0.3
Lower South Total	1,677	27.8
Other		
Choctaw	1	0.0
Indiana	6	0.1
New Jersey	1	0.0
Ohio	6	0.1
Unknown	1	0.0
Other Total	15	0.2
Total	6,043	100.0

Source: ACS Database.

Note: The sum of percentages may not equal 100 due to rounding.

Table 5. Free black emigrants by state

	Number of free black emigrants	Percentage
Upper South		
D.C.	54	1.3
Delaware	3	0.1
Kentucky	88	2.1
Maryland	328	8.0
Missouri	11	0.3
North Carolina	621	15.2
Tennessee	122	3.0
Virginia	1,230	30.0
Upper South Total	2,457	60.0
Lower South		
Alabama	38	0.9
Florida	3	0.1
Georgia	278	6.8
Louisiana	23	0.6
Mississippi	18	0.4
South Carolina	349	8.5
Lower South Total	709	17.3
North/West		
California	1	0.0
Connecticut	49	1.2
Illinois	55	1.3
Indiana	58	1.4
Iowa	5	0.1
Massachusetts	57	1.4
Michigan	1	0.0
New York	269	6.6
New Jersey	36	0.9
Ohio	29	0.7
Pennsylvania	292	7.1
Rhode Island	41	1.0
Wisconsin	7	0.2
North/West Total	900	22.0
Other		
Antigua	1	0.0
Born at sea	6	0.1
Cherokee	1	0.0

	Number of free black emigrants	Percentage
Choctaw	3	0.1
England	2	0.0
Haiti	1	0.0
Unknown	15	0.4
Other Total	29	0.7
Total	4,095	100.0

Source: ACS Database.

Note: The sum of percentages may not equal 100 due to rounding.

Notes

Introduction: American Colonization Society Manumissions and Slavery

1. Sherwood, "Early Negro Deportation Projects," 508; Sherwood, "Formation of the American Colonization Society," 220, 225; Bancroft, "Colonization of American Negroes," 190; Fox, *American Colonization Society*; Staudenraus, *African Colonization Movement*, 113–14, 309. For scholars who continued to emphasize the ACS's antislavery aspects, see P. Campbell, *Maryland in Africa*, 242–43; Degler, *Other South*, 13–46; R. Miller, *"Dear Master"*; Wiley, ed., *Slaves No More*.

2. Litwack, *North of Slavery*, 28–29; Berwanger, *Frontier against Slavery*, 4–5; Voegeli, *Free But Not Equal*, 22–25; Foner, *Free Soil, Free Labor, Free Men*, 269–80; Fredrickson, *Black Image in the White Mind*, 1–34; Berlin, *Slaves without Masters*, 106, 168, 355–60; F. Miller, *Search for Black Nationality*; Sweet, *Black Images of America*, 23–124; Curry, *Free Black in Urban America*, 232–36.

3. Beyan, *American Colonization Society and the Creation of the Liberian State*; McDaniel, *Swing Low, Sweet Chariot*, 47; Moses, ed., *Liberian Dreams*, xvii; Sanneh, *Abolitionists Abroad*, 216, 217.

4. W. Freehling, *Road to Disunion* and *Reintegration of American History*, 138–57; Onuf, "Every Generation Is an 'Independent Nation'"; Egerton, *Rebels, Reformers, and Revolutionaries*, 107–20, 147–59. See also Tallant, *Evil Necessity*, 1–58; Dorsey, *Reforming Men and Women*, 136–94; Clegg, *Price of Liberty*; K. Barnes, *Journey of Hope*.

5. Statistics on ACS emigration come from ACS ship registers. I have used these documents to compile a database of the 10,939 African-Americans known to have moved to Liberia during the antebellum period (hereafter ACS Database). The ship

registers are located in four different sources: first, the ACS's *African Repository*; second, the organization's *Annual Reports* (1818–1910; repr., New York, 1969); third, the U.S. Congress' *Roll of Emigrants that have been sent to the colony of Liberia* (28th Cong., 2d sess., S. Doc. 150); and fourth, handwritten passenger lists in the Records of the American Colonization Society (hereafter RACS), microfilm edition, reel 314, Library of Congress (hereafter LOC). All of the figures on ACS emigrants in this book are drawn from the ACS Database. I would like to thank Antonio McDaniel for generously sharing his own Liberian database with me.

6. On manumission, see Patterson, *Slavery and Social Death*; Whitman, *Price of Freedom*; Nash and Soderlund, *Freedom by Degrees*; Schafer, *Becoming Free, Remaining Free*; Olwell, "Becoming Free"; Parish, "The Edges of Slavery in the Old South"; M. Campbell, "The Price of Freedom."

7. Martha Moderwell to W. McLain, 28 October 1854, reel 74, no. 149, RACS; *African Repository* (May 1860): 147; Mary King to William McLain, 10 March 1864, in Wiley, *Slaves No More*, 249.

8. Another ACS emancipator, Alfred Cuthbert Jr., also sent freedpersons to Liberia aboard the *Mary Caroline Stevens*, but unlike Moderwell, Cuthbert felt stigmatized for his colonizationist sympathies. A. Cuthbert Jr. to W. McLain, 10 July 1855, reel 75, no. 108, RACS; Gifford, "The Cuthbert Conspiracy."

Chapter 1. An Overview of the African Colonization Movement

1. Berlin, *Many Thousands Gone*, 369–70.

2. G. Nash, *Race and Revolution*, 3–23; Berlin, *Many Thousands Gone*, 217–357; Jordan, *White over Black*; D. Davis, *Problem of Slavery in the Age of Revolution*; Frey, *Water from the Rock*.

3. Melish, *Disowning Slavery*, 7–8; Zilversmit, *First Emancipation*, 109–230; McManus, *Black Bondage in the North*, 160–88.

4. Berlin, *Many Thousands Gone*, 233–34; Tise, *Proslavery*.

5. White southerners called for emancipation and expatriation even earlier. In 1691, for example, Virginia required new manumittees to depart the state. This law was repealed in 1782. South Carolina passed a removal statute in 1722. Sherwood, "Early Negro Deportation Projects," 494 (quotation), 495–500; Morgan, *American Slavery, American Freedom*, 337; Wood, *Black Majority*, 102–3; Zilversmit, *First Emancipation*, 16–19; Jordan, *White over Black*, 546 (quotation), 547; G. Nash, *Forging Freedom*, 101–6; Staudenraus, *African Colonization Movement*, 4–5.

6. In 1770, enslaved African-Americans made up just 4 percent of the northern population, compared to 37 percent in the Upper South and 58 percent in the Lower South. G. Nash, *Race and Revolution*, 115–16; G. Nash, *Forging Freedom*, 103; Berlin, *Generations of Captivity*, 272–74.

7. G. Nash, *Race and Revolution*, 59 (quotation).

8. Bruce, "National Identity and African-American Colonization"; G. Nash, *Race and Revolution*, 171–76; Thomas, *Rise to be a People*, 13–21, 72–81.

9. Jordan, *White over Black*, 547–54, G. Nash, *Race and Revolution*, 25–55; Melish, *Disowning Slavery*, 163–209.

10. Berlin, *Many Thousands Gone*, 223; Whitman, *Price of Freedom*, 8–32; Fields, *Slavery and Freedom on the Middle Ground*, 1–22.

11. Jefferson first outlined his emancipation and colonization ideas in 1779. *Notes* was originally published in French in 1784; an authorized English version appeared in 1787. Jefferson, *Notes on the State of Virginia*, xi–xxv, 143 (quotation); Onuf, "Every Generation Is an 'Independent Nation'"; McColley, *Slavery and Jeffersonian Virginia*, 129–30; Jordan, *White over Black*, 321, 546–47, 562–68.

12. Jefferson, *Notes on the State of Virginia*, 87, 137 (first quotation), 138 (second quotation), 143, 163 (final quotations). Jefferson never abandoned his hope that colonization could avert a race war. In 1824, the octogenarian was still peddling the idea. W. Freehling, *Road to Disunion*, 155–57.

13. Jordan, *White over Black*, 547, 552–53, 559 (quotation); Sherwood, "Early Negro Deportation Projects," 489; Alexander, *Colonization on the Western Coast of Africa*, 61–62; G. Nash, *Race and Revolution*, 146–58.

14. G. Nash, *Race and Revolution*, 42–47; Jordan, *White over Black*, 560 (quotation); McColley, *Slavery and Jeffersonian Virginia*, 135.

15. Alexander, *Colonization on the Western Coast of Africa*, 63–70. For a different interpretation of this episode, see Egerton, *Gabriel's Rebellion*, 147–62.

16. Jordan, *White over Black*, 563–65; Alexander, *Colonization on the Western Coast of Africa*, 71–72.

17. Jordan, *White over Black*, 574–77; Berlin, *Slaves without Masters*, 146.

18. Berlin, *Slaves without Masters*, 135–38.

19. Egerton, "'Its Origin Is Not a Little Curious,'" 478 (first quotation), 466 (second and third quotations).

20. Ibid., 469 (quotation), 470. On the contradiction between colonizationists' low estimation of blacks in America and their high expectations for them in Africa, see Fredrickson, *Black Image in the White Mind*, 1–42.

21. Egerton, "'Its Origin Is Not a Little Curious,'" 471–74; Staudenraus, *African Colonization Movement*, 27.

22. American Colonization Society (hereafter ACS), *Annual Reports* (1819): 7–9; Staudenraus, *African Colonization Movement*, 28 (quotation), 29–30.

23. Staudenraus, *African Colonization Movement*, 34, 50–56, 63–66.

24. W. Freehling, *Road to Disunion*, 144–61.

25. Ibid.

26. Staudenraus, *African Colonization Movement*, 68, 79, 84–126; Alexander, *Colonization on the Western Coast of Africa*, 276 (quotation); Clegg, *Price of Liberty*, 44–51.

27. Nearly half of this number went on the Society's first ship, the *Elizabeth*, which sailed from New York in 1820. ACS Database.

28. Ripley, *Black Abolitionist Papers*, 3:1–9; Walker, *David Walker's Appeal*, 64 (quotation); Quarles, *Black Abolitionists*, 6–7. On early African-American opposition to the ACS, see chapter 4.

29. Ripley, *Black Abolitionist Papers,* 3:6; Tyler-McGraw, "Richmond Free Blacks and African Colonization," 209, n. 2; Berlin, *Slaves without Masters,* 204–7.

30. Paxton, *Letters on Slavery,* 5 (first quotation); "Reminiscences of 'College Church' Hampden-Sidney," Eggleston Family Papers, section 30, box 54, Virginia Historical Society (hereafter VHS); ACS Database; G. Barnes, *Anti-Slavery Impulse,* 36 (second quotation).

31. ACS Database; Alexander, *Colonization on the Western Coast of Africa,* 289 (first quotation), 320 (second quotation), 328 (third quotation).

32. Egerton, "Averting a Crisis," 146 (quotation); Howe, *Political Culture of the American Whigs,* 136–37; Staudenraus, *African Colonization Movement,* 170–75.

33. Staudenraus, *African Colonization Movement,* 170–75; Rugemer, "The Southern Response to British Abolitionism," 226–27; Egerton, "Averting a Crisis," 156 (first quotation), 154 (second quotation); Egerton, *Charles Fenton Mercer and the Trial of National Conservatism,* 239 (third quotation).

34. Egerton, *Charles Fenton Mercer and the Trial of National Conservatism,* 239–40.

35. ACS Database; Staudenraus, *African Colonization Movement,* 180 (quotation).

36. W. Freehling, *Road to Disunion,* 178–96; Berlin, *Slaves without Masters,* 203–4; Degler, *Other South,* 79–80.

37. Dew is quoted in Faust, ed., *Ideology of Slavery,* 50. See also W. Freehling, *Road to Disunion,* 190–95.

38. W. Freehling, *Reintegration of American History,* 138–57.

39. Garrison, *Thoughts on African Colonization,* 4 (first quotation), 146 (second quotation); Ripley, *Black Abolitionist Papers,* 3:10.

40. Massachusetts Colonization Society, *American Colonization Society and the Colony at Liberia,* 11.

41. Fredrickson, *Black Image in the White Mind,* 12–21; William H. Starr to Robert Kent and Phillip Jones, 27 August 1851, Kent-Hunter Family Papers, University of Virginia (hereafter UVA).

42. Egerton, *Charles Fenton Mercer and the Trial of National Conservatism,* 242, 244 (quotation), 251; W. Freehling, *Road to Disunion,* 274.

43. W. Freehling, *Road to Disunion,* 275 (first quotation), 307 (second quotation).

44. Ibid., 326 (quotation), 347–48.

45. Staudenraus, *African Colonization Movement,* 208–9.

46. Ibid., 223–25 (quotation on p. 225).

47. Ibid., 232–39.

48. ACS Database; ACS, *Annual Report* (1847): 27–30.

49. Kornblith, "Rethinking the Coming of the Civil War," 84 (quotation).

50. Twenty-two percent of the emigrants for the 1834–47 period were Lower South manumittees.

51. During the 1820s and early 1830s, postmortem liberations were rarities in colonization circles. Seven percent of freedpersons during the 1820–33 period were freed by will. During the 1834–47 period, conversely, 55 percent of the freedpersons heading to Liberia received their liberty upon their owners' demise.

52. *African Repository* (July 1844): 221 (quotation).

53. Berlin, *Slaves without Masters,* 182–216; ACS, *Annual Report* 31 (1848).

54. ACS, *Annual Report* 30 (1847): 7; ACS Database; Ripley, *Black Abolitionist Papers,* 3:20–26, 222 (quotation).

55. Wiley, *Slaves No More,* 4–11; Shick, *Behold the Promised Land,* 19–87; Staudenraus, *African Colonization Movement,* 241.

56. Tallant, *Evil Necessity,* 115–32 (first quotation on p. 132); W. Freehling, *Road to Disunion,* 485 (second quotation), 494; Howe, *Political Culture of the American Whigs,* 133; Harrold, *Abolitionists and the South,* 130–31.

57. W. Freehling, *Road to Disunion,* 504–5.

58. Stowe, *Uncle Tom's Cabin,* 436–37; Litwack, *North of Slavery,* 254–55.

59. Staudenraus, *African Colonization Movement,* 245; Howe, *Political Culture of the American Whigs,* 136.

60. Berlin, *Slaves without Masters,* 351, 355–56; Harrold, *Subversives,* 116–73; W. Freehling, *Road to Disunion,* 511–15, 530 (quotation); Staudenraus, *African Colonization Movement,* 244; Rice, "Eli Thayer and the Friendly Invasion of Virginia," 575–96; McPherson, *Battle Cry of Freedom,* 93–95.

61. ACS Database; *African Repository* (August 1857): 242.

62. Berlin, *Slaves without Masters,* 343–80; ACS Database; Woodson, ed., *Mind of the Negro,* 85 (quotation).

63. Ripley, *Black Abolitionist Papers,* 3:40–57; ACS Database.

64. Clegg, *Price of Liberty,* 263.

65. W. Freehling, *Road to Disunion,* 538–65.

66. McPherson, *Battle Cry of Freedom,* 118–26; Howe, *Political Culture of the American Whigs,* 275–81, 289–92; Foner, *Free Soil, Free Labor, Free Men,* 193–99; W. Freehling, *Road to Disunion,* 560–65.

67. Foner, *Free Soil, Free Labor, Free Men,* 267–80.

68. Faust, *Ideology of Slavery,* 10–20; Berlin, *Slaves without Masters,* 350–51; W. Freehling, *Reintegration of American History,* 204–10.

69. D. Brown, "Attacking Slavery from Within," 541–76; W. Freehling, *Reintegration of American History,* 209; Staudenraus, *African Colonization Movement,* 243, 246, 251.

70. Johannsen, *Lincoln-Douglas Debates,* 51 (quotation); Foner, *Free Soil, Free Labor, Free Men,* 277–79.

Chapter 2. ACS Manumitters: Their Ideology and Intentions

1. Opper, "The Mind of the White Participant," 281 (first quotation); Caspar Morris, *Memoir of Miss Margaret Mercer,* 45–48 (second, third, and fourth quotations on p. 45; fifth and sixth quotations on p. 47). For Morris's own dabbling in slave liberations, see Anne Arundel County Court Records, Manumissions, 1844 folder, Maryland Hall of Records.

2. Cocke, "Plan for Gradual Emancipation," box 184, John Hartwell Cocke Papers (hereafter JHC Papers), UVA.

3. Statistics on the Liberian emigrant population come from the ACS Database.

4. Harrold, *Subversives,* 36–37. Margaret Mercer to Martha Fenton Hunter, 28 April n.d., 8 January n.d., and 12 November 1835, folder 14, box 22, Hunter Family Papers, VHS; William Meade to Mary Lee Custis, 30 May 1825, and Ann R. Page to Mary Lee Custis, n.d., both in Mary Lee (Fitzhugh) Custis Papers, VHS; Charles W. Andrews to John Hartwell Cocke, 24 November 1837, box 89, JHC Papers, UVA.

5. ACS manumitters' residences are drawn from the ACS Database.

6. Clegg, *Price of Liberty,* 7–17, 44–76.

7. Oakes, *Ruling Race*; J. Miller, *Wolf by the Ears*; McCoy, *Last of the Fathers,* 253–322.

8. Snay, *Gospel of Disunion*; Matthews, *Religion in the Old South*; Genovese and Fox-Genovese, "The Divine Sanction of Social Order"; Loveland, *Southern Evangelicals and the Social Order*; Genovese, *"Slavery Ordained by God"*; Maddex Jr., "'The Southern Apostasy' Revisited." On the subject of guilt and slavery, see Foster, "Guilt over Slavery."

9. Mercer, *Popular Lecture on Ethics,* 210 (both quotations).

10. Andrews, *Memoir of Mrs. Ann R. Page,* 45; Wiley, *Slaves No More,* 100.

11. W. Johnson, *Soul by Soul,* 19–44.

12. Cocke, "Plan for Gradual Emancipation," box 184, JHC Papers, UVA; Blackford, *Mine Eyes Have Seen the Glory,* 53; Edwards, ed., *Some Interesting Papers of John McDonogh,* 101–2.

13. Wright, *African Americans in the Early Republic,* 85–124.

14. Edwards, *Some Interesting Papers of John McDonogh,* 67 (first quotation) Nathaniel Hooe to William A. Harrison, 8 November 1832, 8 June 1835 (second quotation), 17 January 1836, and 28 February 1836, all in Nathaniel Harris Hooe Papers, UVA; John Hartwell Cocke, "Plan for Gradual Emancipation," box 184, JHC Papers, UVA (third quotation). See also William George Read to James A. Pearce, 13 April 1844, box 1, Pearce Papers, Maryland Historical Society (hereafter MHS).

15. Opper, "The Mind of the White Participant," 270, 280; Mary Lee Custis to Mary Ann Randolph (Custis) Lee, 8 October 1831, Mary Lee (Fitzhugh) Custis Papers, VHS; Margaret Mercer to Martha Fenton Hunter, 12 November 1835, folder 14, box 22, Hunter Family Papers, VHS.

16. Fredrickson, *Black Image in the White Mind,* 1–42; Albert Heaton to Jesse and Mars Lucas, 29 April 1830 (quotation), Lucas-Heaton Letters, UVA.

17. Paxton, *Letters on Slavery,* 4.

18. Andrews, *Memoir of Mrs. Ann R. Page,* 27; Gimelli, "Louisa Maxwell Cocke," 53–71; Edwards, *Some Interesting Papers of John McDonogh,* 50.

19. Cornelius, *When I Can Read My Title Clear*; Webber, *Deep Like the Rivers.*

20. Edwards, *Some Interesting Papers of John McDonogh,* 51.

21. Nancy Smith McDonogh to John McDonogh, in Wiley, *Slaves No More,* 137.

22. Whitman, *Price of Freedom,* 61–92; Jane C. Washington to "Dear Sir," 7 October 1848, reel 57, no. 16, RACS.

23. Berlin, *Slaves without Masters,* 31; Jackson, "Manumission in Certain Virginia Cities," 310. See also Patterson, *Slavery and Social Death,* 264.

24. *African Repository* (February 1851): 49.

25. Fogel and Engerman, "Philanthropy at Bargain Prices."

26. Cocke quoted in R. Miller, *"Dear Master,"* 150.

27. Edwards, *Some Interesting Papers of John McDonogh,* 48–50.

28. Ann R. Page to Mary Lee Custis, n.d., Mary Lee (Fitzhugh) Custis Papers, VHS (quotation); Elliot Cresson to James Jones, 2 October 1835, Watson Family Papers, Virginia State Library (hereafter VSL).

29. Page quoted in Lee, "Life Is a Sacred Trust," 157–58; Patterson, *Slavery and Social Death,* 240–47.

30. Harrold, *Subversives,* 56; Bogger, *Free Blacks in Norfolk,* 32–51; Berlin, *Slaves without Masters,* 204–7; Thomas Kennedy to William McLain, 28 November 1851, reel 66 B, no. 259, RACS.

31. Klebaner, "American Manumission Laws and the Responsibility for Supporting Slaves"; Berlin, *Slaves without Masters,* 138–39.

32. The foregoing statistics, along with the subsequent figures concerning the manumitters' slaveholdings, occupations, places of birth, and similar data, are drawn from the 1850 free and slave census schedules.

33. Philip Slaughter, *Virginia History of African Colonization,* xiii.

34. Maryland, with its independently operated state colonization society, registered just a handful (3 percent) of such liberations.

35. Gifford, "The African Colonization Movement in Georgia," 1–30.

36. Schwarz, *Migrants against Slavery,* 3–17.

37. Isaac Disheroon to "Dear Sir," 7 February 1852, reel 66 B, no. 185, RACS; A. E. Blunt to W. McLain, 17 February 1852, reel 67, no. 225, RACS.

38. This is not to imply that the manumitters' endeavors were without pecuniary impact: there were enough attempts to block proposed manumissions to demonstrate the falsity of that notion.

39. Anne S. Rice to Unknown, 8 March 1848, reel 55, no. 286, RACS; Anne S. Rice to Unknown, 23 August 1848, reel 56, no. 210, RACS (both quotations).

40. Elizabeth Holderness to W. McLain, 20 March 1855, reel 75, no. 564 1/2, RACS (both quotations).

41. Elizabeth Holderness to W. McLain, 20 March 1855, reel 75, no. 564 1/2, RACS (both quotations).

42. Oakes, *Ruling Race,* 50, 247–50.

43. McMillen, *Southern Women,* 10; Clinton, *Plantation Mistress,* 87–109; Weiner, *Mistresses and Slaves,* 53–71.

44. Fox-Genovese, *Within the Plantation Household,* 34–35, 114–29.

45. Clinton, *Plantation Mistress,* 162.

46. Blackford, *Mine Eyes Have Seen the Glory,* 42.

47. Margaret Mercer to Martha Fenton Hunter, 28 April n.d., folder 14, box 22, Hunter Family Papers, VHS.

48. Approximately half of the women who orchestrated ACS manumissions during

the 1850s were identified by census enumerators as the head of household, a designa-
tion that probably indicated widowhood.

49. K. Wood, "Broken Reeds and Competent Farmers."

50. See, for example, Will of Gray Jenkins Vick, 29 October 1848, box 1, folder 3, Vick-
Phelps Papers, Mississippi Department of Archives and History, and Will of Thomas D.
Bennehan, 28 April 1845, folder 2178A, Series 2.7, Cameron Family Papers, University of
North Carolina at Chapel Hill (hereafter UNC-CH).

51. Catterall, ed., *Judicial Cases*, 2:516 (first two quotations), 3:292 (third and fourth
quotations), 2:392 (fifth quotation).

52. Patterson, *Slavery and Social Death*, 224; Will of James Crawford, 27 June 1850,
reel 313, RACS.

53. See, for example, Will of Jane C. Washington, 17 September 1855, Washington
Family Papers, VSL.

54. *Banks v. Banks* (Tenn., 1865), in Catterall, *Judicial Cases*, 2:581 (quotation); *Newlin v. Freeman* (N.C., 1841), in Catterall, *Judicial Cases*, 2:93; *Thompson v. Newlin* (N.C.,
1851), in Catterall, *Judicial Cases*, 2:163.

55. *Poindexter v. Poindexter* 1858 WL 3940 *2 (Va.).

Chapter 3. Slaves: Negotiating for Freedom

1. Elijah McLean to W. McLain, 25 August 1855, reel 77, no. 254, RACS. See also R. E.
Troy to William McLain, 19 March 1852, reel 67, no. 390, RACS.

2. Tadman, *Speculators and Slaves*, 3–83, 133–78; W. Johnson, *Soul by Soul*, 19–45;
Gutman, *Black Family in Slavery and Freedom*, 318.

3. W. Johnson, "On Agency."

4. Whitman, *Price of Freedom*, 93–118; Parish, "The Edges of Slavery in the Old South,"
106–25.

5. Takagi, *Rearing Wolves to Our Own Destruction*; Wade, *Slavery in the Cities*.

6. Christopher Morris, "The Articulation of Two Worlds," 982–1007. Considering
the secrecy with which slaves guarded their ability to read and write, manumittees'
literacy rates may have been higher still. As ACS emancipator John McDonogh remarked: "It is not to be expected that masters can be in the houses of their slaves,
watching them day and night, to keep them from learning to read:—Finding therefore,
that was the case, I placed the Holy Gospel in the hands of each, as the richest gift I
could bestow on them" (Hoyt, "John McDonogh and Maryland Colonization in Liberia," 447). See also Cornelius, *When I Can Read My Title Clear*, 122–24, and Webber,
Deep Like the Rivers, 131–38.

7. Nancy Smith McDonogh to John McDonogh, 31 May 1844, in Wiley, *Slaves No
More*, 137.

8. Blackford, *Mine Eyes Have Seen the Glory*, 20, 45, 31; Margaret Mercer to Martha
Fenton Hunter, 28 April n.d., box 22, folder 14, Hunter Family Papers, VHS; Will of
Edward Brett Randolph, 9 May 1848, Randolph-Sherman Papers, Mississippi State Uni-

versity; *Elder v. Elder* 1833 WL 2083 (Va.); Gifford, "Emily Tubman and the African Colonization Movement in Georgia"; Mitchell and Mitchell, "The Philanthropic Bequests of John Rex of Raleigh."

9. P. Campbell, *Maryland in Africa,* 104–6; William McKenny to Charles Howard, 28 May 1835, 29 April 1835, 1 June 1835, all in reel 27, Maryland State Colonization Papers, University of Southern Mississippi.

10. Margaret Mercer to Martha Fenton Hunter, 28 April n.d., folder 14, box 22, Hunter Family Papers, VHS; Wiley, *Slaves No More,* 118; John Hartwell Cocke Journal (1863–64), box 170, JHC Papers, UVA.

11. Will of Robert Lusk (1850), reel 314, RACS; "Rosswood," Rosswood (Lorman) Folder, Isaac Ross Papers, Mississippi State University; Huffman, *Mississippi in Africa,* 77–82.

12. Chris Mann to R. R. Gurley, 7 January 1848, reel 54, no. 29, RACS; G. A. Early to W. McLain, 31 January 1855, reel 74, no. 191, RACS; Wiley, *Slaves No More,* 336.

13. *African Repository* (July 1847): 218–19.

14. *Fisher's Negroes v. Dabbs* 1834 WL 996 *6 (Tenn. Err. & App.); *African Repository* (January 1837): 5. See also William McLain to John M. McCalla, 26 March 1841, John Moore McCalla Papers, VHS, and James Goodwin to John R. Kilby, 2 March 1852, folder 1853–April 1854, box 3, John Richard Kilby Papers, Duke University (hereafter DU).

15. R. A. Worrell to "Dear Sir," 15 December 1847, reel 54, no. 277, RACS; R. A. Worrell to James Hall, 31 January 1848, reel 54, no. 156, RACS.

16. Stuckey, *Slave Culture,* 3–98; Fogel and Engerman, *Time on the Cross,* 25; Holsoe, "A Study of Relations between Settlers and Indigenous Peoples in Western Liberia."

17. Andrews, *Memoir of Mrs. Ann R. Page,* 53, 58; R. Miller, *"Dear Master,"* 35; Edwards, *Some Interesting Papers of John McDonogh,* 49–50; *Niles' Weekly Register* 49, no. 1 (21 November 1835): 195.

18. One version of Henderson's report is printed in McDaniel, *Swing Low, Sweet Chariot,* 153–57.

19. R. R. Gurley to M. B. Blackford, 19 May 1830, folder 2, Blackford Family Papers, UNC-CH; R. R. Gurley to Robert Hairston, 6 October 1832, folder 126, box 14, Wilson and Hairston Family Papers, UNC-CH.

20. R. R. Gurley to Mary Blackford, 18 August 1838, folder 5, Blackford Family Papers, UNC-CH; Wilkeson, *To the Emigrants Now Preparing to Embark for Liberia* (27 January 1840), reel 319, RACS.

21. Titus Shropshere to William McLain, 21 May 1848, reel 55, no. 193, RACS; Eve and Samuel Gideon to "Dear Sir," 30 March 1855, reel 75, no. 641, RACS. See also James R. Starks to "Rev and Dear Sir," 21 November 1848, reel 57, no. 188, RACS; William James Henry to "Dear Sir," 6 September 1855, reel 77, no. 399 1/2, RACS; and John Rapier to William McLain, 5 March 1855, reel 75, no. 365, RACS.

22. Walker, *David Walker's Appeal,* xiv-xv.

23. P. Campbell, *Maryland in Africa,* 28, 40; Garrison, *Thoughts on African Coloniza-*

tion, pt. 2, 22–23; Tyler-McGraw, "Richmond Free Blacks and African Colonization," 207–24; William H. Bayne to "Dear Sir," 25 November 1848, reel 57, no. 204, RACS (quotation); Samuel Lewis to William McLain, 15 November 1848, reel 57, no. 162, RACS; Ralph R. Gurley to Benjamin Brand, 21 September 1833, section 7, Benjamin Brand Papers, VHS.

24. P. Campbell, *Maryland in Africa,* 177–78.

25. Pease and Pease, eds., *Antislavery Argument,* 31 (quotation).

26. This figure excludes the 2,195 emigrants who died in Liberia between 1820 and 1843. Of the remaining 2,362 colonists, 528, or 22 percent, departed the colony. These statistics, as well as all subsequent ones, come from the ACS Database.

27. John M Page Sr. to Charles W. Andrews, n.d., in Wiley, *Slaves No More,* 103–4. See also *Examination of Mr. Thomas C. Brown,* 9.

28. ACS Database; Clegg, *Price of Liberty,* 74.

29. Tyler-McGraw, "Richmond Free Blacks and African Colonization," 220; Saillant, "Circular Addressed to the Colored Brethren and Friends in America," 494 (first quotation), 495 (second quotation) .

30. Tyler-McGraw, "Richmond Free Blacks and African Colonization," 221; ACS official quoted in Sallient, "Circular Addressed to the Colored Brethren and Friends in America," 485.

31. *Examination of Mr. Thomas C. Brown,* 7 (first quotation), 8 (second quotation), 9 (third quotation). For a similar tale involving another highly touted colonist, see Gatewood, "'To be truly free,'" 342–44.

32. P. Campbell, *Maryland in Africa,* 44–45.

33. Ibid., 48, 110–11; A. E. Thome to "My Dear Sir," 20 November 1848, reel 57, no. 183, RACS; Samuel Casseday to William McLain, 5 December 1848, reel 57, no. 237, RACS; John Eakin to William McLain, 29 July 1848, reel 56, no. 122, RACS.

34. *Colonization Herald,* November 1853, p. 161.

35. John Calloway to William McLain, 2 June 1855, reel 76, no. 414, RACS.

36. William Kennedy to William McLain, 29 November 1854, reel 74, no. 307, RACS (quotations). See also Montgomery D. Parker to "My Dear Father," 31 July 1846, folder 1846–1891, section A, Montgomery D. Parker Papers, DU, and James H. Minor to James Mansfield Holladay, 28 April 1857, Holladay Family Papers, UVA.

37. Martha Custis Williams to W. McLain, 9 November 1854, reel 74, no. 225, RACS.

38. Samuel Casseday to William McLain, 11 February 1848, reel 54, no. 191, RACS; *Colonization Herald,* November 1853, p. 161.

39. John H. Bruner to W. McLain, 5 September 1855, reel 77, no. 294, RACS; R. W. Bailey to William McLain, 23 September 1848, reel 56, no. 319, RACS.

40. William H. Ruffner to "My Dear Sir," 20 May 1848, reel 56, no. 5, RACS.

41. James Patterson to William W. Rice, 29 September 1851, in Wiley, *Slaves No More,* 179–80; Titus Glover to William W. Rice, 19 January 1856, in Wiley, *Slaves No More,* 181.

42. James W. Wilson to William McLain, 5 August 1858, in Wiley, *Slaves No More,* 245. See also James W. Wilson to William McLain, 29 February 1859, in Wiley, *Slaves No More,* 246.

43. *African Repository* (July 1854): 207–8; "Applications for Emigration to Liberia," reel 314, RACS, (first two quotations); R. Arnold to W. McLain, 7 December 1848, reel 57, no. 250, RACS (third quotation); Varon, *We Mean to Be Counted*, 62. See also N. S. Jarrett to J. McKee, 4 March 1852, folder 21, series 2, John McKee Sharpe Papers, UNC-CH.

44. John L. Andrews to "Dear Sir," 7 November 1854, reel 74, no. 213, RACS; "List of Emigrants by the Barque *Baltimore*," reel 314, RACS; "Emigrants by the *Linda Stewart*," reel 314, RACS; "Emigrants by the *Liberia Packet*" [tenth voyage], reel 314, RACS.

45. Thomas Benning to "Rev. & Dear Sir," 10 June 1848, reel 55, no. 250, RACS.

46. "Purchased emigrants" refers to bondpersons whose freedom was bought, either by themselves or by someone else.

47. J. Packard to William McLain, 11 August 1848, reel 56, no. 163, RACS (first two quotations); Francis H. Cone to "Dear Sir," 13 January 1855, reel 74, no. 76, RACS (third, fourth, and fifth quotations).

48. By "at the same time," I refer to slaveholders whose bondpersons sailed to Liberia on the same ship.

49. Previous paragraph, Berlin, *Slaves without Masters*, 141 (quotation). This paragraph, M. L. Anderson to Dr. Lugenbeel, 23 November 1851, reel 66B, RACS (quotation); M. L. Anderson to William Starr, 25 November 1851, reel 66B, no. 240, RACS.

50. Joseph Bryan to G.W.S. Hall, 5 December 1851, reel 66B, no. 301, RACS.

51. C. Hines, C. C. Jones, and Edward Harden to Unknown, 20 November 1854, reel 74, no. 270, RACS; C. C. Jones to William McLain, 28 December 1854, reel 74, no. 461, RACS; Thomas Mallard to C. Hines, 28 December 1854, reel 74, no. 465, RACS (first quotation); William McLain to J. W. Lugenbeel, 30 December 1854, reel 74, no. 476, RACS (second quotation). See also John H. B. Latrobe to Moses Sheppard, n.d. 1854, in Latrobe-Sheppard Papers, MHS and Will of Lucy A. Coleman, 24 July 1834, McLaughlin-Reed Papers, UVA.

52. Garland Lilly to William McLain, 22 March 1852, reel 67, no. 401, RACS.

53. Alexander Hance to William McKenny, 19 March 1835, in Wiley, *Slaves No More*, 217.

Chapter 4. The Pennsylvania Colonization Society as a Facilitator of Manumission

1. Thomas C. Benning to "Rev. & Dear Sir," 15 January 1848, reel 54, no. 74, RACS.

2. Will of Lucy Peobles, reel 313, RACS (first quotation); William E. Kennedy to William McLain, 20 October 1854, reel 74, no. 92, RACS (second quotation); *African Repository* (May 1856): 132 (third quotation). See also Wilkeson to John Moore McCalla, 3 March 1841, John Moore McCalla Papers, VHS; William McLain to John H. Cocke, 12 August 1854, box 146, JHC Papers, UVA; J. J. Flournoy to W. McLain, 12 May 1848, reel 55, RACS; William Ruffner to "Dear Sir," 14 September 1848, reel 56, no. 281, RACS; R. W. Bailey to William McLain, 9 December 1851, reel 66B, no. 315, RACS.

3. Ralph R. Gurley to James McDowell, 10 March 1830, folder 13, sub-series 1.2, James McDowell Papers, UNC-CH; Alexander Poundfit to Henry Huntington, 7 March 1842, Henry Huntington Papers, DU.

4. For scholars who have imputed visionary qualities to colonization, see Foner, *Free Soil, Free Labor, Free Men,* 280; Donald, *Lincoln,* 166–67; West, *Back to Africa,* 106; Boritt, "Voyage to the Colony of Linconia."

5. Festinger, *Theory of Cognitive Dissonance.*

6. G. Nash, *Forging Freedom,* 223–26, 233–42; Pennsylvania Colonization Society (hereafter PCS), *Annual Report* (1838), 45–49.

7. G. Nash, *Forging Freedom,* 234–42; Bruce, "National Identity and African-American Colonization," 27–28; Pease and Pease, *Antislavery Argument,* 33, 34 (quotation).

8. Statistics on emigration to Liberia come from the ACS Database.

9. PCS, *Constitution of the Pennsylvania Colonization Society,* Article 2; PCS, *Annual Report* (1827), 4 (quotation).

10. PCS, *Annual Report* (1827), 7; PCS, *Annual Report* (1830), 4–5, 7–13.

11. PCS, *Annual Report* (1830), 9.

12. Garrison, *Thoughts on African Colonization,* 42 (first quotation), 50 (second quotation); Pease and Pease, *Antislavery Argument,* 37 (third and fourth quotations).

13. Hershberg, "Free Blacks in Antebellum Philadelphia"; G. Nash, *Forging Freedom,* 250–59, 273–79.

14. Garrison, *Thoughts on African Colonization,* 13, 23, 77, 122.

15. G. Barnes, *Anti-Slavery Impulse,* 36; Staudenraus, *African Colonization Movement,* 216. See also Fladeland, *Men and Brothers,* 209–20.

16. Stuart, *American Colonization Society,* 2; Staudenraus, *African Colonization Movement,* 217.

17. Staudenraus, *African Colonization Movement,* 216–18; Fladeland, *Men and Brothers,* 213–20.

18. Philadelphia Anti-Slavery Society, *Address to the Members of the Philadelphia Anti-Slavery Society,* 15.

19. *Colonization Herald,* 1846, Extra: 2d ed., pp. 6, 7.

20. Kocher, "A Duty to America and Africa," 126; Staudenraus, *African Colonization Movement,* 224–25.

21. Staudenraus, *African Colonization Movement,* 234 (quotation); P. Campbell, *Maryland in Africa,* 51–57.

22. Colonization Society of the City of New York, *Proceedings of the Colonization Society of the City of New York,* 4–11; Kocher, "A Duty to America and Africa," 127–29.

23. Seifman, "The United Colonization Societies of New-York and Pennsylvania and the Establishment of the African Colony of Bassa Cove," 36–40.

24. The figures are from the ACS Database.

25. Young Men's Colonization Society of Pennsylvania, *Annual Report* (1837), 3, 8.

26. Colton, *Colonization and Abolition Contrasted,* 3.

27. *Colonization Herald,* 31 January 1838, p. 17.

28. The new regime also eliminated redundant managers, made the position of treasurer a salaried job, and centralized the administration of Liberia. State colonization societies retained much autonomy under the new system. For example, they were re-

quired to forward to the ACS only a portion of their collections. The Maryland Colonization Society's settlement in Africa did not join Liberia until 1857 (Staudenraus, *African Colonization Movement,* 237–38).

29. *Colonization Herald,* 19 March 1845, p. 11.

30. Pennsylvania Colonization Society Papers, vol. 1, 2 February 1848, Lincoln University, Lincoln University, Pa. (hereafter PCS Papers); *Colonization Herald,* March 1848, p. 143.

31. *Colonization Herald,* January 1849, p. 182; *Colonization Herald,* October 1849, p. 218.

32. *Colonization Herald,* February 1851, p. 30.

33. *Address to the Free Colored People of These United States of America,* 6, 7.

34. Pennsylvania Abolition Society, *Annual Report* (1849), 3.

35. The entire Corpsen story is reported in the *Colonization Herald,* March 1852, p. 83. All quotations are from this article.

36. On the ethical and pragmatic considerations of buying slaves' freedom, see McFeely, *Frederick Douglass,* 143–45.

37. *Colonization Herald,* October 1851, p. 62.

38. PCS, *Addresses Delivered in the Hall of the House of Representatives,* 3–32.

39. Ibid., 40, 47.

40. Minutes of Executive Committee, 6 February 1852, Records of the New Jersey Colonization Society, LOC; Staudenraus, *African Colonization Movement,* 244.

41. Pennsylvania Anti-Slavery Society, *Annual Report* (1852), 45; *Colonization Herald,* January 1854, p. 170.

42. *Colonization Herald,* July 1853, p. 145. See also *Colonization Herald,* December 1853, p. 166.

43. Woodson, *Mind of the Negro,* 150. Augustus Washington of Connecticut, who left the United States with his wife and two children on the same ship as Deputie, also felt stigmatized upon his departure for Liberia (Woodson, *Mind of the Negro,* 136).

44. David McKinney to W. McLain, 5 May 1852, reel 67, RACS.

45. William Nesbit, *Four Months in Liberia,* in Moses, ed., *Liberian Dreams,* 88, 126.

46. Moses, *Liberian Dreams,* 115–24.

47. *Colonization Herald,* March 1856, p. 270. See also ACS, *Information about Going to Liberia.*

48. *Colonization Herald,* January 1854, p. 170; *Colonization Herald,* August 1854, p. 198.

49. *Colonization Herald,* November 1853, p. 161.

50. PCS, *To the Friends of the African Race; Colonization Herald,* March 1853, p. 130, April 1853, p. 134, May 1853, p. 138, and June 1853, p. 142.

51. *Colonization Herald,* October 1854, p. 202, and December 1854, p. 210.

52. Pease, *Statement and Appeal; Colonization Herald,* November 1852, p. 114, September 1851, p. 57, and February 1853, p. 128. For additional solicitations in Pennsylvania, see PCS, *Appeal in Behalf of African Colonization,* and *Colonization Herald,* July 1853, p. 146, February 1855, and April 1856, p. 274.

53. *Colonization Herald,* March 1855, p. 221.

54. Catherine Yeates to W. McLane, 12 August 1854, reel 173, RACS.

55. Huston, "The Experiential Basis of the Northern Antislavery Impulse."

56. Luther Paul to "The Secretary & Treasury of the American Colonization Society," 14 August 1854, reel 173, RACS.

57. Pennsylvania House of Representatives, *Select Committee of the House of Representatives of Pennsylvania on the Subject of Colonization,* 6.

58. Pennsylvania Anti-Slavery Society, *Annual Report* (1851), 61; Foner, *Free Soil, Free Labor, Free Men,* 9, 73, 97–102, 209 (quotation on p. 97).

59. *Colonization Herald,* November 1854, p. 206.

60. William McLain to William Coppinger, 17 November 1854, reel 197, RACS.

61. PCS, *At a Meeting of the Board of Managers of the Pennsylvania Colonization Society,* 2, 3, 9–12.

62. PCS Papers, vol. 2, 10 March 1857, 14 April 1857.

63. PCS Papers, vol. 1, 13 June 1848, 5 September 1848, 14 December 1848; vol. 2, 9 June 1857, 12 January 1858, 9 March 1858, 11 January 1859.

64. Thomas Chester, a twenty-year-old schoolteacher, emigrated aboard the *Banshee* in 1853.

65. PCS Papers, vol. 2, 1 April 1859, 8 November 1859, 10 January 1860, 14 February 1860.

66. PCS, *Annual Report* (1861).

67. Stampp, *America in 1857,* viii.

68. According to Stanley Harrold, in the mid- to late 1850s, abolitionists also lost interest in their southern allies. (*Abolitionists and the South,* 44).

69. Festinger, *Theory of Cognitive Dissonance,* 18. Emphasis in original.

Chapter 5. White Southerners' Responses to ACS Manumissions

1. Dumond, ed., *Letters of James Gillespie Birney,* 1:25.

2. On antislavery and the South, see Finnie, "The Antislavery Movement in the Upper South before 1840"; Stampp, "The Fate of the Southern Anti-Slavery Movement"; Eaton, *Freedom-of-Thought Struggle in the Old South;* Dillon, *Slavery Attacked;* Harrold, *Abolitionists and the South,* 1–44; Harrold, *Subversives,* 1–13; Degler, *Other South,* 13–96.

3. Collectively, these individuals freed 113 bondpersons, with most liberating just one or two slaves. The foregoing statistics on ACS manumissions, along with any subsequent ones, are drawn from the ACS Database. Blackford, *Mine Eyes Have Seen the Glory,* xii, 20.

4. In 1830, bondpersons constituted less than one-quarter of Loudoun County's population. Tyler-McGraw, "'The Prize I Mean Is the Prize of Liberty,'" 355–62; Stevenson, *Life in Black and White.*

5. Paxton, *Letters on Slavery,* 10; "Reminiscences of 'College Church' Hampden-Sidney," section 30, box 54, Eggleston Family Papers, VHS; Coyner, "John Hartwell Cocke of Bremo," 350–52; R. Miller, *"Dear Master,"* 32 (quotation); Varon, *We Mean to Be*

Counted, 64. See also George Junkin Ramsey to "My Dearest Friend," 23 June 1855, box 1, George Junkin Ramsey Papers, DU.

6. Statistics from ACS Database.

7. New-York State Colonization Society, *Emigration to Liberia,* 11–34; Syndor, *Slavery in Mississippi,* 203–38; "Rosswood," Rosswood (Lorman) Folder, Isaac Ross Papers, Mississippi State University; Edwards, *Some Interesting Papers of John McDonogh,* 51, 56; A. Cuthbert Jr. to W. McLain, 10 July 1855, reel 75, no. 108, RACS. See also Affidavit of J. E. Calhoon, 1 December 1851, American Colonization Society Papers, 1851–54, DU, and Benjamin Labaree to James G. Birney, 23 September 1833, folder 1, Benjamin Labaree Papers, UNC-CH. With 6,700 slaves, Jefferson County had the third-largest slave population in Mississippi in 1830; Orleans Parish had 16,639 slaves in 1830, by far the most in Louisiana; in 1850, Putnam County had 7,468 slaves, placing it in the top third among Georgia counties.

8. Andrews, *Memoir of Mrs. Ann R. Page,* 35.

9. Opper, "The Mind of the White Participant," 278–79; Varon, *We Mean to Be Counted,* 63–64; Caspar Morris, *Memoir of Miss Margaret Mercer,* 109–13, 115, 121 (quotation).

10. William Eagleton to William McLain, 29 September 1854, reel 74, no. 472 1/2, RACS.

11. Lumpkin quoted in Wahl, *Bondsman's Burden,* 161.

12. Southern colonizationists' discomfort with publicity flummoxed ACS leaders, who wanted to use emancipators' and freedpersons' testimonials when soliciting funds in the North. Elizabeth Holderness to W. McLain, 20 March 1855, reel 75, no. 564 1/2, RACS (first quotation); A. Cuthbert Jr. to W. McLain, 10 July 1855, reel 75, no. 108, RACS (second quotation); M. Hall to William McLain, 1 September 1848, reel 56, no. 244, RACS (third quotation). See also Wm. Lisle Baker to Wm. McLain, 25 April 1848, reel 55, no. 106, RACS.

13. James H. Laye to William McLain, 3 March 1848, reel 55, no. 265, RACS (quotation); Silas Howe to "Dear Sir," 14 October 1854, reel 74, no. 69, RACS; S. W. Curtis to W. McLain, 3 March 1848, reel 55, no. 265, RACS; Samuel L. Watson to W. McLain, 7 December 1847, reel 54, no. 241, RACS.

14. *African Repository* (April 1852): 109; William Starr to J. W. Lugenbeel, 26 May 1852, reel 67, no. 275, RACS.

15. J. W. Ware to "Dear Sir," 22 December 1851, reel 66 B, RACS.

16. William Kennedy to Wm. McLain, 14 March 1852, reel 67, RACS; William Starr to William McLain, 16 March 1852, reel 67, no. 369, RACS.

17. McLain quoted in Gifford, "The African Colonization Movement in Georgia," 147.

18. William H. Ruffner to "My Dear Sir," 10 December 1847, reel 54, no. 255, RACS.

19. James Paine to J. W. Lugenbeel, 14 October 1854, reel 74, RACS (quotation); James Paine to J. W. Lugenbeel, 16 October 1854, reel 74, no. 73, RACS; *African Repository* (December 1854): 254.

20. William White to W. McLain, 3 August 1855, reel 77, RACS.

21. Statistics drawn from ACS Database.

22. Will of Nathaniel Hooe, 7 November 1844, Nathaniel Hooe Papers, UVA; Diary of William S. Brown, 8 October 1845 and 1 November 1845, Brown-Hunter Papers, UVA.

23. *Mitchell v. Wells* 1859 WL 3634 *15 (Miss. Err. & App.).

24. John Eakin to W. McLain, 29 July 1848, reel 56, no. 122, RACS; Charles Bright to William McLain, 20 March 1848, reel 55, no. 337, RACS; W. A. Baynham to "My Dr. Sir," 11 August 1848, reel 56, no. 159, RACS.

25. The preceding figures come from the ACS Database.

26. Statistics on "multiple manumitters" are drawn from the ACS Database.

27. Andrews, *Memoir of Mrs. Ann R. Page*, 18 (quotation). See also Varon, *We Mean to Be Counted*, 47; Goodwin, "A Liberia Packet," 87.

28. Port of departure trends are drawn from ACS Database. See also J. W. Lugenbeel to W. J. Winston, 8 May 1851, Winston-Brown Family Papers, UVA.

29. Bogger, *Free Blacks in Norfolk*, 40, 53.

30. Screven quoted in Gifford, "The African Colonization Movement in Georgia," 89.

31. *Norfolk and Plymouth Herald*, 17 February 1826, p. 2 (first three quotations). On the *Saluda*, see *Norfolk and Portsmouth Herald*, 8 August 1839, p. 2. On solicitations for aid, see *American Beacon*, 6 February 1826, p. 3; *American Beacon*, 11 February 1826, p. 3; *Norfolk and Plymouth Herald*, 12 January 1829, p. 2; *American Beacon*, 24 January 1829, p. 2; *Richmond Compiler*, 9 October 1828. On ACS advertising, see *American Beacon*, 15 January 1830, p. 1; *American Beacon*, 20 January 1830, p. 2; *American Beacon*, 29 December 1832, p. 3; *American Beacon*, 24 October 1833, p. 3; *Norfolk and Plymouth Herald*, 24 December 1827, p. 3; *Norfolk and Plymouth Herald*, 26 April 1830, p. 3; *American Beacon*, 13 March 1830, p. 3; *Norfolk and Plymouth Herald*, 4 July 1832, p. 3; *American Beacon*, 24 October 1833, p. 3; *Norfolk and Plymouth Herald*, 17 July 1839, p. 3.

32. *New Orleans Daily Picayune*, 10 January 1847, p. 2; *New Orleans Daily Picayune*, 20 April 1849, p. 2; *New Orleans Daily Picayune*, 14 February 1851, p. 1; *New Orleans Daily Picayune*, 1 January 1853 (evening edition), pp. 1, 2.

33. *New Orleans Commercial Bulletin* 11 [July?] 1843, reprinted in the *African Repository* (July 1843): 224. See also Schafer, *Becoming Free, Remaining Free*, 152.

34. Dumond, *Letters of James Gillespie Birney*, 1:73–74. For Birney's abandonment of colonization and adoption of abolitionism, see James G. Birney to Theodore D. Weld, 21 July 1834, and James G. Birney to Lewis Tappan, 2 February 1835, both in James G. Birney Papers, LOC.

35. Silas Howe to W. McLain, 5 January 1848, reel 54, no. 18, RACS. See also Silas Howe to W. McLain, 10 January 1848, reel 55, no. 6, RACS.

36. Thomas C. Benning to "Rev. & Dear Sir," 7 March 1848, reel 55, no. 283, RACS; McLain quoted in Gifford, "The African Colonization Movement in Georgia," 76.

37. *Baltimore Sun*, 20 July 1851, p. 1 (first quotation); P. Campbell, *Maryland in Africa*, 28; *Norfolk and Plymouth Herald*, 17 February 1826, p. 2 (second quotation); Dumond, *Letters of James Gillespie Birney*, 1:71; *African Repository* (January 1845): 10; *African Repository* (June 1848): 162–63.

38. Noah Fletcher to William McLain, 29 April 1848, reel 55, no. 114, RACS; *Baltimore Sun*, 2 August 1849, p. 2; Thomas C. Benning to "Rev. & Dear Sir," 8 March 1848, reel 55, no. 289, RACS; Thomas C. Benning to "My Dear Sir," 31 March 1848, reel 55, no. 54, RACS.

39. *Norfolk and Plymouth Herald*, 17 February 1826, p. 2; William McLain to J. W. Lugenbeel, 3 January 1855, reel 74, no. 16, RACS; Gifford, "The African Colonization Movement in Georgia," 87; John Ker to Isaac Wade Ross, 7 January 1849, Wade (Isaac Ross) Letters, Mississippi Department of Archives and History; William H. Douthat to William P. Palmer, 5 October 1855, folder 2, section 5, Palmer Family Papers, VHS; John McPhail to Benjamin Brand, 3 December 1832, section 7, Benjamin Brand Papers, VHS.

40. Tise, *Proslavery*, 53–54; Turnbull quoted in Egerton, "Averting a Crisis," 149.

41. Georgia General Assembly, *Report Adopted by the Legislature of Georgia on African Colonization*, 8.

42. Tise regards Dew's tract not so much as the first systematic defense of slavery, but rather as the first great proslavery criticism of colonization (*Proslavery*, 69–74). Drew Gilpin Faust also sees an ambiguous, transitional quality to Dew's work (*Ideology of Slavery*, 22).

43. Quoted in Faust, *Ideology of Slavery*, 50.

44. Quoted in ibid., 45.

45. Quoted in ibid., 46.

46. Ibid., 73.

47. Quoted in ibid., 128–29.

48. Ibid., 179.

49. Quoted in ibid., 190, 132–33.

50. Hammond insisted that slaveholders simply desired peace and stability. "The only thing that can create a mob . . . here is the appearance of an abolitionist, whom the people assemble to chastise," claimed Hammond. "And this is no more of a mob," he continued, "than a rally of shepherds to chase a wolf out of their pastures." At times, white southerners thought ACS emancipators suspiciously lupine (Faust, *Ideology of Slavery*, 179).

51. The only significant exception was David Christy's essay "Cotton Is King," in which the author generally endorsed colonization (*Cotton Is King*, 133). E. N. Elliott also penned a piece, "Slavery in the Light of International Law," for the anthology and took the opportunity to denounce colonization, if only in passing. (*Cotton Is King*, 737).

52. McKitrick, ed., *Slavery Defended*; Faust, *Ideology of Slavery*, 239–99; Fitzhugh, *Cannibals All!*

53. *Southern Quarterly Review* 3, issue 5 (January 1851): 281.

54. *De Bow's Review* 7, issue 4 (October 1849): 314.

55. Ibid. 10, issue 3 (March 1851): 331.

56. Ibid. (June 1848): 487.

57. Ibid. (September 1855): 309.

58. Ibid. (April 1856): 460 and (September 1856): 270.

59. *De Bow's Review* (August 1853): 129.

60. Ibid. (September 1856): 265.

61. Ibid. (July 1857): 87–90 and (July 1858): 7.

62. *De Bow's Review* 26, issue 4 (April 1859): 415–29; *De Bow's Review* 27, issue 1 (July 1859): 55–73; *De Bow's Review* 27, issue 3 (September 1859): 336–44; *De Bow's Review* 27, issue 4 (October 1859): 392–402; *De Bow's Review* 27, issue 5 (November 1859): 583–94. The essays were published as *African Colonization Unveiled*.

63. *De Bow's Review* 26, issue 4 (April 1859): 426.

64. Ibid., 421.

65. Varon, *We Mean to Be Counted*, 68.

66. *De Bow's Review* 26, issue 4 (April 1859): 423 (both quotations).

67. Ibid. 27, issue 1 (July 1859): 65 (both quotations). To prove his point, Ruffin took the unusual step of singling out two liberators and assessing how slaves had responded to their emancipatory endeavors. According to Ruffin, John McDonogh's bondpersons had been rendered useless by the prospect of freedom. G.W.P. Custis's slaves, he asserted, had become equally indolent.

Chapter 6. ACS Manumissions and the Law

1. For overviews of slave law, see T. Morris, *Southern Slavery and the Law*; Tushnet, *American Law of Slavery*; A. E. Nash, "Reason of Slavery"; Genovese, *Roll, Jordan, Roll,* 25–49. See also Mitchell, "Off to Africa—with Judicial Blessings."

2. T. Morris, *Southern Slavery and the Law*, 392–99; Jordan, *White over Black,* 347–49.

3. Berlin, *Slaves without Masters,* 15–50.

4. Whitman, *Price of Freedom,* 140–57; Bogger, *Free Blacks in Norfolk,* 32–51; A. G. Freehling, *Drift toward Dissolution,* 114 (quotation).

5. Georgia also required manumitters to acquire legislative permission. Klebaner, "American Manumission Laws and the Responsibility for Supporting Slaves," 433–53; Finkelman, *State Slavery Statutes*; Lang, *Defender of the Faith,* 75–76.

6. Berlin, *Slaves without Masters,* 92, 173, 215–16; A. G. Freehling, *Drift toward Dissolution,* 117.

7. Ames, *State Documents on Federal Relations,* 196; Carey, *Letters on the Colonization Society,* 17–18; Patton, "The Progress of Emancipation in Tennessee," 99.

8. Georgia General Assembly, *Report Adopted by the Legislature of Georgia on African Colonization,* 7 (first quotation); Staudenraus, *African Colonization Movement,* 170 (second quotation), 184–87. See also *American Colonization Society v. Gartrell* 1857 WL 2072 *8–10 (Ga.).

9. Berlin, *Slaves without Masters,* 138–39; Schafer, *Becoming Free, Remaining Free,* 6; Richard Henderson to Alexander H. H. Stuart, 28 October 1837, box 3, Stuart-Baldwin Papers, UVA.

10. *Elder v. Elder* 4 Leigh 261–62 (1833) (first quotation); *Fisher's Negroes v. Dabbs* 1834

WL *6 (Tenn. Err. & App.); *Cox v. Williams* 1845 WL 1150 *2 (N.C.) (second quotation); Yanuck, "Thomas Ruffin and North Carolina Slave Law," 470.

11. Catterall, *Judicial Cases,* 2:360 (first quotation); *Ross v. Vertner* 1840 WL 2435 *21 (Miss. Err. & App.) (second quotation); Catterall, *Judicial Cases,* 3:12, 14–15; *Vance v. Crawford* 1848 WL 1510 *10 (Ga.) (third quotation).

12. *Vance v. Crawford* 1848 WL 1510 *11 (Ga.).

13. Jenny Bourne Wahl argued that economic considerations also contributed to more state usurpations of slaveholders' property rights, including the right of manumission (*Bondsman's Burden,* 145, 163–66).

14. *Trotter v. Blocker* 1838 WL 1294 *13 (Ala.).

15. Wahl, *Bondsman's Burden,* 150 (first quotation); *Adams v. Bass* 1855 WL 1641 *11 (Ga.) (second quotation).

16. T. Morris, *Southern Slavery and the Law,* 378 (first quotation); *Leech v. Cooley* 1846 WL 2949 *3 (Miss. Err. & App.) (second quotation); *Mahorner v. Hooe* 1848 WL 1937 *20 (Miss. Err. & App.) (third quotation); *Mitchell v. Wells* 1959 WL 3634 *16 (Miss. Err. & App.) (fourth quotation). See also *Shaw v. Brown* 1858 WL 3074 (Miss. Err. & App.), and Finkelman, *Imperfect Union,* 289, 232–33.

17. Schafer, *Becoming Free, Remaining Free,* 8 (first quotation), 9-12, 13 (second quotation).

18. Statistics from ACS Database.

19. *Smith v. Adam* 1858 WL 4848 *4 (Ky.). See also *Elisha (of color) ex parte* 1858 WL 4846 *3 (Ky.); *Winn v. Sam Martin (of color)* 1863 WL 2544 (Ky.); Post, "Kentucky Law Concerning Emancipation or Freedom of Slaves," 363–64.

20. *Adams v. Bass* 1855 WL 1641 *24 (Ga.); *Sanders v. Ward* 1858 WL 1914 *13 (Ga.) (quotation).

21. *Sanders v. Ward* 1858 WL 1914 *7 (Ga.) (both quotations). See also Robert Harper to "My Dear Sir," 23 July 1858, folder 1852–1858, box 6, Alexander H. Stephens Papers, DU.

22. *Bailey v. Poindexter* 1858 WL 3940 *40 (Va.).

23. Goodell, *American Slave Code in Theory and Practice,* 339 (quotation), 341–52.

24. Cobb, *Inquiry into the Law of Negro Slavery in the United States of America,* 287 (both quotations), 290–91.

25. *African Repository* (August 1854): 253 (first quotation); *African Repository* (October 1854): 313 (second quotation).

26. Shaw, *Legal History of Slavery in the United States,* 76–105; Berlin, *Slaves without Masters,* 138–39; T. Morris, *Southern Slavery and the Law,* 379.

27. Patterson, *Slavery and Social Death,* 209–61.

28. *Nancy v. Snell* 1838 WL 2186 *2 (Ky.); *State v. Dorsey* 1848 WL 3018 *2 (Md.).

29. O'Neall quoted in T. Morris, *Southern Slavery and the Law,* 373; *Trotter v. Blocker* 1838 WL 1294 *12 (Ala.).

30. *Ford v. Ford* 1846 WL 1497 *2 (Tenn.).

31. *Leech v. Cooley* 1846 WL 2949 *3 (Miss. Err. & App.); *Cox v. Williams* 1845 WL 1150 *2 (N.C.); *Thompson v. Newlin* 1851 WL 1300 *7 (N.C.); *Tongue v. Negroes Crissy, Rhody, et al.* 1855 WL 3801 *8 (Md.).

32. *Wood v. Humphreys* 1855 WL 3474 *4, *11 (Va.); T. Morris, *Southern Slavery and the Law*, 31–36.

33. T. Morris, *Southern Slavery and the Law*, 374 (quotation), 377–78; *Cameron v. Commissioners* 1841 WL 844 *3 (N.C.); Mitchell and Mitchell, "The Philanthropic Bequests of John Rex of Raleigh," 278.

34. *Young v. Vass* (Va., 1855) in Catterall, *Judicial Cases*, 1:233–35; *Prater's Administrator v. Darby* 1854 WL 437 *8 (Ala.).

35. *Evans v. Kittrell* 1859 WL 585 *3 (first quotation) (Ala.); *American Colonization Society v. Gartrell* 1857 WL 2072 *4 (second quotation) (Ga.); *Hunter v. Bass, American Colonization Society v. Bass* 1855 WL 1639 *2 (third and fourth quotations) (Ga.).

36. *Maund v. M'Phail* 1839 WL 2067 (Va.); *Wade v. American Colonization Society* 1846 WL 3004 *20 (Miss. Err. & App.); *Vance v. Crawford* 1848 WL 1510 *11 (Ga.).

37. *American Colonization Society v. Gartrell* 1857 WL 2072 *4–5, *10 (Ga.); *Lewis v. Lusk* 1858 WL 4592 *14 (Miss. Err. & App.) (first quotation); *Wade v. American Colonization Society* 1846 WL 3004 *20 (Miss. Err. & App.) (second quotation). See also *Lusk v. Lewis* 1856 WL 4022 *4 (Miss. Err. & App.) and *Walker v. Walker* 1858 WL 1980 *6 (Ga.).

38. *Leech v. Cooley* 1846 WL 2949 *3 (Miss. Err. & App.) (first quotation); *Wooten v. Becton* (N.C., 1851), in Catterall, *Judicial Cases*, 2:163–64; *Atwood's Heirs v. Beck, Administrator* (Ala., 1852), in Catterall, *Judicial Cases*, 3: 183–85; *Drane v. Beall* 1857 WL 1791 *15 (second quotation) (Ga.). In *Mitchell v. Wells*, Harris opined that the order of the words did make a difference: "I should also differ with the court in the construction of the language . . . by the *rule of inversion* applied to it, were that a question before me" (1859 WL 3634 *5 [Miss. Err. & App.]).

39. *Elder v. Elder* 1833 WL 2083 *6 (Va.); *John or Jack v. Moreman, Stith &c* 1847 WL 2920 *1 (Ky.); *Hayden v. Burch* 1850 WL 3288 *1, *4 (Md.); *Cox v. Williams* 1845 WL 1150 *2–3 (N.C.); *Thompson v. Newlin* 1851 WL 1300 (N.C.); *Redding v. Long and Findley* 1858 WL 1858 *3 (N.C.).

40. *Isaac v. McGill* 1848 WL 1908 *2 (Tenn.).

41. *Roser v. Marlow* (Ga., 1837), in Catterall, *Judicial Cases*, 3:14–15; Riley, "A Contribution to the History of the Colonization Movement in Mississippi," 413; *Executors of Henderson v. Heirs* 1856 WL 4575 *2 (La.).

42. Catterall, *Judicial Cases*, 3:127; *Carroll v. Brumby* 1848 WL 301 *3 (Ala.); *Creswell's Executor v. Walker* 1861 WL 362 *3, *5 (quotation) (Ala.).

43. *Forward's Adm'r v. Thamer* 9 Grattan 537–40 (Va., 1853); *Osborne v. Taylor* 12 Grattan 117, 128 (Va., 1855); *Bailey v. Poindexter* 1858 WL 3940 *35 (first two quotations), *38 (third quotation) (Va.); *Williamson v. Coalter* 1858 WL 3952 *3 (Va.).

44. *Cleland v. Waters* 1855 WL 1788 *5 (Ga.) (first quotation); *Curry v. Curry* 1860 WL 2130 *4 (Ga.) (second and third quotations). See also *Miller v. Gaskins* 1864 WL 1117 *4 (Fla.).

45. *Cameron v. Commissioners* 1841 WL 844 *3 (N.C.); Mitchell and Mitchell, "The Philanthropic Bequests of John Rex of Raleigh," 278; *Leech v. Cooley* 1846 WL 2949 *3

(Miss. Err. & App.); *Alvany (a free woman of color) v. Powell* 1853 WL 1495 *3 (N.C.) (quotation).

46. *Nicholas v. Burruss* 1833 WL 2087 *3 (Va.); *Nancy (a woman of color) v. Snell* 1838 WL 2186 *2 (Ky.) (first two quotations); *Snead v. David* 1840 WL 2582 *6 (Ky.) (third quotation); T. Morris, *Southern Slavery and the Law,* 391 (fourth and fifth quotations).

47. *Elder v. Elder* 1833 WL 2083 *4 (Va.); *Hogg v. Capehart* (N.C., 1857), in Catterall, *Judicial Cases,* 2:208; Yanuck, "Thomas Ruffin and North Carolina Slave Law," 470; *Harry v. Green* (Tenn., 1848), in Catterall, *Judicial Cases,* 2:537; *Boon v. Lancaster (next friend)* 1854 WL 2114 *4 (Tenn.); *Elisha (of color) Ex Parte* 1858 WL 4846 *3 (Ky.); *Graham v. Sam and others* 1847 WL 2843 *4 (Ky.). See also Francis Scott Key to Alexander Randall, 15 December 1831, Alexander Randall Papers, DU.

48. *Jordan v. Bradley* (Ga., 1830), in Catterall, *Judicial Cases,* 3:12; *Thorton v. Chisholm* 1856 WL 1918 *3 (Ga.) (first quotation); *Drane v. Beall* 1857 WL 1791 *16 (Ga.) (second quotation).

Chapter 7. Liberia: Freedpersons' Experiences in Africa

1. Shick, *Behold the Promised Land*; Liebenow, *Liberia*; Huberich, *Political and Legislative History of Liberia*; Temperly, "African-American Aspirations and the Settlement of Liberia."

2. Garrison, *Thoughts on African Colonization,* 13. All statistics in this chapter concerning the freedperson population come from the ACS Database.

3. On the occupational distribution of the American slave population, see Fogel, *Without Consent or Contract,* 47, 50; Stampp, *Peculiar Institution,* 49–50; Fogel and Engerman, *Time on the Cross,* 39–40; Stevenson, *Life in Black and White,* 186–87; Wade, *Slavery in the Cities,* 28–38; Ransom and Sutch, *One Kind of Freedom,* 15–16, 224, 232–34.

4. Webber, *Deep Like the Rivers,* 131; Genovese, *Roll, Jordan, Roll,* 563; Wade, *Slavery in the Cities,* 91–92, 173–75; Ransom and Sutch, *One Kind of Freedom,* 15, 17; Thompson, *Sociology of the Black Experience,* 168; Woodson, *Education of the Negro Prior to 1861,* 3, 13–15, 227–28; J. Williamson, *After Slavery,* 210.

5. Burin, "'If the rest stay, I will stay—If they go, I will go.'"

6. Jacob Gibson to John H. Latrobe and William McKenney, 31 August 1833, in Wiley, *Slaves No More,* 216. See also Samson Ceasar to David S. Haselden, 7 February 1834, Samson Ceasar Letters, UVA.

7. Mars Lucas to Townsend Heaton, 12 March 1830; Mars Lucas to Townsend Heaton, 19 June 1830 (quotation), both in Lucas-Heaton Letters, UVA. See also Tyler-McGraw, "'The Prize I Mean Is the Prize of Liberty.'"

8. *African Repository* (July 1847): 218.

9. Peter Ross and Robert Carter to John Ker, 23 March 1848, in Wiley, *Slaves No More,* 157; Hannibal Ross to John Ker, 26 March 1848, in Wiley, *Slaves No More,* 158; Sarah J. Woodson to Catherine E. Wade, 11 May 1848, in Wiley, *Slaves No More,* 159; Sarah J. Woodson to Catherine E. Wade, 1 April 1850, in Wiley, *Slaves No More,* 160 (quotation).

10. Sarah J. Woodson to Catherine E. Wade, 1 April 1850, in Wiley, *Slaves No More,* 161.

11. Ibid.

12. McDaniel, *Swing Low, Sweet Chariot,* 84, 86.

13. Ibid., 86.

14. Ibid., 115.

15. Ibid., 112–15; ACS, *Information about Going to Liberia,* 5 (quotation).

16. Almost all of the interior settlements were within ten miles of the coast and were situated on rivers. John B. Pinney to "To All Who See these Presents," 9 October 1834, folder 1/5, Wheeden and Whitehurst Family Papers, UNC-CH; Cornelia Gainshaw to William McLain, 7 July 1848, reel 56, RACS; John Hartwell Cocke to William McLain, 18 December 1847, reel 54, no. 298, RACS; W. H. Ruffner to "My Dear Sir," 10 December 1847, reel 54, no. 255, RACS; McDaniel, *Swing Low, Sweet Chariot,* 157.

17. McDaniel, *Swing Low, Sweet Chariot,* 104 (first quotation); *Examination of Mr. Thomas C. Brown,* 8 (second quotation).

18. ACS, *Information about Going to Liberia,* 9 (quotations).

19. William McLain to Lugenbeel, 13 November 1848, reel 238, no. 101, RACS.

20. William McLain to Joseph Corker, 14 February 1849, reel 238, no. 106, RACS. See also James Adger Jr. to W. McLain, 23 November 1848, reel 57, no. 195, RACS.

21. Henry B. Stewart to William McLain, 20 October 1849, in Wiley, *Slaves No More,* 282 (both quotations).

22. William McLain to Edmund Jennings Lee, 24 March 1858, Edmund Jennings Lee Papers, DU. White missionaries in Liberia also had to cope with sickness and poverty, and like freedpersons, they responded by requesting aid from their acquaintances in the United States. See, for example, Susan H. Benham to Sarah Ann Round, 8 February 1846 and 27 January 1847, both in section 3, Round Family Papers, VHS.

23. On manumitters' supposed impoverishment, see Blackford, *Mine Eyes Have Seen the Glory,* xvi, 57; Andrews, *Memoir of Mrs. Ann R. Page,* 29–31; Opper, "The Mind of the White Participant," 265; Caspar Morris, *Memoir of Miss Margaret Mercer,* 120.

24. Albert Heaton to Jesse and Mars Lucas, 29 April 1830, Lucas-Heaton Letters, UVA; Tyler-McGraw, "'The Prize I Mean Is the Prize of Liberty,'" 359. In one instance, an emancipator's remaining slaves were alleged to have stolen $2,500 from their owner and sent it to their compatriots in Liberia (C. Johnson to John Marron, 11 September 1854, American Colonization Society Papers, 1851–54, DU).

25. D. W. Whitehurst, "Ship Jupiter" [newspaper clipping], 19 August 1834, folder 1/5, Wheeden and Whitehurst Family Papers, UNC-CH; Horace Ross to Ralph R. Gurley, 3 June 1860, in Wiley, *Slaves No More,* 174.

26. Diana Skipwith to Sally Cocke, 7 May 1838, in Wiley, *Slaves No More,* 42.

27. ACS, *Information about Going to Liberia,* 6–7.

28. Lucy Clay to Brutus J. Clay, 19 August 1857, in Wiley, *Slaves No More,* 273; McDaniel, *Swing Low, Sweet Chariot,* 72.

29. McDaniel, *Swing Low, Sweet Chariot,* 68; Staudenraus, *African Colonization*

Movement, 152–55; Syfert, "The Origins of Privilege," 110; Akpan, "The Liberian Economy in the Nineteenth Century," 2–6.

30. George Crawford to John Moore McCalla, 25 September 1836, John Moore McCalla Papers, VHS; Peter Ross and Robert Carter to John Ker, 23 March 1848, in Wiley, *Slaves No More,* 158.

31. McDaniel, *Swing Low, Sweet Chariot,* 69.

32. Although indigenous peoples cultivated rice, the crop never flourished among the colonists. Seaborn Evans to Josiah Sibley, 19 September 1853, in Wiley, *Slaves No More,* 263; Moses, *Liberian Dreams,* 95.

33. James P. Skipwith to John H. Cocke, 11 February 1859, in Wiley, *Slaves No More,* 92; G. Brown, *Economic History of Liberia,* 133–34; Titus Glover to William C. Rice, 16 January 1869, in Wiley, *Slaves No More,* 187 (quotation).

34. Akpan, "The Liberian Economy in the Nineteenth Century," 11; Syfert, "The Origins of Privilege," 120–21.

35. Peyton Skipwith to John H. Cocke, 10 February 1834, in Wiley, *Slaves No More,* 36; Robert Leander Sterdivant to John H. Cocke, 11 June 1846, in Wiley, *Slaves No More,* 63; Abraham Blackford to Mary B. Blackford, 14 February 1846, in Wiley, *Slaves No More,* 24.

36. Edward James Patterson to William W. Rice, in Wiley, *Slaves No More,* 185 (quotation); Wilson Coalman to James Minor, 23 August 1859, James Hunter Terrell Papers, UVA.

37. Peyton Skipwith to John H. Cocke, 11 November 1839, in Wiley, *Slaves No More,* 52.

38. William C. Burke to Ralph R. Gurley, 26 July 1858, in Wiley, *Slaves No More,* 202; William C. Burke to Ralph R. Gurley, 31 August 1860, in Wiley, *Slaves No More,* 210.

39. Sion Harris to William McLain, 20 May 1849, in Wiley, *Slaves No More,* 227.

40. John M. Page Jr. to Charles W. Andrews, 7 May 1849, in Wiley, *Slaves No More,* 110. See also Henry Chaver Jr. to Ellis Malone, 2 August 1857, Ellis Malone Papers, DU.

41. Wiley, *Slaves No More,* 156 (quotation).

42. James W. Wilson to William McLain, 5 August 1858, in Wiley, *Slaves No More,* 245 (first quotation); John H. Faulcon to John H. Cocke, 30 September 1853, in Wiley, *Slaves No More,* 80.

43. Abraham Blackford to Mary B. Blackford, 9 September 1844, in Wiley, *Slaves No More,* 21–22.

44. Jacob Harris to N. M. Gordon, 4 July 1848, in Wiley, *Slaves No More,* 261.

45. Wiley, *Slaves No More,* 103, 137, 132, 95.

46. Peyton Skipwith to John Hartwell Cocke, 22 April 1840, in R. Miller, *"Dear Master,"* 75; Diana James Skipwith to Sally Cocke, 6 March 1843, in Wiley, *Slaves No More,* 57; Akpan, "Black Imperialism"; Holsoe, "A Study of the Relations between Settlers and Indigenous Peoples in Western Liberia."

47. Samson Ceasar to Henry F. Westfall, 2 June 1834, Samson Ceasar Letters, UVA.

48. Robert Leander Sterdivant to John H. Cocke, 11 June 1846, in Wiley, *Slaves No More,* 62; McDaniel, *Swing Low, Sweet Chariot,* 72–73.

49. Jacob Gibson to John H. Latrobe and William McKenney, 31 August 1833, in Wiley, *Slaves No More*, 216.

50. R. Miller, "'Home as Found,'" 103.

51. Lucy Clay to Brutus J. Clay, 29 September 1853, in Wiley, *Slaves No More*, 266 (quotation); Lucy Clay to Brutus J. Clay, 19 August 1857, in Wiley, *Slaves No More*, 273–74.

52. Horace Ross to Ralph R. Gurley, 3 June 1860, in Wiley, *Slaves No More*, 174; Clegg, *Price of Liberty*, 226.

53. It is possible—even likely—that such provisions were adopted as a means of preventing the dissolution of wealth among the first families of Liberia. See Lebsock, *Free Women of Petersburg*, 57–58.

54. McDaniel, *Swing Low, Sweet Chariot*, 77–78, 82, 88–100.

55. Matilda Skipwith Lomax to John H. Cocke, 30 September 1850, in Wiley, *Slaves No More*, 71.

56. Matilda Skipwith Lomax to John H. Cocke, 19 May 1852, in Wiley, *Slaves No More*, 75.

57. Matilda Richardson to John Hartwell Cocke, 23 February 1861, in R. Miller, *"Dear Master,"* 122 (quotation), 21.

58. Seaborn Evans to Josiah Sibley, 19 September 1853, in Wiley, *Slaves No More*, 263.

Conclusion

1. Dixon, *African Americans and Haiti*, 177–216; Crummell, *Future of Africa*; Moses, *Alexander Crummell*; James McCune Smith to Henry Highland Garnet, 5 January 1861, in Ripley, *Black Abolitionist Papers*, 5:105.

2. W. Freehling, *Reintegration of American History*, 220–52. See also Crofts, *Reluctant Confederates*; Link, *Roots of Secession*.

3. Simpson, ed., *Think Anew, Act Anew*, 104; W. Freehling, *Reintegration of American History*, 233 (quotation), 245.

4. Quarles, *Lincoln and the Negro*, 68–77.

5. Simpson, ed., *Think Anew, Act Anew*, 104; Quarles, *Lincoln and the Negro*, 102–6 (Lincoln quotation on p. 106).

6. *Congressional Globe*, 37th Cong., 2d Sess.; Appendix, p. 1; *Congressional Globe*, 37th Cong., 2d Sess., 1774–76; 1806–7; 1815, 2499–503, 2530–36.

7. Donald, *Lincoln*, 354–76; Quarles, *Lincoln and the Negro*, 125–52; Simpson, ed., *Think Anew, Act Anew*, 113–15, 117 (quotation).

8. Berlin et al., *Free At Last*, xxix–xxx.

9. *Report of the Select Committee on Emancipation and Colonization*; Simpson, ed., *Think Anew, Act Anew*, 129–31.

10. Quarles, *Lincoln and the Negro*, 110–33 (Welles quotation on p. 133); Bancroft, "The Colonization of American Negroes"; M. Johnson, ed., *Abraham Lincoln, Slavery, and the Civil War*, 209–28; Boritt, "Voyage to the Colony of Linconia," 619–32.

11. M. Johnson, *Abraham Lincoln, Slavery, and the Civil War,* 218–19; H. Ford Douglas to Frederick Douglass, 8 January 1863, in Ripley, *Black Abolitionist Papers,* 5:167 (first quotation); Quarles, *Lincoln and the Negro,* 114; Ripley, *Black Abolitionist Papers,* 5:65 (second quotation); Simpson, ed., *Think Anew, Act Anew,* 145 (third quotation).

12. Fields, *Slavery and Freedom on the Middle Ground,* 121–22; W. Freehling, *Reintegration of American History,* 237–38; Berlin, *Generations of Captivity,* 245–71.

13. Perman, *Emancipation and Reconstruction,* 12–27; Quarles, *Lincoln and the Negro,* 191–94.

14. Boritt, "Journey to the Colony of Linconia," 623 (Hay quotation); Quarles, *Lincoln and the Negro,* 193 (Usher quotation), 194; Lane, *Speech of Hon. J. H. Lane of Kansas, in the Senate of the United States, February 16, 1864.*

15. Quarles, *Lincoln and the Negro,* 222–23.

16. Cohen, *At Freedom's Edge,* 138–66 (quotation on p. 141); Hahn, *Nation under Our Feet,* 317–63; K. Barnes, *Journey of Hope;* Murza, "The American Colonization Society and Emigration to Liberia, 1863–1905."

17. Clegg, *Price of Liberty,* 249–70 (quotation on p. 268).

Bibliography

Manuscript Sources

Duke University
    American Colonization Society Papers, 1851–54
    Henry Huntington Papers
    John Richard Kilby Papers
    Edmund Jennings Lee Papers
    Ellis Malone Papers
    Montgomery D. Parker Papers
    George Junkin Ramsey Papers
    Alexander Randall Papers
    Alexander H. Stephens Papers
Indiana University Archives of Traditional Music Liberian Collections
    Holsoe Collection
Library of Congress
    James G. Birney Papers
    Records of the American Colonization Society
    Records of the New Jersey Colonization Society
Lincoln University
    Pennsylvania Colonization Society Papers
Maryland Hall of Records
    Anne Arundel County Court, Manumission Records
Maryland Historical Society
    Latrobe-Sheppard Papers
    Pearce Papers

Mississippi Department of Archives and History
    Vick-Phelps Papers
    Wade (Isaac Ross) Papers
Mississippi State University
    Randolph-Sherman Papers
    Isaac Ross Papers
University of North Carolina–Chapel Hill
    Blackford Family Papers
    Cameron Family Papers
    Benjamin Labaree Papers
    James McDowell Papers
    John McKee Sharpe Papers
    Wheeden and Whitehurst Family Papers
    Wilson and Hairston Family Papers
University of Southern Mississippi
    Maryland State Colonization Papers
University of Virginia
    Albemarle County Will Book
    Brown-Hunter Papers
    Samson Ceasar Letters
    John Hartwell Cocke Papers
    Holladay Family Papers
    Nathaniel Harris Hooe Papers
    Kent-Hunter Family Papers
    Lucas-Heaton Letters
    McLaughlin-Reed Papers
    Stuart-Baldwin Papers
    James Hunter Terrell Papers
    Winston-Brown Family Papers
Virginia Historical Society
    Benjamin Brand Papers
    Mary Lee (Fitzhugh) Custis Papers
    Eggleston Family Papers
    Hunter Family Papers
    John Moore McCalla Papers
    Palmer Family Papers
    Round Family Papers
Virginia State Library
    Washington Family Papers
    Watson Family Papers

Published Sources

Address to the Free Colored People of these United States of America. Philadelphia, 1845.
Akpan, M. B. "Black Imperialism: Americo-Liberian Rule over the African Peoples of Liberia, 1841–1964." *Canadian Journal of African Studies* 7, no. 2 (1973): 217–36.

————. "The Liberian Economy in the Nineteenth Century: The State of Agriculture and Commerce." *Liberian Studies Journal* 6, no. 1 (1975): 1–24.

Alexander, Archibald. *A History of Colonization on the Western Coast of Africa.* 1846. Reprint, New York: Negro Universities Press, 1969.

American Colonization Society. *African Repository.* Washington, D.C.: American Colonization Society, 1825–92.

————. *Annual Reports of the American Society for the Colonizing the Free People of Colour of the United States.* 1818–1910. Reprint, New York: Negro Universities Press, 1969.

————. *Information about Going to Liberia: With Things Which Every Emigrant Ought to Know: Report of Messrs. Fuller and Janifer: Sketch of the History of Liberia: and the Constitution of the Republic of Liberia.* Washington, D.C.: C. Alexander, 1852.

Ames, Herman V., ed. *State Documents on Federal Relations: The States and the United States.* 1911. Reprint, New York: De Capo Press, 1970.

Andrews, C. W. *Memoir of Mrs. Ann R. Page.* New York: Protestant Episcopal Society for the Promotion of Evangelical Knowledge, 1856. Reprint, New York: Garland Publishing, 1987.

Bancroft, Frederic. "The Colonization of American Negroes, 1801–1865." In *Frederic Bancroft: Historian,* edited by Jacob E. Cooke. Norman: University of Oklahoma Press, 1957.

Barnes, Gilbert Hobbs. *The Anti-Slavery Impulse, 1830–1844.* N.p.: American Historical Association, 1933. Reprint, New York: Harcourt, Brace, and World, 1964.

Barnes, Kenneth C. *Journey of Hope: The Back-to-Africa Movement in Arkansas in the Late 1800s.* Chapel Hill: University of North Carolina Press, 2004.

Berlin, Ira. *Generations of Captivity: A History of African-American Slaves.* Cambridge: Belknap Press of Harvard University Press, 2003.

————. *Many Thousands Gone: The First Two Centuries of Slavery in North America.* Cambridge: Belknap Press of Harvard University Press, 1998.

————. *Slaves without Masters: The Free Negro in the Antebellum South.* New York: New Press, 1974.

Berlin, Ira, Barbara J. Fields, Steven F. Miller, Joseph P. Reidy, and Leslie S. Rowland, eds. *Free at Last: A Documentary History of Slavery, Freedom, and the Civil War.* New York: New Press, 1992.

Berwanger, Eugene H. *The Frontier against Slavery: Western Anti-Negro Prejudice and the Slavery Extension Controversy.* Urbana: University of Illinois Press, 1967.

Beyan, Amos. *The American Colonization Society and the Creation of the Liberian State.* Lanham, Md.: University Press of America, 1991.

Blackford, L. Minor. *Mine Eyes Have Seen the Glory: The Story of a Virginia Lady Mary Berkeley Minor Blackford, 1802–1896, Who Taught Her Sons to Hate Slavery and to Love the Union.* Cambridge: Harvard University Press, 1954.

Bogger, Tommy L. *Free Blacks in Norfolk, Virginia, 1790–1860: The Darker Side of Freedom.* Charlottesville: University Press of Virginia, 1997.

Boritt, Gabor S. "The Voyage to the Colony of Linconia: The Sixteenth President, Black Colonization, and the Defense Mechanism of Avoidance." *Historian* 37, no. 4 (August 1975): 619–32.

Brown, David. "Attacking Slavery from Within: The Making of *The Impending Crisis.*" *Journal of Southern History* 70, no. 3 (August 2004): 541–76.

Brown, George W. *An Economic History of Liberia.* Washington, D.C.: Associated Publishers, 1941.

Bruce, Dickson D., Jr. "National Identity and African-American Colonization, 1773–1817." *Historian* 58, no. 1 (autumn 1995): 15–28.

Burin, Eric. "'If the rest stay, I will stay—If they go, I will go': How Slaves' Familial Bonds Affected American Colonization Society Manumission." In *Manumission in the Atlantic World,* edited by Jack Greene, Randy Sparks, and Rosemary Brana-Shute. Columbia: University of South Carolina Press, forthcoming.

Campbell, Marvis C. "The Price of Freedom: *On Forms of Manumission.* A Note on the Comparative Study of Slavery." *Review/Revista Interamericana* 6, no. 2 (summer 1976): 239–52.

Campbell, Penelope. *Maryland in Africa: The Maryland State Colonization Society, 1831–1857.* Urbana: University of Illinois Press, 1971.

Carey, M. *Letters on the Colonization Society; and on Its Probable Results.* 4th ed. Philadelphia: L. Johnson, 1832.

Carroll, Kenneth. "Religious Influences on the Manumission of Slaves." *Maryland Historical Magazine* 56, no. 2 (June 1961): 176–97.

Catterall, Helen T., ed. *Judicial Cases Concerning American Slavery and the Negro.* Washington, D.C.: Carnegie Institute of Washington, 1926.

Clegg, Claude A., III. *The Price of Liberty: African Americans and the Making of Liberia.* Chapel Hill: University of North Carolina Press, 2004.

Clinton, Catherine. *The Plantation Mistress: Woman's World in the Old South.* New York: Pantheon Books, 1982.

Cobb, Thomas R. *An Inquiry into the Law of Negro Slavery in the United States of America.* N.p.: T. and J. W. Johnson, 1858. Reprint, New York: Negro Universities Press, 1969.

Cohen, William. *At Freedom's Edge: Black Mobility and the Southern White Quest for Racial Control, 1861–1915.* Baton Rouge: Louisiana State University Press, 1991.

Colonization Society of the City of New York. *Proceedings of the Colonization Society of the City of New York.* New York: Wm. A. Mercein and Son, 1835.

Colton, Calvin. *Colonization and Abolition Contrasted.* Philadelphia: Robert B. Davidson, 1839.

Cornelius, Janet Duitsman. *When I Can Read My Title Clear: Literacy, Slavery, and Religion in the Antebellum South.* Columbia: University of South Carolina Press, 1991.

Coyner, M. Boyd, "John Hartwell Cocke of Bremo: Agriculture and Slavery in the Antebellum South." PhD diss., University of Virginia, 1961.

Crofts, Daniel W. *Reluctant Confederates: Upper South Unionists in the Secession Crisis.* Chapel Hill: University of North Carolina Press, 1989.

Crummell, Alexander. *The Future of Africa: Being Addresses, Sermons, etc., etc., Delivered in the Republic of Liberia.* New York: Scribner, 1862.

Curry, Leonard P. *The Free Black in Urban America, 1800–1850: The Shadow of the Dream.* Chicago: University of Chicago Press, 1981.

Davis, Charles S., ed. "Liberian Letters from a Former Georgia Slave." *Georgia Historical Quarterly* 24, no. 3 (September 1940): 253–56.

Davis, David Brion. *The Problem of Slavery in the Age of Revolution, 1770–1823.* Ithaca, N.Y.: Cornell University Press, 1975.

Degler, Carl. *The Other South: Southern Dissenters in the Nineteenth Century.* New York: Harper and Row, 1974. Reprint, Gainesville: University Press of Florida, 2000.

Dillon, Merton L. *Slavery Attacked: Southern Slaves and their Allies, 1619–1865.* Baton Rouge: Louisiana State University Press, 1990.

Dixon, Chris. *African Americans and Haiti: Emigration and Black Nationalism in the Nineteenth Century.* Westport, Conn.: Greenwood Press, 2000.

Donald, David Herbert. *Lincoln.* London: Jonathan Cape, 1995.

Dorsey, Bruce. "A Gendered History of African Colonization in the Antebellum United States." *Journal of Social History* 34, no. 1 (fall 2000): 77–103.

———. *Reforming Men and Women: Gender in the Antebellum City.* Ithaca, N.Y.: Cornell University Press, 2002.

Dumond, Dwight L., ed. *Letters of James Gillespie Birney, 1831–1857.* Vol. 1. N.p.: American Historical Association, 1938. Reprint, Peter Smith, 1968.

Eaton, Clement. *The Freedom-of-Thought Struggle in the Old South.* Durham: Duke University Press, 1940. Reprint, New York: Touchstone, 1964.

Edwards, James T., ed. *Some Interesting Papers of John McDonogh.* McDonogh, Md.: Boys of McDonogh School, 1898.

Egerton, Douglas R. "Averting a Crisis: The Proslavery Critique of the American Colonization Society." *Civil War History* 43, no. 2 (June 1997): 142–56.

———. *Charles Fenton Mercer and the Trial of National Conservatism.* Jackson: University Press of Mississippi, 1985.

———. *Gabriel's Rebellion: The Virginia Slave Conspiracies of 1800 and 1802.* Chapel Hill: University of North Carolina Press, 1993.

———. "'Its Origin Is Not a Little Curious': A New Look at the American Colonization Society." *Journal of the Early Republic* 5 (winter 1985): 463–80.

———. *Rebels, Reformers, and Revolutionaries: Collected Essays and Second Thoughts.* New York: Routledge, 2002.

Elliott, E. N., ed. *Cotton Is King, and Pro-Slavery Arguments: Comprising the Writings of Hammond, Harper, Christy, Stringfellow, Hodge, Bledsoe, and Cartwright, on this Important Subject.* Augusta, Ga.: Pritchard, Abbott, and Loomis, 1860.

Examination of Mr. Thomas C. Brown, A Free Colored Citizen of S. Carolina, as to the Actual State of Things in Liberia in the Years 1833 and 1834, at the Chatham Street Chapel, May 9th and 10th, 1834. New York: S. W. Benedict, 1834.

Faust, Drew Gilpin, ed. *The Ideology of Slavery: Proslavery Thought in the Antebellum South, 1830–1860.* Baton Rouge: Louisiana State University Press, 1981.

Festinger, Leon. *A Theory of Cognitive Dissonance.* 1957. Reprint, Stanford, Calif.: Stanford University Press, 1985.

Fields, Barbara Jeanne. *Slavery and Freedom on the Middle Ground: Maryland during the Nineteenth Century.* New Haven: Yale University Press, 1985.

Finkelman, Paul. *An Imperfect Union: Slavery, Federalism, and Comity.* Chapel Hill: University of North Carolina, 1981.

———. *State Slavery Statutes.* Frederick, Md.: University Publications of America, 1989.

Finnie, Gordon E. "The Antislavery Movement in the Upper South before 1840." *Journal of Southern History* 35, no. 3 (August 1969): 319–42.

Fitzhugh, George. *Cannibals All! or Slaves Without Masters.* 1857. Reprint, edited by C. Vann Woodward. Cambridge: Harvard University Press, 1960.

Fladeland, Betty. *Men and Brothers: Anglo-American Antislavery Cooperation.* Urbana: University of Illinois Press, 1972.

Fogel, Robert William. *Without Consent or Contract: The Rise and Fall of American Slavery*. New York: W. W. Norton, 1989.

Fogel, Robert William, and Stanley L. Engerman. "Philanthropy at Bargain Prices." *Journal of Legal Studies* 3, no. 2 (June 1974): 377–402.

———. *Time on the Cross: The Economics of American Negro Slavery*. New York: W. W. Norton, 1974.

Foner, Eric. *Free Soil, Free Labor, Free Men: The Ideology of the Republican Party before the Civil War*. New York: Oxford University Press, 1970.

Foster, Gaines M. "Guilt over Slavery: A Historiographical Analysis." *Journal of Southern History* 56, no. 4 (November 1990): 665–94.

Fox, Early. *The American Colonization Society, 1817–1840*. Baltimore: Johns Hopkins University Press, 1919.

Fox-Genovese, Elizabeth. *Within the Plantation Household: Black and White Women of the Old South*. Chapel Hill: University of North Carolina Press, 1988.

Fredrickson, George M. *The Black Image in the White Mind: The Debate on Afro-American Character and Destiny, 1817–1914*. New York: Harper and Row, 1971.

Freehling, Alison Goodyear. *Drift toward Dissolution: The Virginia Slavery Debates of 1831–1832*. Baton Rouge: Louisiana State University Press, 1982.

Freehling, William W. *The Reintegration of American History: Slavery and the Civil War*. New York: Oxford University Press, 1994.

———. *The Road to Disunion: Secessionists at Bay, 1776–1854*. New York: Oxford University Press, 1990.

Frey, Sylvia R. *Water from the Rock: Black Resistance in a Revolutionary Age*. Princeton, N.J.: Princeton University Press, 1991.

Garrison, William Lloyd. *Thoughts on African Colonization*. Boston: Garrison and Knapp, 1832. Reprint, New York: Arno Press, 1968.

Gatewood, Willard B., Jr. "'To be truly free': Louis Sheridan and the Colonization of Liberia." *Civil War History* 29, no. 4 (December 1983): 332–48.

Genovese, Eugene D. *Roll, Jordan, Roll: The World the Slaves Made*. New York: Pantheon, 1974.

———. *"Slavery Ordained by God": The Southern Slaveholders' View of Biblical History and Modern Politics*. Gettysburg, Pa.: Gettysburg College 24th Annual Robert Fortenbaugh Memorial Lecture, 1985.

Genovese, Eugene D., and Elizabeth Fox-Genovese. "The Divine Sanction of Social Order: Religious Foundations of the Southern Slaveholders' World View." *Journal of the American Academy of Religion* 55, no. 2 (summer 1987): 211–34.

Georgia General Assembly. *Report Adopted by the Legislature of Georgia on African Colonization, February 8, 1828*. Washington: Gales and Seaton, 1828.

Gifford, James M. "The African Colonization Movement in Georgia, 1817–1860." PhD diss., University of Georgia, 1977.

———. "Black Hope and Despair in Antebellum Georgia: The William Moss Correspondence." *Prologue* 8, no. 3 (fall 1976): 152–62.

———. "The Cuthbert Conspiracy: An Episode in African Colonization." *South Atlantic Quarterly* 79, no. 3 (summer 1980): 312–20.

———. "Emily Tubman and the African Colonization Movement in Georgia." *Georgia Historical Quarterly* 59, no. 1 (spring 1975): 10–24.

Gimelli, Louis B. "Louisa Maxwell Cocke: An Evangelical Plantation Mistress in the Antebellum South." *Journal of the Early Republic* 9, no. 1 (spring 1989): 53–71.

Goldin, Claudia Dale. "The Economics of Emancipation." *Journal of Economic History* 33, no. 1 (March 1973): 66–85.

Goodell, William. *The American Slave Code in Theory and Practice: Its Distinctive Features Shown by Its Statutes, Judicial Decisions, and Illustrative Facts.* N.p.: American and Foreign Anti-Slavery Society, 1853. Reprint, New York: Negro Universities Press, 1968.

Goodwin, Mary F. "A Liberia Packet." *Virginia Magazine of History and Biography* 59, no. 1 (January 1951): 72–88.

Gutman, Herbert G. *The Black Family in Slavery and Freedom, 1750–1925.* New York: Vintage, 1976.

Hahn, Steven. *A Nation under Our Feet: Black Political Struggles in the Rural South from Slavery to the Great Migration.* Cambridge: Belknap Press of Harvard University Press, 2003.

Harrold, Stanley. *The Abolitionists and the South, 1831–1861.* Lexington: University Press of Kentucky, 1995.

———. *Subversives: Antislavery Community in Washington, D.C., 1828–1865.* Baton Rouge: Louisiana State University Press, 2003.

Hershberg, Theodore. "Free Blacks in Antebellum Philadelphia: A Study of Ex-Slaves, Freeborn, and Socioeconomic Decline." *Journal of Social History* 5 (winter 1971–72): 183–209.

Holsoe, Svend E. "A Study of Relations between Settlers and Indigenous Peoples in Western Liberia, 1821–1847." *African Historical Studies* 4, no. 2 (1971): 331–62.

Howe, Daniel Walker. *The Political Culture of the American Whigs.* Chicago: University of Chicago Press, 1979.

Howington, Arthur F. "'A Property of Special and Peculiar Value': The Tennessee Supreme Court and the Law of Manumission." *Tennessee Historical Quarterly* 44 (1985): 302–17.

———. "'Not in the Condition of a Horse or an Ox': *Ford v. Ford*, the Law of Testamentary Manumission, and the Tennessee Courts' Recognition of Slave Humanity." *Tennessee Historical Quarterly* 34, no. 3 (fall 1975): 249–63.

Hoyt, William D., Jr. "John McDonogh and Maryland Colonization in Liberia, 1834–35." *Journal of Negro History* 24, no. 4 (October 1939): 440–53.

Huberich, Charles Henry. *The Political and Legislative History of Liberia.* 2 vols. New York: Central Book, 1947.

Huffman, Alan. *Mississippi in Africa: The Saga of the Slaves of Prospect Hill Plantation and Their Legacy in Liberia Today.* New York: Gotham Books, 2004.

Huston, James L. "The Experiential Basis of the Northern Antislavery Impulse." *Journal of Southern History* 56, no. 4 (November 1990): 609–40.

Jackson, Luther Porter. "Manumission in Certain Virginia Cities." *Journal of Negro History* 15, no. 1 (January 1930): 278–314.

Jefferson, Thomas. *Notes on the State of Virginia.* Edited by William Harwood Penden. Chapel Hill: Institute of Early American History and Culture, University of North Carolina Press, 1954.

Johannsen, Robert W., ed., *The Lincoln-Douglas Debates of 1858.* New York: Oxford University Press, 1965.

Johnson, Michael P., ed. *Abraham Lincoln, Slavery, and the Civil War: Selected Writings and Speeches.* Boston: Bedford/St. Martin's, 2001.

Johnson, Walter. "On Agency." *Journal of Social History* 37, no. 1 (2003): 113–24.

————. *Soul by Soul: Life inside the Antebellum Slave Market.* Cambridge: Harvard University Press, 1999.

Jordan, Winthrop D. *White over Black: American Attitudes Toward the Negro, 1550–1812.* 1968. Reprint, Baltimore: Penguin Books, 1969.

Kautzsch, Alexander. "Liberian Letters and Virginia Narratives: Negation Patterns in Two New Sources of Earlier African American English." *American Speech* 75, no. 1 (2000): 34–53.

Kerr, Norwood Allen. "The Mississippi Colonization Society, 1831–1860." *Journal of Mississippi History* 43, no. 1 (February 1981): 1–30.

Klebaner, Benjamin Joseph. "American Manumission Laws and the Responsibility for Supporting Slaves." *Virginia Magazine of History and Biography* 63, no. 4 (October 1955): 443–53.

Kocher, Kurt Lee. "A Duty to America and Africa: A History of the Independent African Colonization Movement in Pennsylvania." *Pennsylvania History* 51, no. 2 (April 1984): 118–53.

Kornblith, Gary J. "Rethinking the Coming of the Civil War: A Counterfactual Exercise." *Journal of American History* 90, no. 1 (June 2003): 76–105.

Lane, J. H. *Speech of Hon. J. H. Lane of Kansas, in the Senate of the United States, February 16, 1864, on the special order, being Senate bill no. 45, to set apart a portion of the state of Texas for the use of persons of African descent.* Washington, D.C.: Gibson Brothers Printers, 1864.

Lang, Meredith. *Defender of the Faith: The High Court of Mississippi, 1817–1875.* Jackson: University Press of Mississippi, 1977.

Lebsock, Suzanne. *The Free Women of Petersburg: Status and Culture in a Southern Town, 1784–1860.* New York: W. W. Norton, 1985.

Lee, Deborah A. "Life Is a Sacred Trust: Ann R. Page and the Antislavery Movement in the Upper South." PhD diss., George Mason University, 2002.

Liebenow, J. Gus. *Liberia: The Evolution of Privilege.* Ithaca, N.Y.: Cornell University Press, 1969.

Link, William A. *Roots of Secession: Slavery and Politics in Antebellum Virginia.* Chapel Hill: University of North Carolina Press, 2003.

Litwack, Leon F. *North of Slavery: The Negro in the Free States, 1790–1860.* Chicago: University of Chicago Press, 1961.

Loveland, Anne C. *Southern Evangelicals and the Social Order, 1800–1860.* Baton Rouge: Louisiana State University, 1980.

Maddex, Jack P., Jr. "'The Southern Apostasy' Revisited: The Significance of Proslavery Christianity." *Marxist Perspectives* 2 (fall 1979): 132–42.

Massachusetts Colonization Society. *American Colonization Society and the Colony at Liberia.* Boston: Perkins and Marvin, 1832.

Matthews, Donald. *Religion in the Old South.* Chicago: University of Chicago Press, 1977.

McColley, Robert. *Slavery and Jeffersonian Virginia.* Urbana: University of Illinois Press, 1964.

McCoy, Drew R. *The Last of the Fathers: James Madison and the Republican Legacy.* Cambridge: Cambridge University Press, 1989.

McDaniel, Antonio. *Swing Low, Sweet Chariot: The Mortality Cost of Colonizing Liberia in the Nineteenth Century.* Chicago: University of Chicago Press, 1995.

McFeely, William S. *Frederick Douglass.* New York: W. W. Norton, 1991.

McKitrick, Eric L., ed. *Slavery Defended: The Views of the Old South.* Englewood Cliffs, N.J.: Prentice-Hall, 1963.

McManus, Edgar J. *Black Bondage in the North.* Syracuse, N.Y.: Syracuse University Press, 1973.

McMillen, Sally. *Southern Women: Black and White in the Old South.* 2d ed. Wheeling, Ill.: Harlan Davidson, 2002.

McPherson, James M. *Battle Cry of Freedom: The Civil War Era.* New York: Oxford University Press, 1988.

Melish, Joanne Pope. *Disowning Slavery: Gradual Emancipation and "Race" in New England.* Ithaca, N.Y.: Cornell University Press, 1998.

Mercer, Margaret. *Popular Lecture on Ethics, or Moral Obligation.* Petersburg, Va.: Edmund and Julian C. Ruffin, 1841.

Miller, Floyd. *The Search for Black Nationality: Black Emigration and Colonization, 1787–1863.* Urbana: University of Illinois Press, 1975.

Miller, John C. *The Wolf by the Ears: Thomas Jefferson and Slavery.* New York: Free Press, 1977.

Miller, Randall M., ed. *"Dear Master": Letters of a Slave Family.* Ithaca, N.Y.: Cornell University Press, 1978. Reprint, Athens: University of Georgia Press, 1990.

———. "'Home as Found': Ex-Slaves and Liberia." *Liberian Studies Journal* 6, no. 2 (1975): 92–108.

Mitchell, Memory F. "Freedom Brings Problems: Letters from the McKays and the Nelsons in Liberia." *North Carolina Historical Review* 70, no. 4 (October 1993): 431–65.

———. "Off to Africa—with Judicial Blessings." *North Carolina Historical Review* 53, no. 3 (July 1976): 265–87.

Mitchell, Memory F., and Thornton W. Mitchell. "The Philanthropic Bequests of John Rex of Raleigh, Part I." *North Carolina Historical Review* 49, no. 3 (July 1972): 254–79.

Morgan, Edmund S. *American Slavery, American Freedom: The Ordeal of Colonial Virginia.* New York: Norton, 1975.

Morris, Caspar. *Memoir of Miss Margaret Mercer.* Philadelphia: Lindsay and Blakiston, 1848.

Morris, Christopher. "The Articulation of Two Worlds: The Master-Slave Relationship Reconsidered." *Journal of American History* 85, no. 3 (December 1998): 982–1007.

Morris, Thomas D. *Southern Slavery and the Law, 1619–1860.* Chapel Hill: University of North Carolina Press, 1996.

Moses, Wilson Jeremiah. *Alexander Crummell: A Study of Civilization and Discontent.* New York: Oxford University Press, 1989.

———, ed. *Liberian Dreams: Back-to-Africa Narratives from the 1850s.* University Park: Pennsylvania State University Press, 1998.

Murza, Peter John. "The American Colonization Society and Emigration to Liberia, 1865–1904." Master's thesis, University of Wisconsin, 1972.

Nash, A. E. Keir. "Reason of Slavery: Understanding the Judicial Role in the Peculiar Institution." *Vanderbilt Law Review* 32 (January 1979): 7–218.

Nash, Gary B. *Forging Freedom: The Formation of Philadelphia's Black Community, 1720–1840.* Cambridge: Harvard University Press, 1988.

———. *Race and Revolution.* Madison: Madison House, 1990.

Nash, Gary B., and Jean R. Soderlund. *Freedom by Degrees: Emancipation in Pennsylvania and Its Aftermath.* New York: Oxford University Press, 1991.

New-York State Colonization Society. *Emigration to Liberia. One-thousand Applicants for a Passage to Liberia in 1848. An Appeal in Behalf of Two-hundred Slaves Liberated by Captain Isaac Ross. A Brief History of the Ross Slaves.* New York: D. Fanshaw, 1848.

Oakes, James. *The Ruling Race: A History of American Slaveholders.* New York: Alfred A. Knopf, 1982.

Olwell, Robert. "Becoming Free: Manumission and the Genesis of a Free Black Community in South Carolina, 1740–1790." *Slavery and Abolition* 17, no. 1 (1996): 1–19.

Opper, Peter Kent. "The Mind of the White Participant in the African Colonization Movement, 1816–1840." PhD diss., University of North Carolina, 1972.

Onuf, Peter S. "Every Generation Is an 'Independent Nation': Colonization, Miscegenation, and the Fate of Jefferson's Children." *William and Mary Quarterly* 57 (January 2000): 153–70.

Parish, Peter. "The Edges of Slavery in the Old South: Or, Do Exceptions Prove Rules?" *Slavery and Abolition* 4, no. 2 (September 1983): 106–25.

Patterson, Orlando. *Slavery and Social Death: A Comparative Study.* Cambridge: Harvard University Press, 1982.

Patton, James W. "The Progress of Emancipation in Tennessee." *Journal of Negro History* 17, no. 1 (January 1932): 67–102.

Paxton, J. *Letters on Slavery, addressed to the Cumberland Congregation, Virginia.* Lexington, Ky.: Abraham T. Skillman, 1833.

Pease, J. Morris. *A Statement and Appeal in Behalf of the Redemption from Slavery of the Wife and Seven Children of the Rev. Hardy Mobley, and Their Settlement in Western Africa as a Missionary Family.* Philadelphia, 1855.

Pease, William H., and Jane H. Pease, eds. *The Antislavery Argument.* Indianapolis: Bobbs-Merrill, 1965.

Pennsylvania Abolition Society. *Annual Report of the Association of Friends for the Promoting the Abolition of Slavery, and Improving the Condition of the Free People of Color.* Philadelphia: Merrihew and Thompson, 1849.

Pennsylvania Anti-Slavery Society. *Annual Reports.* Philadelphia: Merrihew and Thompson, 1851–52.

Pennsylvania Colonization Society. *Addresses Delivered in the Hall of the House of Representatives, Harrisburg, Pa., on Tuesday Evening, April 6, 1852, by William V. Pettit, Esq. and Rev. John P. Durbin, D.D.* Philadelphia: W. F. Geddes, 1852.

———. *Annual Reports of the Board of Managers of the Pennsylvania Colonization Society.* Philadelphia, 1829–61.

———. *Appeal in Behalf of African Colonization.* Philadelphia, 1856.

———. *At a Meeting of the Board of Managers of the Pennsylvania Colonization Society.* Philadelphia, 1857.

———. *To the Friends of the African Race.—An Appeal in Behalf of the Pennsylvania Colonization Society.* Philadelphia, 1853.

Pennsylvania House of Representatives. *The Select Committee of the House of Representatives of Pennsylvania on the Subject of Colonization.* Harrisburg, Pa., 1854.

Perman, Michael. *Emancipation and Reconstruction.* 2d ed. Wheeling, Ill.: Harlan Davidson, 2003.

Philadelphia Anti-Slavery Society. *Address to the Members of the Philadelphia Anti-Slavery Society to Their Fellow Citizens.* Philadelphia: W. P. Gibbons, 1835.

———. *Annual Reports.* Philadelphia: n.p., 1835.

Post, Edward M. "Kentucky Law Concerning Emancipation or Freedom of Slaves." *Filson Club Quarterly* 59, no. 3 (July 1985): 344–67.

Quarles, Benjamin. *Black Abolitionists.* New York: Oxford University Press, 1969.

———. *Lincoln and the Negro.* New York: Oxford University Press, 1962.

Ransom, Roger L., and Richard Sutch. *One Kind of Freedom: The Economic Consequences of Emancipation.* New York: Cambridge University Press, 1977.

Report of the Select Committee on Emancipation and Colonization. Washington, D.C.: Government Printing Office, 1862.

Rice, Otis K. "Eli Thayer and the Friendly Invasion of Virginia." *Journal of Southern History* 37, no. 4. (November 1971): 575–96.

Riley, Franklin L. "A Contribution to the History of the Colonization Movement in Mississippi." *Publications of the Mississippi Historical Society* 9 (1906): 331–414.

Ripley, C. Peter, ed., *The Black Abolitionist Papers.* 5 vols. Chapel Hill: University of North Carolina Press, 1985–92.

Rugemer, Edward B. "The Southern Response to British Abolitionism: The Maturation of Proslavery Apologetics." *Journal of Southern History* 70, no. 2 (May 2004): 221–49.

Saillant, John. "Circular Addressed to the Colored Brethren and Friends in America: An Unpublished Essay by Lott Cary, Sent from Liberia to Virginia, 1827." *Virginia Magazine of History and Biography* 104, no. 4 (autumn 1996): 481–504.

Sanneh, Lamin. *Abolitionists Abroad: American Blacks and the Making of Modern West Africa.* Cambridge: Harvard University Press, 1999.

Schafer, Judith Kelleher. *Becoming Free, Remaining Free: Manumission and Enslavement in New Orleans, 1846–1862.* Baton Rouge: Louisiana State University Press, 2003.

Schwarz, Philip J. "Emancipators, Protectors, and Anomalies: Free Black Slaveowners in Virginia." *Virginia Magazine of History and Biography* 95 (1987): 317–38.

———. *Migrants against Slavery: Virginians and the Nation.* Charlottesville: University of Virginia Press, 2001.

Scott, Anne F. *The Southern Lady: From Pedestal to Politics, 1830–1930.* 1970. Reprint, Charlottesville: University Press of Virginia, 1995.

Seifman, Eli. "The United Colonization Societies of New-York and Pennsylvania and the Establishment of the African Colony of Bassa Cove." *Pennsylvania History* 35, no. 1 (January 1968): 23–44.

Sellers, Charles J., Jr. "The Travail of Slavery." In *The Southerner as American,* edited by Charles J. Sellers Jr., 40–71. Chapel Hill: University of North Carolina Press, 1960.

Shaw, Robert B. *A Legal History of Slavery in the United States.* Potsdam, N.Y.: Northern Press, 1991.

Sherwood, Henry Noble. "Early Negro Deportation Projects." *Mississippi Valley Historical Review* 2, no. 4 (March 1916): 484–508.

———. "The Formation of the American Colonization Society." *Journal of Negro History* 2, no. 3 (July 1917): 209–28.

Shick, Tom W. *Behold the Promised Land: A History of Afro-American Settler Society in Nineteenth-Century Liberia.* Baltimore: Johns Hopkins University Press, 1980.

Simpson, Brooks D., ed., *Think Anew, Act Anew: Abraham Lincoln on Slavery, Freedom, and Union.* Wheeling, Ill.: Harlan Davidson, 1998.

Slaughter, Philip. *The Virginia History of African Colonization.* 1855. Reprint, Freeport, N.Y.: Books for Libraries Press, 1970.

Smith, John David, ed. *Emigration and Migration Proposals*. New York: Garland Publishing, 1993.

Smith, W. Wayne. "A Marylander in Africa: The Letters of Henry Hannon." *Maryland Historical Magazine* 69, no. 4 (winter 1974): 398–404.

Snay, Mitchell. *Gospel of Disunion: Religion and Separatism in the Antebellum South*. New York: Cambridge University Press, 1993.

Sowle, Patrick. "The North Carolina Manumission Society, 1816–1834." *North Carolina Historical Review* 42, no. 1 (January 1965): 46–69.

Stampp, Kenneth M. *America in 1857: A Nation on the Brink*. New York: Oxford University Press, 1990.

———. "The Fate of the Southern Anti-Slavery Movement." *Journal of Negro History* 28, no. 1 (January 1943): 10–22.

———. *The Peculiar Institution: Slavery in the Ante-Bellum South*. New York: Vintage, 1956.

Staudenraus, P. J. *The African Colonization Movement, 1816–1865*. New York: Columbia University Press, 1961.

Stevenson, Brenda E. *Life in Black and White: Family and Community in the Slave South*. New York: Oxford University Press, 1996.

Stowe, Harriet Beecher. *Uncle Tom's Cabin*. 1852. Reprint, New York: Harper and Row, 1965.

Stuart, C. *American Colonization Society*. N.p., 1831.

Stuckey, Sterling. *Slave Culture: Nationalist Theory and the Foundations of Black America*. New York: Oxford University Press, 1987.

Sweet, Leonard I. *Black Images of America, 1784–1870*. New York: W. W. Norton, 1976.

Syfert, Dwight N. "The Origins of Privilege: Liberian Merchants, 1822–1847." *Liberian Studies Journal* 6, no. 2 (1975): 109–28.

Syndor, Charles Sackett. *Slavery in Mississippi*. 1933. Reprint, Gloucester, Mass.: Peter Smith, 1965.

Tadman, Michael. *Speculators and Slaves: Masters, Traders, and Slaves in the Old South*. Madison: University of Wisconsin Press, 1989.

Takagi, Midori. *Rearing Wolves to Our Own Destruction: Slavery in Richmond, 1782–1865*. Charlottesville: University of Virginia Press, 1999.

Tallant, Harold D. *Evil Necessity: Slavery and Political Culture in Antebellum Kentucky*. Lexington: University Press of Kentucky, 2003.

Temperly, Howard. "African-American Aspirations and the Settlement of Liberia." *Slavery and Abolition* 21, no. 2 (August 2000): 67–92.

Thomas, Lamont D. *Rise to be a People: A Biography of Paul Cuffee*. Urbana: University of Illinois Press, 1986.

Thompson, Daniel C. *Sociology of the Black Experience*. Westport, Conn.: Greenwood Press, 1974.

Tise, Larry E. *Proslavery: A History of the Defense of Slavery in America, 1701–1840*. Athens: University of Georgia Press, 1987.

Tushnet, Mark V. *The American Law of Slavery, 1810–1860: Considerations of Humanity and Interest*. Princeton, N.J.: Princeton University Press, 1981.

———. "Approaches to the Study of the Law of Slavery." *Civil War History* 25, no. 4 (December 1979): 329–38.

Tyler-McGraw, Marie. "Richmond Free Blacks and African Colonization, 1816–1832." *Journal of American Studies* 21, no. 2 (August 1987): 207–24.

———. "'The Prize I Mean Is the Prize of Liberty': A Loudon County Family in Liberia." *Virginia Magazine of History and Biography* 97, no. 3 (July 1989): 355–74.

United States Congress. *Roll of Emigrants that have been sent to the colony of Liberia, Western Africa, by the American Colonization Society and its Auxiliaries, to September, 1843, & c.* 28th Cong., 2d sess., S. Doc. 150.

Varon, Elizabeth R. "Evangelical Womanhood and the Politics of the African Colonization Movement." In *Religion and the Antebellum Debate over Slavery,* edited by John R. McKivigan and Mitchell Snay. Athens: University of Georgia Press, 1998.

———. *We Mean to Be Counted: White Women and Politics in Antebellum Virginia.* Chapel Hill: University of North Carolina Press, 1998.

Voegeli, V. Jacque. *Free But Not Equal: The Midwest and the Negro during the Civil War.* Chicago: University of Chicago Press, 1967.

Wade, Richard C. *Slavery in the Cities: The South, 1820–1860.* New York: Oxford University Press, 1964.

Wahl, Jenny Bourne. *The Bondsman's Burden: An Economic Analysis of the Common Law of Southern Slavery.* New York: Cambridge University Press, 1998.

Walker, David. *David Walker's Appeal, in Four Articles; Together with a Preamble, to the Coloured Citizens of the World, but in Particular, and Very Expressly, to those of the United States of America.* 1829. Reprint, New York: Hill and Wang, 1995.

Webber, Thomas L. *Deep Like the Rivers: Education in the Slave Quarter Community, 1831–1865.* New York: W. W. Norton, 1978.

Weiner, Marli Frances. *Mistresses and Slaves: Plantation Women in South Carolina, 1830–1880.* Urbana: University of Illinois Press, 1997.

Welter, Barbara. "The Cult of True Womanhood, 1800–1860." *American Quarterly* 18, no. 2 (summer 1966): 151–74.

West, Richard. *Back to Africa: A History of Sierra Leone and Liberia.* London: Jonathan Cape, 1970.

Whitman, T. Stephen. *The Price of Freedom: Slavery and Manumission in Baltimore and Early National Maryland.* 1997. Reprint, New York: Routledge, 2000.

Wight, Willard C., ed. "Two Letters from Liberia." *Journal of Negro History* 44, no. 4 (October 1959): 379–84.

Wiley, Bell I., ed. *Slaves No More: Letters from Liberia, 1833–1869.* Lexington: University Press of Kentucky, 1980.

Wilkeson, Samuel. *To the Emigrants Now Preparing to Embark for Liberia.* N.p., 1840.

Williamson, Joel. *After Slavery: The Negro in South Carolina During Reconstruction, 1861–1877.* Chapel Hill: University of North Carolina Press, 1965.

Wood, Kirsten E. "Broken Reeds and Competent Farmers: Slaveholding Widows in the Southeastern United States, 1783–1861." *Journal of Women's History* 13, no. 2 (summer 2001): 34–57.

Wood, Peter H. *Black Majority: Negroes in Colonial South Carolina from 1670 through the Stono Rebellion.* New York: Knopf, 1974.

Woodson, Carter G. *Education of the Negro Prior to 1861: A History of the Education of the Colored People of the United States from the Beginning of Slavery to the Civil War.* 1915. Reprint, New York: Arno Press, 1968.

————, ed. *The Mind of the Negro as Reflected in Letters Written during the Crisis, 1800–1860*. Washington, D.C.: Association for the Study of Negro Life and History, 1926.

Wright, Donald R. *African Americans in the Early Republic, 1789–1831*. Wheeling, Ill.: Harlan Davidson, 1993.

Yanuck, Thomas. "Thomas Ruffin and North Carolina Slave Law." *Journal of Southern History* 21, no. 4 (November 1955): 456–75.

Young Men's Colonization Society of Pennsylvania. *Annual Report of the Board of Managers of the Young Men's Colonization Society of Pennsylvania*. Philadelphia: William Stavely, 1837.

Zilversmit, Arthur. *The First Emancipation: The Abolition of Slavery in the North*. Chicago: University of Chicago Press, 1967.

Index

Page numbers in *italics* refer to tables.

Abolition: Lincoln and, 164; Upper South manumitters' views of, 39–40
Abolitionists: ACS and, x; African-American, 26; demands of, ix; divisions among, 89–90; PCS and, 84–86, 87–88
ACS. *See* American Colonization Society (ACS)
Adams, Hugh, 108
Adams, John Quincy, 17
Adams, Nehemiah, 117
Adams v. Bass (Ga.), 128
African-Americans: abolition and, 26; ACS and, 82, 89; colonization movement and, 83–84, 92; emigration, interest in, 160–61; in North, 16; population of, 24–25, 80; views of colonization, 8–9, 16–17. *See also* Free blacks; Slaves
African Civilization Society, 160
African Repository (monthly): Gurley and, 23; letters published in, 71; reaction to, 106
Agriculture: in Liberia, 150–52
Alabama, 126, 137
Allen, Richard, 82
Alvany v. Powell (N.C.), 138–39

American and Foreign Anti-Slavery Society, 89
American Anti-Slavery Society, 84
American Colonization Society (ACS): African-Americans and, 16–17, 82, 89; constituency of, 15–16; constitution of, 24; demise of slavery and, 166–67; fiscal management of, 24, 79–80, 86; goals of, 1; historiography of, 2; manumissions and, 17; origins of, ix–x, 13–14; public image of, 23–24; self-promotion of, 112–13
—agents of: and conveying of freedpersons, 109; as informants about Liberia, 64–65, 68–69; and letters from Liberia, 71–72; as returnees from Liberia, 106–7
American Colonization Society v. Gartrell (Ga.), 135
The American Slave Code (Goodell), 129–30
Anaconda Plan, 161
Anderson, Franklin, 66
Anderson, M. L., 75
Andrews, Eliza, 74
Andrews, Ephraim, 74
Anti–free black policies, 126–30

Appeal (Walker), 83
Atchison, David, 31

Bacon, Harry, 77
Bailey, R. W., 72
Bailey v. Poindexter (Va.), 129, 137
Bain, George, 91
Banks, Anna J., 55
Barnet, Jack, 76
Barnet, John, 76
Bassa Cove, Liberia, 87, 148
Bayne, William H., 65
Bell, John, 33, 82
Benezet, Anthony, 8
Benning, Henry L., 128, 134
Benning, Thomas, 74, 79
Benton, Thomas Hart, 31
Berlin, Ira, 9, 76
Bethune, George M., 82
Bibb, Henry, 30
Bibb, Richard, 60
Birney, James G., 84, 112
Blackford, Abraham, 153, 155
Blackford, Lucy, 101
Blackford, Mary, 39, 51, 60, 101
Blair, Frank, Jr., 31, 33
Blair, James, 22
Bledsoe, Albert Taylor, 117
Border South: in Civil War, 161–62, 164–65
Bradley, James, 62, 140
Branagan, Thomas, 9
Branch, John, 18
Bratton, Dorothea, 107–8
Breckinridge, John, 82
Breckinridge, John C., 33
British Anti-Slavery Society, 85
British West Indies, 18
Britton, E. H., 117
Brockenbrough, William, 126
Brown, Anderson, 48–49
Brown, Ann, 74
Brown, Daniel, 74
Brown, Edmund, 108
Brown, Henry "Box," 30
Brown, Thomas C., 68
Bruner, John, 71–72
Bryce, Archibald, 19–20

Buchanan, James, 32
Buchanan, Thomas, 82
Burke, William C., 153–54
Butler, Benjamin, 162

Cabell, William, 136
Caldwell, Elias B., 14
Calhoun, John C., 23
Calloway, John, 70
Cameron v. Commissioners (N.C.), 133, 138
Cape Mount, Liberia, 153
Cape Palmas, Liberia, 66
Carney, Charity, 74
Carney, Mingo, 74
Carr, Dabney, 139–40
Carroll v. Brumby (Ala.), 137
Cartwright, Samuel A., 117
Cary, Lott, 16–17, 67, 68
Cassava, 152
Catron, John, 125
Catterall, Helen T., 137
Ceasar, Samson, 156
Chain migration, 109–10
Charity: manumissions viewed as, 133
Charles et al. v. Hunnicutt (Va.), 133
Charleston, S.C., 68, 112–13
Chesapeake region, 9–13
Chester, Thomas W., 98
Civil War: Anaconda Plan for, 161; Border South in, 161–62, 164–65; colonization and, 160
Claget, Charity, 66
Clay, Clement, 22
Clay, Henry: ACS and, 1, 14, 28; colonization and, 27, 38; Distribution Bill of, 22; Gag Rule controversy and, 23; on Liberia, 17; presidential campaign of, 25
Clay, Lucy, 157
Clay, Mary, 157
Clay, Sidney P., 61, 157
Clayton, Alexander M., 132, 134, 135
Cleland v. Waters (Ga.), 137
Clinton, Catherine, 50
Coalman, Wilson, 153
Cobb, Thomas R.: *An Inquiry into the Law of Negro Slavery in the United States of America,* 130
Cocke, John Hartwell, 38, 44, 61, 63, 102

Coffee, 152

Cognitive dissonance, 81, 99

Coker, Daniel, 16–17

Cole, Henry, 98

Coles, Edward, 47

Collier, Henry W., 132

Colonization: African-American views of, 8–9, 16–17, 83–84, 92; agency of slaves and, xi; Civil War and, 160, 163–64, 165; constituencies in favor of, 13; as force in America, 1; free blacks and, 26; historiography of, x; "purchased" emigrants and, 92; as racist ideology, 21–22; Republican Party and, 31–32; in Revolutionary era, 8; slavery and, 2, 22–23, 82–83, 84; support for, x; viability of, 20–21; views on, in Virginia, 11, 12. See also Opponents of colonization; Pennsylvania Colonization Society (PCS)

Colonization and Abolition Contrasted (Colton), 87

Colonization Herald (journal), 89, 91, 94, 98

Colton, Calvin, 82, 87

Commerce: in Liberia, 152–54

Commercial Bulletin (newspaper), 112

Communications network: transatlantic, 4, 69–70. See also Letters

Compromise of 1850, 28

Concise View of the Critical Situation (Seabrook), 114

Confiscation Act, 162

Conjunctive emancipations, 4–5, 75–77, 108

Connecticut, 7

Coppinger, William, 97

Corker, Joseph, 149

Cornish, Samuel, 16

Corpsen family, 90–91

Cotton Is King (Elliott), 117

Cox v. Williams (N.C.), 125, 132, 136

Craighead, William, 10

Crawford, James, 54

Crawford, William, 14

Cresson, Elliot, 82, 85

Creswell's Executor v. Walker (Ala.), 137

Crummell, Alexander, 160

Curry v. Curry (Ga.), 138

Cuthbert, Alfred, Jr., 97, 102

Cy pres: doctrine of, 133–34

Daily Picayune (newspaper), 112

Daniel, William, 129, 137

De Bow's Review (journal), 118

Delany, Martin, 30

Delaware, 162

Democratic Party, 31

Deputie, Charles, 94

Dew, Thomas R.: Review of the Debate in the Virginia Legislature of 1831 and 1832, 20, 115–16

"Diffusion" theory, 15

Disheroon, Isaac, 47

Distribution Bill, 22

District of Columbia Emancipation Act, 162

Doddridge, Philip, 13

Domestic emancipations, 12, 121–24, 125

Douglas, Stephen, 28, 31, 33

Douglass, Frederick, 160

Douglass, William, 16

Drane v. Beall (Ga.), 135, 140

Dred Scott verdict, 32

Durbin, John P., 93

Eagleton, William, 104

Early, J., 61

Education: in Liberia, 156; for manumission, 41–42, 59

Egalitarianism, 6

Elder, Herbert, 139

Elder v. Elder (Va.), 125, 136, 139–40

Election cases, 57–58, 62–63, 77–78, 135–38

Elliott, E. N.: Cotton Is King, 117

Emancipation Proclamation, 164

Emancipators. See Manumitters

Embarkation dates, 114

Emigrants, free black: by state, 172–73

Emigration: 1816–1830, 13–19; 1820–1860, 169, 170; 1831–1847, 19–27; 1848–1860, 27–33; Civil War and, 165; by free blacks, 16, 29–30; government assistance and, 25; patterns of, 25–26; postbellum era and, 166

Evans, Seaborn, 152, 159

Evans v. Kittrell (Ala.), 133–34

Everett, Edward, 28

Ewing, Ephraim M., 131

Executors of Henderson v. Heirs (La.), 137

Expatriation movement, 30

Fairfax, Ferdinando, 10–11, 14

Familial aspects of emigration: choice and, 57, 77–78; dependents, traveling with, 143–44; free black kin and, 73–75; slave kin and, 75–77, 156–57

Faulcon, John H., 155

Federal funding of ACS: J. Q. Adams administration, 17–18; Buchanan administration, 32; Fillmore administration, 28–29; importance of, 25; Jackson administration, 18, 22; Monroe administration, 14–15

Festinger, Leon, 81, 99

Fillmore, Millard, 28

Finley, Robert, 14

Fiscal management issues, 24

Fisher, Peter, 62

Fisher's Negroes v. Dabbs (Tenn.), 125

Fitzhugh, George, 117

Ford v. Ford (Tenn.), 132

Foreign emancipations, 122, 125–26, 128–29

Forten, James, 82

Forten, Sarah L., 26

Forward's Adm'r v. Thamer (Va.), 137

Four Months in Liberia (Nesbit), 94

Frazier v. Frazier (S.C.), 125

Free blacks: anti–free black policies, 126–30; colonization and, 26; deportation of, 19–20, 89; ACS's dockside visibility and, 113; emigrants, by state, 172–73; immigration of, 124; kinship ties with slaves and, 73–75; in Liberia, 151, 152; mistrust of, 7–8; northern, 30; PCS and, 98–99; as returnees from Liberia, 67; southern, 19, 29–30, 95–96, 122–23; as threat, ix; as topic of complaint, 65; in Virginia, 12

Freedom: giving and receiving, 131–35

Freedom's Journal (newspaper), 16

Freehling, William, 20–21

Freeman, Sarah, 55

Fugitive Slave Law, 28, 30, 92, 161

Fuller, James, 35–36

Fuller, Thomas, 106

Gabriel: insurrection plot of, 11

Gag Rule controversy, 23

Garnet, Henry Highland, 30, 160

Garrison, William Lloyd, 16, 21–22, 39, 84, 85

Gass, John, 53

Gaston, William, 132

Gender norms: southern, 49–53

Georgia: anti–free black policies in, 128–29; colonization and, 124; domestic emancipations and, 123; election cases and, 137–38; hiring out of slaves and, 140; manumitters from, 46; Savannah, 111–12, 113; testamentary bequests of slaves to ACS and, 135

Gibson, Jacob, 144, 156

Gibson, James, 105

Gideon, Francis, 75

Gloucester, John, 82

Glover, Titus, 72, 152

Goodell, William: The American Slave Code, 129–30

Goodwin, Henry B., 60

Gordon, Betsy, 95

Gordon v. Blackman (S.C.), 53–54

Grain Coast, 146, 153

Great Britain, 85

Green, Nathan, 136

Green, Samuel B., 137

Greener, Jacob, 16

Griffith, David, 90, 92

Grimké, Sarah, 82

Gurley, Ralph R., 16, 23–24, 64, 100

Haiti: African-Americans and, 160; diplomatic relationships with, 162–63; expedition to, 165; Lincoln and, 164; Quakers and, 37

Hamilton, James, Jr., 23

Hamlin, Hannibal, 33

Hammond, James Henry: on C. Mercer, 18; Two Letters on Slavery, 116

Hance, Alexander, 69, 78

Harper, Robert G., 66

Harper, William: Memoir on Slavery, 116

Harris, Catherine, 74

Harris, Jack, 74

Harris, King Joe, 87

Harris, Samuel, 72

Harris, Sion, 69

Harris, William L., 127

Hawes, Aylett, 86–87

Hay, John, 165
Hayden v. Burch (Md.), 136
Hayne, Robert Y., 18
Heaton, Albert, 101, 149–50
Heaton, Townsend, 101
Hébert, Paul Octave, 127–28
Help: appeals to former owners for, 149–50
Helper, Hinton Rowan: *The Impending Crisis,* 32
Hemphill, Joseph, 82
Herbert, Edward, 90, 91, 92
Herbert, Elizabeth, 90, 92
Herndon, Thaddeus, 95
Hines, C., 77
Historiography: of American Colonization Society, 2; of manumission and colonization, x
Hodge, Charles, 117
Holderness, Elizabeth, 49
Holly, James T., 30
Holt, George, 105
Hooe, Nathaniel, 39, 109
Hopkins, Samuel, 8
Hughes, Henry, 117
Hunt, Gilbert, 68

The Impending Crisis (Helper), 32
Indigenous peoples: in Liberia, 155–56
Ingersoll, Joseph R., 82
Inheritance of slaves: by ACS, 134–35; of property, 138–39
An Inquiry into the Law of Negro Slavery in the United States of America (Cobb), 130
Inskeep, Sarah, 105
Isaac v. McGill (Tenn.), 136

Jackson, Andrew, 18, 22
James, Diana Skipwith, 156
James, Frederick, 67
Jefferson, Thomas, 9–10, 11, 13
Johnson, William Cost, 23
Johnston, Job, 53–54
John v. Moreman (Ky.), 136
Jones, Absalom, 82
Jones, Walter, 24
Jordan, Peter, 62
Jordan v. Bradley (Ga.), 125, 140

Kansas-Nebraska Act, 31
Kendall, Isaac, 98
Kennedy, William, 70, 107
Kentucky, 27, 128
Key, Francis Scott, 14, 24
Keys, Solomon, 105
King, Alfred, 3, 4
King, Martin Luther, Jr., 166–67
King, Mary, 3, 4
King, Rufus, 18
Kornblith, Gary, 25

Lee, Mary Custis, 39, 71
Leech v. Cooley (Miss.), 132, 135, 138
Legal issues: ACS and, 107–8, 130, 132–33; antebellum era, 126–31; election cases, 135–38; giving and receiving freedom, 131–35; inheritances and hiring out, 138–40; overview of, 121–22, 131; Revolutionary era to 1840, 122–26. *See also specific cases*
Lenoir v. Sylvester (S.C.), 132
Letters: education for manumission and, 41–42; from Liberia, 70–73
Lewis, Mildred M., 75
Lewis, Samuel, 65
Lewis v. Lusk (Miss.), 135
Liberator (newspaper), 21, 39
Liberia: ACS origins and, ix–x; ACS reports on, 64–65; agriculture in, 150–52; aid to, 148–50; American informants on, 63–66; Bassa Cove, 87, 148; Cape Mount, 153; Cape Palmas, 66; commerce in, 152–54; constitution of, 141, 153, 155; demographics and, 142–44; diplomatic relations with, 162–63; emigration to, 17, 141; experiences in, 142; free blacks in, 67, 151, 152; as "hard country," 26–27; "Hard Times" and, 159; immunity and acclimatization, 146–48; independence of, 27, 141; initial attitudes toward, 144–46; investigations of, 69, 70, 97; letters from, 70–73; manumitters' views of, 40; missionaries in, 196n.22; mortality rates in, 141; Nesbit and, 94; PCS and, 97; religion in, 155; returnees from, 66–70, 72–73, 106–7, 144–45; slavery and, 153–54; social and political dynamics of, 30, 154–59; sources of information on, 63,

Liberia—*continued*
145–46; Stockton and, 15; symbolic significance of, 22; upland communities in, 147–48
Lincoln, Abraham, 32–33, 160, 161–67
Lomax, Matilda Skipwith, 158
Louisiana, 111, 112, 127–28
Louisiana Territory, 11–12
Love, George, 95
Lower South: antimanumission policies in, 126–29, 130–31; colonization and, 124; election cases in, 136–38; manumitters from, 46–47; migration to, 46–47; reaction to manumission in, 105–6
Lucas, Jesse, 144
Lucas, Mars, 144
Lugenbeel, J. W., 155
Lumpkin, Joseph Henry: on cy pres principle, 134; on election cases, 137–38; on foreign emancipation, 125, 128–29; on inheritance of slaves by ACS, 134–35; on postmortem manumissions, 104–5

Madison, James, 10
Malaria, 64, 146–47
Mallard, Thomas, 77
Manumission: ACS and, 17; agency of slaves and, xi, 131–40; assessing terms of, 58–63; "experimentalist," 48–49, 103–4; historiography of, x; location of, 100–103; method of, 103–5; PCS and, 83, 96–97; from plantation to port, 105–10; ports of departure and, 110–14; proximity to enterprise of, 114–20; rural, 36, 59, 101–2, 108; by state, *171*; urban, 101, 102. *See also* Testamentary liberations
Manumission programs: emigration and, 44–45; selection of slaves for, 43–44; slaves' reaction to, 59–60; training, 41–43, 59–60
Manumitters: advice on Liberia from, 63–64; age of, 45–46, 47, 54; appeals for help to, 149–50; choice left to slaves by, 57–58, 62–63, 77–78, 135–38; 1820–1840, 35–45; 1841–1860, 45–56; gender of, 48–53; multiple, 110; origins of, 46–47; by state, *170*; Upper South, 35–40; wealth of, 47–48
Maryland, 20, 36, 103–4
Maryland Colonization Journal, 71

Maryland Colonization Society, 66, 68
Massachusetts, 7
Mathes, E. L., 72
Maund v. M'Phail (Va.), 134
McDaniel, Antonio, 148
McDonogh, John, 60; advice on Liberia from, 63; legacy of, 32; manumission by, 102; on manumission program, 41–42, 44
McDonogh, Nancy Smith, 42
McGill, James, 104, 136
McGill, Robin, 104
McLain, William: on Bacon, 77; Coppinger and, 97; on fiscal issues, 79; on litigation, 107; reprimand of emigrants by, 148–49; on secrecy, 113
McLean, Elijah, 57
McPherson, George, 67
Memoir on Slavery (Harper), 116
Mercer, Charles Fenton, 1, 13–14, 18, 22, 38
Mercer, John Francis, 38
Mercer, Margaret: choice made by slaves of, 60, 67; dilemma of, 34; "experimentalist" approach of, 103–4; opposition to, 115; on Smith, G., 39; on society, 38; southern gender norms and, 51
Migration: from Upper South to Lower South, 46–47
Militia Act, 163
Minor, Dabney, 13
Missionaries: in Liberia, 196n.22
Mississippi, 127, 135
Missouri Compromise, 31
Missouri Crisis, 15
Mobley, Hardy, 95
Moderwell, Martha, 3–5
Moncure, Richard, 129, 137
Monroe, James, 11, 14–15
Morris, John, 107
Murray, Daniel, 35–36

Nancy v. Snell (Ky.), 131, 139
Nash, Gary, 8
Natural rights rhetoric, 6
Nesbit, William, 94, 152
New Hampshire, 7
New Jersey, 7
New Orleans, 111, 112
New York, 7

Nicholas v. Burruss (Va.), 139
Norfolk, Va., 110–11, 112
North Carolina, 36–37
Notes on the State of Virginia (Jefferson), 9–
    10, 13
Nott, Josiah, 118
Nullification Crisis, 22–23

O'Neall, John Belton, 125, 127, 132
Opponents: of abolition, 7
—of colonization: African-Americans as, 83–
    84, 92; in 1820s, 18; as informants on Liberia,
    65–66; proslavery arguments and, 114–20
Orr, James L., 29
Osborne v. Taylor (Va.), 137

Packard, J., 75
Page, Ann R.: choice made by slaves of, 60;
    colonization and, 44; on Liberia, 63; as re-
    peat emancipator, 110, 115; slavery and, 38
Page, John M., Sr., 66
Paine, James, 108
Paine, Thomas, 8
Parkham, John D., 60
Parrish, John, 9
Patterson, Edward James, 153
Patterson, James, 72
Paul, Luther, 96
Paxton, John, 17, 101–2, 115
PCS. *See* Pennsylvania Colonization Society
    (PCS)
Pearson, Richmond, 138–39
Peele, Sandy, 66
Peele, William, 66
Pennsylvania: gradual emancipation in, 7
Pennsylvania Abolition Society, 8, 83, 90
Pennsylvania Anti-Slavery Society (PASS), 85–
    86, 90
Pennsylvania Colonization Society (PCS):
    abolitionists and, 84–86, 87–88; ACS and,
    80, 83, 86, 88; colonization movement and,
    88–89; contributions to, 96; 1816–1839, 81–
    88; 1840–1861, 88–99; emigration of free
    blacks and, 98–99; funds for ACS and, 80,
    83; goals of, 80–81; Liberia and, 97; manu-
    missions abetted by, 83, 96–97; positive
    outlook of, 94–95; reorganization of, 97–
    98; southern free blacks and, 95–96; south-

ern partners of, 87, 92, 97; state funding
    for, 93–94
Pettit, William V., 93
Phelps, Amos A., 21, 84
Pinney, J. B., 82
Plantation mistress: role of, 49–53
Poindexter, Edward, 55, 77–78
Polk, James K., 25
Pollard, Edward A., 117
Population: of African-Americans, 24–25, 80;
    enslaved, 176n.6; of free blacks in South,
    122–23; sent to ACS colony, 2, 142–44
Ports: conveying freedpersons to, 108–10; of
    departure, 110–14
Postmortem liberations. *See* Testamentary
    liberations
A Practical Treatise on the Law of Slavery
    (Wheeler), 130
Prater's Administrator v. Darby (Ala.), 133
Pratt, Thomas, 28
Preliminary Emancipation Proclamation, 164
Press: ACS's use of, 112
Proslavery arguments, 114–20
Prout, Jacob, 68, 69
Public image issues, 23–24
Public policy and statutory law: antebellum
    era, 126–31; overview of, 121–22; Revolu-
    tionary era to 1840, 122–26
"Purchased" emigrants: ACS and, 77, 83;
    Corpsen family and, 90–92; definition of,
    185n.46; southern counties and, 75

Quakers, 36–37, 82

Racism: Garrison on, 21–22; Liberia and, 40,
    155, 159
Ragland, William, 53
Randolph, Edward Brett, 60, 63
Randolph, John, 14
Redding v. Long (N.C.), 136
Reed, Margaret, 102, 146
Religious instruction: for manumission, 41,
    59–60
Religious liberty: in Liberia, 155
Repeat emancipators, 110
Republican Party, 31–32
*Review of the Debate in the Virginia Legisla-
    ture of 1831 and 1832* (Dew), 20, 115–16

Rhode Island, 7

Rice, Anne, 48–49, 102

Rice, William, 72

Richardson, Francis DuBose, 127–28

Richardson, James, 158

Richmond, Va., 67–68

Roberts, Joseph Jenkins, 16–17, 30, 164

Rollins, James A., 166

Roser v. Marlow (Ga.), 125, 136

Ross, Horace, 150

Ross, Isaac, 102, 146, 150

Ross, Peter, 151

Ross v. Vertner (Miss.), 125

Roye, Edward J., 30

Ruffin, Edmund, 118–20

Ruffin, Thomas, 125, 136

Ruffner, William, 72, 107–8

Rural manumissions, 36, 59, 101–2, 108

Russwurm, John, 16

Sanders v. Ward (Ga.), 128, 129

Savannah, Ga., 111–12, 113

Schafer, Judith Kelleher, 36

Scott, Winfield, 161

Screven, James P., 111

Seabrook, Whitemarsh B.: *Concise View of the Critical Situation*, 114

Sea Islands, S.C., 165

Second Confiscation Act, 163

Second Great Awakening, 37

Select Committee on Emancipation and Colonization, 162, 163

Ship registers, 175n.5

Short, William, 82

Sierra Leone, 11, 66

Skipwith, George, 44

Skipwith, Peyton, 153, 155

Slaughter, Philip, 46

Slave agency: election cases, 135–38; giving and receiving freedom, 131–35; inheritances and hiring out, 138–40; issues, xi; overview of, 131

Slavery: in Border States, 164–65; in Chesapeake region, 9–13; colonization and, 2, 22–23, 82–83, 84; founding of ACS and, 14; Garrison on, 21–22; in Liberia, 153–54; manumitters' views of, 37–39; PCS and, 80; proslavery arguments, 114–20; Revolutionary era and, 6–7; in Upper South, 29. See

also "Purchased" emigrants

Slaves: American informants on Liberia and, 63–66; assessment of terms of manumission by, 58–63; choice left to, by manumitters, 57–58, 62–63, 77–78, 135–38; familial considerations of, 57, 73–78; hiring out, 108, 139–40; influence on ACS operations, 21; inheritance of, by ACS, 134–35; and letters from Liberia, 70–73; and returnees from Liberia, 66–70; runaway, 113; as sources of information on Liberia, 63, 145–46; and southern gender norms, 51

Slave Trade Act, 14, 18

Smart, William, 61

Smith, Gerrit, 39, 84

Smith, James McCune, 160–61

Smith v. Adam (Ky.), 128

Snead v. David (Ky.), 139

Society. *See* American Colonization Society (ACS)

South. *See* Lower South; Upper South

South Carolina: *African Repository* and, 106; Charleston, 68, 112–13; colonization and, 124; domestic emancipations and, 123; Nullification Crisis, 22–23; Sea Islands, 165; testamentary liberations in, 127

Southern gender norms, 49–53

Southern Quarterly Review (journal), 117

Speed, Henry, 38

Spence, Ara, 131

Stampp, Kenneth, 99

Starnes, Ebenezer, 126–27

Starr, William, 106, 107

State: free black emigrants by, *172–73*; manumittees by, *171*; manumitters by, *170*. *See also specific states*

State v. Dorsey (Md.), 131

Sterdivant, Robert Leander, 153

Steven, John, 32

Stewart, Henry B., 149

Stewart, Maria W., 16

Stockton, Robert, 15, 141

Stowe, Harriet Beecher: *Uncle Tom's Cabin*, 28

Stringfellow, Thornton, 117

Stuart, Charles, 85

Stuart, Robert, 108

Stuckey, Sterling, 63

Sullivan, James, 9

Swamp theory of malaria, 147

Tappan, Arthur, 84, 89
Tappan, Lewis, 89
Taylor, John, 14
Tennessee, 20, 128
Testamentary liberations: bans on, 127; challenges to, 53–54, 55–56; contingencies of, 54–55; growth of, 25, 29, 53; reaction to, 104–5; rise in, 4; slaves' reaction to, 61–62; widows receiving credit for, 52–53
Thomas v. Wood (Md.), 139
Thompson v. Newlin (N.C.), 132
Thornton, William, 9
Thornton v. Chisholm (Ga.), 140
Thoughts on African Colonization (Garrison), 21, 84
Training programs: for manumission, 41–45, 59–60
Transportation, 114
Trials, 107–8, 130, 132–33
Trotter v. Blocker (Ala.), 126, 132
Trump, George M., 18
Tubman, Emily, 60
Tucker, Beverly, 27–28
Tucker, Henry St. George, 125
Tucker, St. George, 10–11
Turnbull, Robert J., 18, 114–15
Turner's Rebellion, 19, 39
Two Letters on Slavery (Hammond), 116

Uncle Tom's Cabin (Stowe), 28
Upper South: antimanumission policy and, 129; election cases in, 136; inheritances and, 139; manumitters from, 35–40, 46; migration to Lower South from, 46–47; slavery in, 29
Urban centers: reaction to manumissions in, 101, 102
Usher, J. P., 165

Van Buren, Martin, 25
Vance v. Crawford (Ga.), 125, 134
Vass, Philip E., 133
Vaux, Robert, 82
Vermont, 7
Virginia: chain migration in, 109–10; domestic emancipations in, 123; election cases in, 137; legislative debates of 1831–1832, 19–20; manumitters from, 36; Norfolk, 110–11, 112; *Notes on the State of Virginia* (Jefferson), 9–10; reaction to manumissions in, 101–2; Richmond, 67–68
Vocational training: for manumission, 42–43

Wade v. The American Colonization Society (Miss.), 134, 135
Walker, David, 16, 65, 83
Walker, George J., 3
Ward, Samuel Ringgold, 30
Ware, J. W., 106
War of 1812, 12
Washington, Bushrod, 14
Watkins, William, 16
Watson, James, 73
Watson, William, 73
Webster, Daniel, 1, 14, 28
Webster, Noah, 9
Weld, Theodore Dwight, 21
Welles, Gideon, 164
West Virginia, 165
Wheeler, Jacob D.: *A Practical Treatise on the Law of Slavery*, 130
Whig Party, 31
White, William, 108
Whitman, T. Stephen, 36
Widows: in Liberia, 157–58; as manumitters, 52–53
Wilkeson, Samuel, 24
Williams, Peter, 16
Williamson v. Coalter (Va.), 137
Wilson, James W., 73, 155
Wirt, William, 14–15
Women: in Liberia, 157–58; as manumitters, 48–53; slaveholding, 3
Woodson, Lewis, 16
Woodson, Sarah, 146
Worrell, Moore, 62
Wright, Elizur, Jr., 21

Yeates, Catherine, 96
Young Men's Colonization Society of Pennsylvania (YMCSP), 86–87
Young v. Vass (Va.), 133

Eric Burin is associate professor of history at the University of North Dakota.

CPSIA information can be obtained
at www.ICGtesting.com
Printed in the USA
BVHW071512280620
582416BV00003B/273

9 780813 032733